Continuants

Their Activity, Their Being and Their Identity

Twelve Essays

David Wiggins

OXFORD
UNIVERSITY PRESS

OXFORD
UNIVERSITY PRESS

Great Clarendon Street, Oxford, OX2 6DP,
United Kingdom

Oxford University Press is a department of the University of Oxford.
It furthers the University's objective of excellence in research, scholarship,
and education by publishing worldwide. Oxford is a registered trade mark of
Oxford University Press in the UK and in certain other countries

© in this volume David Wiggins 2016

The moral rights of the author have been asserted

First Edition published in 2016

Impression: 1

All rights reserved. No part of this publication may be reproduced, stored in
a retrieval system, or transmitted, in any form or by any means, without the
prior permission in writing of Oxford University Press, or as expressly permitted
by law, by licence or under terms agreed with the appropriate reprographics
rights organization. Enquiries concerning reproduction outside the scope of the
above should be sent to the Rights Department, Oxford University Press, at the
address above

You must not circulate this work in any other form
and you must impose this same condition on any acquirer

Published in the United States of America by Oxford University Press
198 Madison Avenue, New York, NY 10016, United States of America

British Library Cataloguing in Publication Data

Data available

Library of Congress Control Number: 2016935438

ISBN 978–0–19–871662–4

Printed in Great Britain by
Clays Ltd, St Ives plc

Links to third party websites are provided by Oxford in good faith and
for information only. Oxford disclaims any responsibility for the materials
contained in any third party website referenced in this work.

Preface

In response to my editor Peter Momtchiloff's suggestion that I make selections, subject by subject, from among the papers I have written over the last four and a half decades, I decided to begin with the topics of substance and identity. These are among my longest-standing interests in philosophy. Out of a much much larger number of pieces about these two subjects—one part of my contribution to the publishing mania that has afflicted our times—I have chosen barely one third. Some such as Chapters 6 and 7 are given here in more or less their original state. That might have been a wise policy to follow everywhere. But where identity is concerned I still aspire to do more exact justice to the Aristotelian insight from which I once began. Fidelity to this aspiration has demanded a more energetic policy of local repair and improvement. All too often the essays repeat one another at certain points or redeploy some of the same well-worn examples. But, holding paramount the self-sufficiency and independent accessibility of each and every essay, I have been unable to do very much to reduce this overlap. To those who would have preferred a different policy I can only apologize.

At the end of the book there is a would-be complete bibliography of the writings that I published between 1964 and 2016. The simple effort of continuing this from an earlier bibliography that I take from *Identity Truth and Value: Essays for David Wiggins*, edited by Sabina Lovibond and Stephen Williams (see Wiggins 1996d), has reinforced and renewed my gratitude to them—for this as for much else. (Any corrections or additions to the bibliography will be noted in subsequent collections.) Another debt is to Gareth Jenkins for his technical, moral, and philosophical support in the production of this collection. A further debt of gratitude is owed to Hilla Wait, Colin Cook, and Daniel Drury in the Library of Philosophy and Theology, Oxford, and to Naomi van Loo, the College Librarian of New College, and her colleagues.

Oxford, July 2015

Contents

Sources	viii
Introduction	ix
1. Identity, Individuation, and Substance	1
2. On Being in the Same Place at the Same Time	33
3. Substance	41
4. The Person as Object of Science, as Subject of Experience, and as Locus of Value	71
5. Sameness, Substance, and the Human Person	87
6. Heraclitus' Conceptions of Flux, Fire, and Material Persistence	99
7. The Concept of the Subject Contains the Concept of the Predicate	128
8. Putnam's Doctrine of Natural Kind Words and Frege's Doctrines of Sense, Reference, and Extension: Can They Cohere?	150
9. The *De Re* 'Must', Individuative Essentialism, and the Necessity of Identity	165
10. Mereological Essentialism and Chisholm on Parts, Wholes, and Primary Things	191
11. Sortal Concepts: A Reply To Xu	201
12. Activity, Process, Continuant, Substance, Organism	211
Bibliography of David Wiggins's writings	221
Bibliography of other writings referred to	227
Index	235

Sources

Versions of these essays were originally published in the following places, and are reproduced by kind permission:

'Identity, Individuation and Substance': *European Journal of Philosophy*, 2012
'On Being in the Same Place at the Same Time': *Philosophical Review*, 1968
'Substance': *Philosophy: A Guide Through the Subject*, ed. A. C. Grayling, Oxford University Press 1995
'The Person as an Object of Science, as Subject of Experience, and as Locus of Value': *Persons and Personality*, ed. A. R. Peacocke, Blackwell 1987
'Sameness, Substance, and the Human Animal': *The Philosophers' Magazine*, 2000
'Heraclitus' Conceptions of Flux, Fire, and Material Persistence': *Language and Logos: Essays for G. E. L. Owen*, ed. M. Nussbaum and M. Schofield, Cambridge University Press 1982
'The Concept of the Subject Contains the Concept of the Predicate': *On Being and Saying: Essays for Richard Cartwright*, ed. J. J. Thomson, MIT Press 1987
'Putnam's Doctrine of Natural Kind Words and Frege's Doctrines of Sense, Reference, and Extension: Can They Cohere?': *Meaning and Reference*, ed. A. W. Moore, Oxford University Press 1993
'The *De Re* Must': *Truth and Meaning*, ed. G. Evans and J. McDowell, Clarendon Press 1976
'Mereological Essentialism: Asymmetrical Essential Dependence and the Nature of Continuants': *Grazer Philosophische Studien*, 1979
'Sortal Concepts: A Reply to Xu': *Mind and Language*, 1997
'Activity, Process, Continuant, Substance, Organism': *Philosophy*, vol. 91, 2016, pp. 269–80.

Full publication details may be found in the Bibliography.

Introduction

1

Forty-four years ago I published a short monograph called *Identity and Spatio-Temporal Continuity*,[1] henceforth *ISTC*, in which I contended that the identity between x and y—or the persistence of x in the shape of y—cannot in general be determined without reference to what x is and what y is, the fundamental thing-kind of each. I recently discovered that, in placing such emphasis on the question *x and y are the same what?*, I was repeating something I had said in an entry for *Analysis* Problem number 11 (1957). I did not win the competition, but it was a consolation (I now recall) that, in his report, Arthur Prior who was the judge made honourable mention of my deployment of that question. In *ISTC* I contended also that a proper concern with that same question, so soon as it was married with a concern for the indiscernibility of identicals, logically excluded the very idea, which was championed at that time by Peter Geach, of relative identity. The point of the *same what* question was not to make room for relative identity but to focus attention upon the question what thing or things—and what sort of things—were being inquired about.

Once *ISTC* was in print, I started putting one or two things right. From this process, once it was begun, arose *Sameness and Substance*,[2] henceforth *S&S*, and later *Sameness and Substance Renewed*,[3] henceforth *S&SR*. In the present collection the first essay summarizes, clarifies or extends *S&SR*. A summary of this paper is given at Section 2 which ensues here. Section 3 describes the contents of Chapters 2 to 12. Sections 4 and 5 give explanations which are perfectly essential to the understanding of all the essays in this book. Sections 6 to 8 treat less immediate matters which arise from recent controversy.

2

Chapter 1, 'Identity, Individuation, and Substance' (much revised), takes off from the problem of finding a proper content for the relation of identity as it holds or

---

[1] David Wiggins, *Identity and Spatio-Temporal Continuity* (Oxford: Blackwell, 1967).
[2] David Wiggins, *Sameness and Substance* (Oxford: Blackwell, 1980).
[3] David Wiggins, *Sameness and Substance Renewed* (Cambridge: Cambridge University Press, 2001).

fails to hold among ordinary things or substances. The necessary conditions of identity are straightforward, the sufficient conditions less so. The search is for a ground of identity more serviceable than the Leibnizian Identity of Indiscernibles (independently suspect) and strong enough to underwrite the indiscernibility of identicals and all the formal properties of the relation. At the level of metaphysics and epistemology alike the key to this problem rests, I claim, with a *sortalist* position.

Sortalism is the position which insists, as I have said already, that, where it is asked whether x and y are the same, it has to be asked *what are they*—what kind of thing is x and what kind of thing is y? In the case of substances and the like, any sufficiently specific answer to that question will bring with it a principle of activity or behaviour putatively common to x and to y and carrying with it implicit reference to a mode of being characteristic of a particular kind of thing. It is in the light of this sort of information that I suggest that questions of persistence or non-persistence through change—as of 'continuity'/'unity'/'unitariness'—will have in cases of difficulty to be adjudicated. These contentions are illustrated by reference to deliberately familiar examples such as the human zygote, the Ship of Theseus and Shoemaker's Brown/Brownson.

The first of these examples is representative of a mass of unproblematical cases. The problems presented by the second arise partly (it is claimed) from an incompleteness in our conceptions of the relevant sort—of the *what the thing in question is*. That incompleteness (whose diminution will depend—in the presence of some concretely given or imagined example of an artefact—upon further and closer specification of the relevant and particular kind or sort) need not prevent us from knowing perfectly well, in the ordinary and everyday sense, what thing we are referring to. In the third case, that of Brown/Brownson, where Brown's brain replaces the brain in the body of Robinson, my claim is that philosophy ought to pay much greater heed both to the kind of thing that Brownson is supposed to be and to the kind of possibility that can be credited to putative cases of brain transplant and the rest. Simple logical possibility is not enough. The authority of logic is limited to the exclusion of outright contradiction. Nor is the capacity of an alleged or putative survivor to utter the word 'I' sufficient to eke out the near total vacuity of bare logical possibility.

By any account, the cases of the zygote, of the ship of Theseus, and of Brownson are markedly dissimilar. The sortalist account may not differ very much from other accounts of these differences, but it lends a particular importance to the distinction between an artefact-kind such as *ship* and a natural kind such as *human being*. The principle of activity (and of passivity, perhaps one might add) for the case of a ship depends centrally upon the capacity of the thing in question to enable the carriage of people or goods over lake, sea, or river. In the characterization of the artefact-kind *ship* nothing corresponds to the need that we encounter in the case of natural things possessed of a *phusis* of their own to mount enquiries which may in some cases stretch down towards the principles of zoology, botany, biochemistry, chemistry, or physics. (See Chapter 8.) In the case of artefacts, that which is disputable lies elsewhere, in the elaboration of the sortal conception to which an artefact may owe its creation or preservation. In the Brown/Brownson case, our difficulties arise in part from a further controversy, one concerning the status—whether natural, artificial (!) or other—of the subject that is in question.

Chapter 1 stands in continuity with *Sameness and Substance Renewed*. But at some points it supersedes or supplants theses or formulations proposed there. For instance, the work done or attempted in *S&SR* by the *Only a and b* rule that I defended there passes now to the Adequacy Requirement, which says that whatever grounds the identity of x with y must itself ground their indiscernibility. (See section 4 with footnote 16.) For a further addition to *S&SR*, which said almost nothing about sortal concepts such as *bar of soap* or *piece of clay*, see Chapter 1, footnote 14. This addition was conceived as a partial response to David Lewis's paper 'Many, but almost one'.[4]

3

Chapter 2, the earliest essay, to which I attach here a critical commentary, considers the possibility or impossibility of the co-occupation by distinct things of the same place at the same time. It lays particular emphasis upon the distinction between a proper substance and an aggregation of material components.

Chapter 3 ('Substance', revised) expounds the Aristotelian doctrines from which sortalism derives. It defends them, not without the help of Leibniz, against multiple misunderstandings and misconceptions of the category of substance. It asserts the indispensability to us of that category.

The fourth and fifth chapters (both revised) are concerned with persons as a special case of substances, and with some of the immediate practical and ethical consequences of the sortalist understanding of persons and their identity.

The essays in the second half of the collection are concerned with the views of other philosophers from Heraclitus to the present day. Chapters 6 (unrevised) and 7 (unrevised) record some of the contributions made to our subject by

---

[4] David Lewis, 'Many, but almost one', in Keith Campbell, John Bacon, and Lloyd Reinhardt (eds), *Ontology, Causality and Mind: Essays on the philosophy of D. M. Armstrong* (Cambridge: Cambridge University Press, 1993), pp. 23–37.

Heraclitus and Leibniz. Chapters 8 to 12 relate to twentieth-century philosophers and to some distinctively twentieth-century preoccupations. Chapter 8 (revised slightly) seeks to align Hilary Putnam's account of the semantics of natural kind terms with Frege's account of sense and reference. It defends and endorses the result. Chapter 9 (partly new) reconsiders, among other things, Saul Kripke's argument for the necessity of identity—this in the light of a variety of attacks by contingency theorists such as Ayer and Quine. My eagerness to defend that necessity amounts of course to a serious tribute to Quine's power and authority. Chapter 10 is a critical exposition (now abbreviated and reorganized) of Roderick Chisholm's account of primary things, his mereological essentialism, and his defence of the principle that all the proper parts of a thing are essential to it. Chapter 11 (revised) is a sortalist commentary on Fei Xu's account of how particular substances can be singled out. It emphasizes the central importance of the determinable concept *object of some kind or other (to be determined)*.

Chapter 12 is a response to John Dupré's suggestion that an ontology of processes will provide a better framework for interpreting science than any ontology of substances. In response, after giving grounds to doubt that an ontology of pure processes can muster the resources to answer the individuative questions presented by the biological sciences themselves, I defend a plural ontology of process, activity, event *and* continuant.

4

It will be useful if I explain immediately that, in these essays, my policy is to use the word 'concept' to stand for the reference/Bedeutung of an expression that can be predicated.[5] I follow Frege's usage. See the diagram for Chapters 4 and 8, which I have based on that which Frege drew for Husserl in the letter of 1894 where he explained the distinction he proposed of sense from reference. More or less, a concept is a property. It belongs at the level of Bedeutung or reference.[6] At the level of sense, and where many philosophers and lay persons now use the word 'concept', I use the words 'conception' and/or 'idea' (in the colloquial, not the imagistic sense). As a result, I have sometimes to speak of a thinker's conception (or idea) of a concept. This is ungainly but it says what I mean. I remark further that,

---

[5] Throughout Chapter 8 I have to follow another injunction however—namely, to follow the usage that Leibniz employs in the various texts there discussed. Remarkably often this coincides with Frege's usage and my usage, but not always. In Chapter 11 I have had to compromise at some points with Fei Xu's discrepant usage.

[6] Where there is need to refer to the concept itself that a predicate or predicative expression stands for, it is a useful option to italicize the expression, thus: the concept *man*. But in this book italics are not confined to that role.

where our conceptions are of a sortal concept or of a kind of thing, they will comprise a mass of individuatively useful information that quickly outruns the narrowly semantic. Not least, the conception of a thing-kind may specify the principle of activity or way of behaving characteristic of the instances of the kind.

Let me add to the foregoing that the conceptions I speak of are not always conceptions of concepts. Conceptions can be of particular objects or substances, of stuffs, of kinds or sorts, or of abstract things—indeed of everything that belongs to the realm of Bedeutung. And conceptions can be of things such as events which have a different relation to time from the relation that substances have to it. (Cf. S&SR, p. 31 note 13.)

5

The general background to all the essays given here is a simple philosophical realism: the claim (to be defended somewhere else in philosophy) that that which we confront and try to describe—and that whose workings we seek earnestly to understand—is a mind-independent reality. We are not cut off from all success in that endeavour. This is to say that, even where the observer contributes a particular perspective or slant upon that reality, the reality that is revealed is not by that token a construct or creation of the knowing mind or of the effort of cognition. It goes without saying (let me add) that the claim that such a reality is mind-independent is not intended to exclude from the multitude of things that that reality comprises all objects and kinds that *owe their existence* to mind itself or the minds of their makers or users. It is true that questions about artefacts present special difficulties. In Chapter 1, section 16, I address these at some length, qualifying simple realism at one point by a concession to a kind of constructivism. (What else could one expect?) But this takes nothing away from the objectivity of the identity or individuation of the artefacts that we refer to in thought or speech. The difficulties in question are not such as to motivate philosophical idealism.

Philosophical realism so stated needs to be distinguished carefully from another kind of realism, which Hilary Putnam calls *metaphysical* realism. This is the doubtful contention that any 'given ... system of things can be described in exactly one way, *if* the description is complete and correct ... That [correct] way ... fix[es] exactly one ontology and one ideology (in Quine's sense of those words), ... [it fixes] exactly one domain of individuals and one domain of [properties] of those individuals'.[7] I concur entirely with Putnam's rejection of such claims, and I note

---

[7] See Hilary Putnam, *Philosophy in an Age of Science: Physics, Mathematics, and Skepticism*, ed. Mario De Caro and David Macarthur (Cambridge, MA: Harvard University Press, 2012), ch. 2, esp. p. 62.

that the 'conceptual realism' proposed in Chapter 5 of S&S and S&SR was all of a piece with a similar rejection. (See, for instance, S&SR pp. 151–5, 159–60, 172–3.)

The first avowed metaphysical realist was perhaps Plato, who stressed (*Phaedrus* 265e) the equal importance in philosophical classification and in carving of 'dividing where the joints are'. This is a telling metaphor and a telling anticipation also of some of the metaphysical utterances of present-day proponents of the 'new metaphysics'. But it falls well short of justifying the metaphysical position that Putnam distinguishes from philosophical realism. Carving belongs with eating, one definite purpose, or with anatomy, another definite purpose. Maybe there is always a best way to carve for purposes of eating and a best way to carve in the cause of scientific anatomy. But, as is evident from Plato's own example, not all carvings and not all singlings out or classifyings (even at a given location) will serve the same theoretical or practical purpose. Consider the case of the Mississippi. (I owe the example, but not my take on it, to Chisholm.) Shall we say that it is the stream that rises in northern Minnesota? Or is it a causally connected hydrological system fed from a stream that rises in northern Minnesota, another that begins in Pittsburgh (the Ohio) or further back in Allegheny, and yet another stream coming from another source that gives rise to the river that goes under the name Monongahela? (See Chapter 11, section 13.) If the question is worth asking, then the answer surely depends on what particular practical or theoretical purpose is at issue. It is this purpose that will determine which of these several things must concern us. Again, consider the plant *Thymus praecox*, which propagates itself both by seed and by suckers or shoots that it sends forth below ground level. The result may be a whole colony of genetically identical wild thyme plants. Is the fundamental thing here (the 'unitary substance'?) the whole colony or is it the individual plant? When the plant sends out a shoot, does it simply propagate *itself*, or should we think of it as contributing its propagule to the larger whole that is or will be the colony? Or is the only fundamental thing really a concrete universal—the genotype? Nothing in the philosophical realism that I avow prevents me from saying that what thing or system or subsystem you should attend to depends on the question (botanical, ecological, evolutionary, ...) that concerns you. (See also Chapter 1, section 22.) According to what that question is, you may attend to these things or to those different things. However palpable the things we refer to may be—no matter how strong their claim to be 'there anyway'—they will often require the one who notices or finds or observes them to be attending—optically or in thought, or in both ways at once—to *this* sort of thing or to *that* sort of thing. The mind recognizes by the exercise of conceptions the thing that is there to be recognized, but, aside from the cases where familiar objects simply obtrude themselves upon our perception, there are contexts where the things in question can only impinge upon a mind which is party to the right sort of enquiry, the right sort of concern or the right readiness to look for *this* or *that* kind of thing. (See for instance Chapter 1, section 10, note 21.)

So much for preliminaries. The sections that ensue (6–8) will chiefly concern the polemics in which the sortalist position has involved me—the polemics *and* the pacifics. The reader may want to go straight to Chapter 1, to which the way is now clear.

6

Let me now relate my affirmation of realism and denial of metaphysical realism to the 'conceptual realism' I defended in Chapter 5 of *S&S* and *S&SR*. My aim in what follows will be to propitiate one of the sternest critics of my sortalist approach to identity and individuation. The critic is Michael Ayers, from whom I now transcribe (but abbreviate) four claims [1] [2] [3] [4] which he makes in volume II of his book about Locke:[8]

[1] Substances or material objects characteristically have a kind of natural or given individuality, unity and continuity which non-substances [most artefacts] cannot have.

[2] The individuality of substances is real and prior to their individuation by us. The noun-predicates which serve to say 'what they are' simply place such individuals in classes according to affinity, origin, or structure.

[3] The individuality of non-substances, on the other hand, is posterior to our individuating them and to the predicates or concepts through which they are sliced out of reality...

[4] Any attempt to maintain a significant distinction... between the mass of matter and the living body or the *person* and the *man* is doomed to failure.

In response to these claims, I begin with that which seems most incontrovertible of all, namely [2]. But first let it be clear what Ayers intends in [2]. His concern there is with what he takes to be the central cases of substances and scarcely at all with artefacts—except in so far as those are as impressively and unproblematically 'unitary' as a lump of lead or a one pound weight (say). Contrast a steam engine, which is at best (he says) only 'notionally unitary' (see his page 127).

---

[8] See Michael Ayers, *Locke*, vol. II: *Ontology* (London: Routledge, 1991), p. 295. See also his 'Ordinary Objects, Ordinary Language, and Identity', *The Monist*, 88 (2005).

On these terms and while I reserve my own position about artefacts, I can concur wholeheartedly in [2]. I agree with it, and am ready to show that I am entitled to do so. On the same terms, I can agree with the first half of Ayers's [1]. By my conceptualist-realist account, the truth that is embodied in [2] may be further expounded as follows (I shall transcribe now, but abridge, from S&SR, Chapter 5):

A conceptualism that aspires to the title of a modest and sober realism must keep at arm's length any such sense as the sense in which horses, leaves, sun and stars could be supposed to be [the products of their individuation by human beings]... And it must hold a nice balance, adjusted to what is in fact a subtly reciprocal relation, between (1) the extent to which the conceptions that we bring to bear in order to distinguish, articulate and individuate things in nature are our [contrivance] and (2) the extent to which these conceptions make reference to concepts [i.e. sortal properties] that we find [in the external world] or permit nature itself to discover to us [or impress upon us].... Conceptualism properly conceived [contrast the position which is propounded by Kolakowski as quoted at S&SR pp. 168–9]... must insist that natural things and [the concepts they fall under] existed independently of whether our conceptions of them were destined to be fashioned or the things themselves were destined to be discovered [that answer to] these concepts... Our claim [is] only that what sortal concepts [better, what conceptions of what sortal concepts] we can bring to bear upon experience determines what we can find there—just as the size and mesh of a net determine, not what fish are in the sea, but which ones we shall catch.[9]

On this basis I am well placed to accept the first sentence of Ayers's [2]. The second sentence of [2] covers very well the case of natural substances, but as it stands, it applies less readily to most artefact-kinds. That is what Ayers intends. In Chapter 1 I recognize the sort of difficulties that Ayers sets out for artefacts, but I give the case for accepting artefacts as substances. I offer to pay the price for this acceptance by making a concession to constructivism that coheres with the artefactual subject-matter. See section 16 of Chapter 1. This concession need not complicate my acceptance of that which Ayers intends by [2] or his claims concerning the things that he prefers to accept as substances.

I need not quarrel too much with [3] but, even though Ayers and I differ over what things are to count as substances, I do need to distance myself from one of Ayers's ways of stating (p. 113) the difference he sees between his position and a conceptualist position such as my own: 'For the conceptualist all beings are concept-relative, for the realist some beings are concept-relative, but others,

---

[9] S&SR, pp. 149–52. There are similar formulations in S&S at pp. 138–40. Since Ayers makes no explicit reference to S&S, I have preferred the later and clearer version from S&SR. The differences do not bear on any point that is in dispute.

substances, are not'. Even if I were entirely content with [3], I could not quite bring myself to say that the pencil I am writing with—the pencil *itself*—was concept-relative, or that the much controverted ship of Theseus—the ship itself— was concept-relative. But Ayers was not forced or obliged to make his point in that way. In this matter, I want chiefly to insist first that nothing Ayers says discredits the sortalist account of identity in its application to substances or to anything else. I insist also that there are all sorts of similarities between the way in which we understand the natural world and the way in which we understand the man-made world.

Artefacts quite apart, Ayers in his justification of [3] enlarges also upon all the differences between natural substances and occurrences/events/processes. There I am entirely on his side (see *S&SR* p. 31 note 13), but I demur somewhat where he gives the impression that the differences that interest him depend on our speaking of human thinkers 'slicing [such] non-substances out of reality'. Frequently occurrences/events/processes *force* themselves upon us (just as natural substances can) and *then* we make sense of them. Think of a hurricane or a mudslide.

I come now to Ayers's [4]. In harmony with his views, Chapters 4 and 5 here register my own rejection of the distinction between persons and human beings. But the distinction or non-distinction between a mass of matter and a substance is a different question. As Chapter 2 makes plain, the distinction that first interested me was between the substance (e.g. the tree) and the aggregate of cellulose-molecules (or whatever) that constitute it. By reference to such examples, thinking of aggregates simply as quantities and deploying Leibniz's Law, I convinced myself that aggregates are not substances and substances are not aggregates. It would be much harder to show that aggregates are not even things. In 1968, the question I ought to have made it clearer I was left with was the philosophical or logical basis for the conviction that two *substances* cannot be in the same place at the same time. In regard to this question, I should like to concur in Ayers's thought that, if two substances were in the same place at the same time, they would place conflicting demands upon the disposition of the matter supposedly common to them. An aggregate does not place such demands and on these terms it seems it *can* co-occupy a space with a substance. I revert to these matters, however, at the end of the commentary that I append to the paper that is reprinted as the first part of Chapter 2.

7

Finally, I want to signal my agreement with the following passage from Michael Ayers's illustrious work. I agree with it provided only that the passage be read in the way that Ayers himself intended for it to be read where, following a usage different from mine, he wrote 'concept':

Any 'principle of individuation of a particular substance is to be sought not in a concept, but in reality, as the causal principle of a unity which is material and real, not imposed and ideal'.[10]

Knowing Ayers's usage of 'concept', I read this as denial that our *conception* of the concept that a thing falls under itself can itself lend either reality or a principle of individuation to a natural thing. Where natural things are concerned, I agree entirely. Indeed the conception, in the case where all is well with it, is itself a creature (in part) of that which it is a conception of, namely the thing itself and the kind to which the thing belongs.[11] It is these that impinge on the perceiver. If there is a residue of disagreement, it arises from Ayers's optimism and my own markedly lesser optimism concerning the *autonomous* usefulness—*in advance* of any answer at all to the '*what is it?*' question—of the notions of unity, unitariness, continuity, wholeness, etc. In this matter, I have long taken myself to be in closer agreement with something that Leibniz says. See Chapter 1, section 9 and footnote 17. 'Continuity alone, in and of itself, does not constitute substance, any more than multitude or number constitutes it. There has already to be *something or other* that is numbered [as a unity], or given over again, or continuous.' This is the truth that I have tried to find a way for us to live with.[12]

8

It is sometimes objected against the sortalist account of identity that it implies (first) that one cannot refer to a thing or single it out in experience unless one knows already what it is; and implies (secondly) that one can never tell whether a thing persists unless one knows already what it is. These would be devastating objections if they were upheld. I must respond to both.

What did I say to provoke the first of these charges? Here, for good or ill, is something I said about singling a thing out in experience: 'for a thinker to single out or individuate a substance, there must be something about what he does, something about his rapport with x or his relational state towards x, which

---

[10] Ayers, *Locke*, ii, p. 228.

[11] Cf. Leibniz: 'Nonne ipsi conceptus formantur ex rebus', Gerhardt, II, p. 182. (Are not our concepts/conceptions themselves formed from or shaped by the objects of which they are concepts/conceptions?) For the case of artefacts, we need the more complicated story that I try to tell in Chapter 1, section 16.

[12] Unity, unitariness, continuity wholeness...are surely determinables (see section 8, third paragraph) with a multitude of determinations. Whenever necessary, sortalism prompts us to make such determinations explicit.

sufficiently approximates to this: the thinker's singling *x* out as a thing of some kind or other *f* such that membership in *f* entails or implies some correct answer (known or unknown)[13] to the question "what is *x*?"' (*S&SR*, p. 7).

In giving this formulation in *S&SR*, I ought to have been more careful to allow for the distinction between simply perceiving a thing while taking it for what it is and the further development of this understanding that it takes for its possessor to grasp and even anticipate the way in which an object such as the one in question comes into being, changes and persists through change. I ought also to have emphasized in the way I do in the ensuing chapters how a thinker can refer to a thing in thought or speech even while fumbling, guessing or struggling to get a closer fix. I ought also to have elaborated upon the way in which, even in fumbling, etc., a thinker will bring to bear the general idea of *object of kind f*—the idea, that is, of the determinable *object of some kind or other to be determined*. In Chapter 11 and elsewhere I call the content thus italicized a formal concept. Among the *determinations* of this determinable will be sortal concepts which count as sufficient to answer Aristotle's question *what is it?*

It may assist to illustrate just one of these possibilities of singling out by an example reminiscent of discussions which long ago ensued upon the posthumous publication of J. L. Austin's *Sense and Sensibilia* (Oxford: Oxford University Press, 1962). Peter and Paul are walking across hill and dale in search of a house they have been lent for the night but know only by the description given to them by the owner X. As they reach the top of a hill and look down into the next valley, one says to the other 'Can you make out that dot in the distance, to the right of what looks like a poplar? I wonder whether that's the cottage.' It proves in due course that he is right. In the sense intended, the dot was indeed X's cottage. Of course this last is no ordinary identity-statement. Peter and Paul were not going to spend the night in a dot. But, applying the formal concept *object* by reference to the dot that each made out, Peter and Paul did single out the cottage in question.[14] They found it. Even before they were sure they had found it, they had already singled it out.

Now the second objection. Suppose someone asks you to look after a small object that you don't recognize as belonging to any kind that you are familiar

---

[13] It does not matter how *articulately* he knows this. All he needs is clear indistinct (or effective, untheorized) knowledge. Cf. *S&SR* pp. 80–5; Leibniz, 'Meditationes de Cognitione, Veritate et Ideis', Gerhardt, IV, p. 442; Chapter 1 in the present collection, section 8; and Chapter 3, section 9.1.

[14] 'Dot', like 'blob', 'smudge', 'streak'..., belongs to the phenomenal language we sometimes use in the struggle to situate ourselves or to identify things. It is inessential of course, often or usually, to that struggle. But it offers striking confirmation of the role of the formal or determinable concept. See also Chapter 11.

with. Suppose you put the object on the mantelpiece and take it down again five weeks later when your friend asks for it back. Suppose it hasn't changed or been interfered with. Then, on this basis alone,[15] and without finding out any more about the object, or knowing quite what it is, you can be sure that *for every kind f*, if the object belongs to *f*, then the object you give back to your friend is the same *f* as the one that he entrusted to you. (Even for the solemn purposes of philosophy it may be useful to remember that, just as we can tell that *someone* has stolen our watch without knowing who has taken it, we can tell, if we still have the watch, that *everyone* is such as to be innocent of stealing it.)

9

To conclude this introduction, let me mention a question about identity that is almost entirely foreign to the concerns of this book. Suppose that Pierre, gloomy, desperate, and at sea with the world or himself, asks himself 'Who am I?' Suppose that Pierre knows perfectly well where he is, where he lives, where he was born, who his mother, father, and brother are, yet he still feels at the mercy of nameless forces. Suppose he is helplessly uncertain what work to look for or what life to pursue, uncertain where he fits into the scheme of things, uncertain where or with what larger collective 'us' he belongs. If so, then his question about who he is differs markedly from the sort of question that metaphysicians ask (and different also from the questions asked by one who has really and truly 'lost his mind').

What is the relation of Pierre's question to the metaphysical-cum-logical questions that will concern us in this book? Well, Pierre needs to ask himself what he in his particularity is to aspire to be or to become or to make of himself. But he knows well enough already who has to answer these questions. He knows full well who that is. His real perplexity might then be understood as being about *what* he is—or *what* he is to be—rather than about *who* he is.[16] Another aspect of Pierre's plight suggests that he should ask himself to what cause or métier or collective *we* he owes his allegiance or loyalty. Again, however, he knows full well who this question is about. And he knows who has to answer it.

Questions of the kind which trouble Pierre are not the questions that engage metaphysics or logic. The concern of metaphysics or logic is with the individuation, among a multitude of other things, of enquirers such as Pierre. The concern is with what it takes to single out such a being and to track his existence

---

[15] If it *has* been interfered with, there may be doubts. For some alterations might entail that the original object is no longer. That will depend on what it is.

[16] To put it another way, this is a question of *qualis?* not *quis?*

in the world at large—both after and before Pierre 'finds himself'. The concern is with the identification and singling out of substances—substances of this or that kind.

Pierre's sort of question and our sorts of questions are equally real, but such different questions that it ought to be almost impossible to confuse them.

1

Identity, Individuation, and Substance

1

My subject is identity and individuation. By identity I mean being the same as. By individuation I mean something done by a thinker. Among acts of individuation I include (1) singling out something which is a *g* (a donkey, say) as a *g*; (2) distinguishing that *g* from other *g*s; (3) singling something out when coming upon it again and recognizing it as that *g*, the same *g* again.[1] It will appear in due course how I take identity and individuation to be connected. By a substance I intend, with tradition, something singular or individual, a single particular object or individual thing. Unlike a universal/type/sort/kind/clone/character, a substance does not have specimens or instances. Nothing falls under it, exemplifies it or instantiates it.[2]

The approach I shall commend to questions of identity and individuation will be a sortalist one, claiming among other things that the identity of *x* and *y* is to be determined by reference to some fundamental kind *f* that *x* and *y* each exemplify. This approach is prefigured in Aristotle's question, definitive of his category of substance, *ti esti* or *what is it?* Contrast the question, definitive of his category of quality, *what is it like?* It is no longer wise to assume, however, as I once was apt to do, that everyone with a serious interest in the metaphysics of identity will know Aristotle's distinction or be eager to read such texts as

---

[1] Some of the acts included in this list, like others I might adjoin, go beyond the dictionary definition of 'individuate'. No matter. The word itself does no distinctive philosophical work here beyond suggesting some of the questions to be pursued and answers to be proposed.

In due course the adjective 'individuative' will appear as qualifying thoughts or notions or terms, connoting various relations that such things can have to the business of individuation by a thinker confronting the world of substances. Such a thinker is finding his way in the world, needless to say, not creating it.

[2] It can of course be copied, but that is different.

Categories, Chapters 1–5. Nor can the other Aristotelian resonances by which I once set such store be relied upon any longer to enlighten or remind. If they have any effect, it is rather to cast doubt on my claim to have arrived at a general account—an account not at odds with anything that modern science reveals to us—of the identity and individuation of objects which are extended in space and persist through time.

So putting to one side the insights of Aristotle—who will enter now only at the point where the argument simply forces our attention onto him—we shall proceed here more simply and single-mindedly, starting from the bare logic of the identity relation and setting the still underestimated requirements of that logic in authority over the judgements of same and other into which we are constrained by the effort to make sense of the world of perpetual alteration in which we have to find our way.

2

In partial illustration of the extent and nature of the perpetual alteration aforesaid, let me set the scene for our enquiry by drawing from a work of science which was as important in its day as it was lucid of expression:

[In the living animal] the large and complex molecules and their component units are constantly involved in rapid chemical reactions... Part of the pool of newly formed small molecules constantly re-enters vacant places in the large molecules to restore the fats, the proteins, and the nucleoproteins... Components of an animal are rapidly degraded into specific molecular groupings which may wander from one place to another. The chemical reactions must be balanced so delicately that, through regeneration, the body components remain constant in total amount and in structure.... All regeneration reactions must be enzymatic in nature. The large molecules, such as the fats and the proteins, are, under the influence of lytic enzymes, constantly being degraded to their constituent fragments. These changes are balanced by synthetic processes which must be coupled to other chemical reactions, such as oxidation or dephosphorylation. After death, when the oxidative systems disappear, the synthetic processes also cease, and the unbalanced degradative reactions lead to the collapse of the thermodynamically unstable structural elements. In general, every regeneration reaction involving an increase in free energy must be coupled with another process. In order to maintain structure against its tendency to collapse, work has to be done. The replacement of a brick fallen from a wall requires energy, and in the living organism energy debts are paid by chemical reactions...[3]

---

[3] R. Schoenheimer, *The Dynamic State of Body Constituents* (Cambridge, MA: Harvard University Press, 1942), pp. 62–4.

In other words:

All constituents of living matter, whether functional or structural, of simple or of complex constitution, are in steady state of rapid flux.[4]

Heraclitus, the first Western thinker to recognize the cosmic significance of change, is commonly reputed to have denied, precisely on the basis of the processes of change, all possibility of identity through change. But he did not deny it:

Upon those who step into the same rivers different and again different waters flow. The waters scatter and gather, come together and flow away, approach and depart.[5]

On the whole view I take of Heraclitus, it was the maintenance or perpetuation of the world order—and *within* that order the persistence through time of changeable things such as rivers ('the same rivers')—that Heraclitus chiefly set out to describe, redescribe, and explain. However obscurely, his account of these matters anticipates Schoenheimer's.[6] But one will understand these accounts best if one does not misconstrue the common sense of identity.

3

We begin upon that common sense by setting forth the logical nature of the relation. First we have the obvious truth where everybody begins, the reflexivity of identity:

For all x, x is the same thing as x.

In second place, we have Leibniz's principle, the Indiscernibility of Identicals. This requires that, if x is the same thing as y, then x and y have all the same properties:

If x is identical with y, then x is F if and only if y is F.[7]

---

[4] Schoenheimer, *The Dynamic State of Body Constituents*, p. 3.
[5] Fragments 12 and 91, as reunited by Geoffrey Kirk in *Heraclitus: The Cosmic Fragments*, intro. and trans. G. S. Kirk (Cambridge: Cambridge University Press, 1954).
[6] Compare fragment 125 which puts one in mind of the last portion of our first extract from Schoenheimer and the work that maintains structure: 'The barley drink disintegrates and loses its nature unless it is constantly stirred.' (Texts for this and other citations from Heraclitus are given as B12, B91, B125 in H. Diels and W. Kranz, *Die Fragmente der Vorsokratiker* (6th edn, Berlin: Weidermann, 1952). On the interpretation of Heraclitus, see Chapter 6.) Compare also J. Z. Young, quoted at *S&S*, p. vii.
[7] Cf. W. V. Quine, 'Review of Milton K. Munitz (ed.), *Identity and Individuation*', *Journal of Philosophy*, 69 (1972), p. 490. Here Quine interprets 'F' by specifying the intended replacements for this letter. He also explains the reason why this formal version is better than the informal version, to which I resort so often in the text, in terms of properties.

4   IDENTITY, INDIVIDUATION, AND SUBSTANCE

From these two principles, taken together, there follow the symmetry and transitivity of identity. Suppose $x = y$ and $y = z$. Then x has any property that y has. But y is z. So x is z. That gives transitivity. Now symmetry. Suppose $x = y$. Then y has any property that x has. One of x's properties is being the same as x. (Contrast the property of being the same as itself. Everything has *that* property.) So y too has the property of being the same as x. So y is x. That gives symmetry.

There are three further consequences. The first is the necessity of identity:

If x is the same thing as y, then x is necessarily the same thing as y.

Proof: x is necessarily x. So, by the Indiscernibility principle, the object y has the same property as x has, namely the property of being necessarily the same thing as x.[8]

In the displayed version given in the text, the 'is' is intended timelessly. But it may help against misunderstandings that prompt doubts concerning identities among things that change through time if I spell out the Indiscernibility principle in another way:

If x is identical with y (simply identical, whether tensedly or timelessly) then, if and only if x is, was, or will be F, y is, was, or will be F.

[8] In answer to questions that may be raised about the possibility of a referential opacity created by 'necessarily', see *S&SR*, pp. 115 ff. See also Chapter 9.

Timothy Williamson, afforcing earlier work of Prior and Kripke (see *S&SR*, pp. 116-17), explains how, by the addition of one further principle beyond the two we have started with here—namely the so-called Brouwersche principle: *if not p, then necessarily not necessarily p*—we may obtain the necessity of difference as well as that of identity. See Timothy Williamson, 'The Necessity and Determinacy of Distinctness', in Sabina Lovibond and S. G. Williams (eds), *Essays for David Wiggins: Identity, Truth and Value* (Oxford: Blackwell, 1996) pp. 1-17, reported at *S&SR*, p. 117, as follows:

Begin with the necessity of identity as we find it in Barcan and Kripke (H and P being, say, Hesperus and Phosphorus);

$(H=P) \rightarrow \Box(H=P)$

Contraposing this, we have

Not $\Box(H=P) \rightarrow$ Not$(H=P)$.

Being proven from a theorem, this is a theorem. So we have the necessity of it:

$\Box($Not $\Box(H=P) \rightarrow$ Not$(H=P))$.

And then, by the modal principle $\Box(A \rightarrow B) \rightarrow (\Box A \rightarrow \Box B)$, we have

$\Box($Not $\Box(H=P)) \rightarrow \Box(Not(H=P))$.

But by the Brouwersche principle, we have

Not$(H=P) \rightarrow \Box($Not $\Box(H=P))$.

In which case, by virtue of the last two formulae and the transitivity of $\rightarrow$, we have

Not$(H=P) \rightarrow \Box($Not$(H=P))$.

In other words, if Hesperus is different from Phosphorus, then it is necessary that Hesperus be different from Phosphorus.

The same scheme of argument guarantees the determinacy of the relation of identity:[9]

If x is the same thing as y, then x is
absolutely and determinately the same thing as y

For x is absolutely and determinately the same thing as x. (Any fuzziness attaching supposedly to x or to true conceptions of x will pair off exactly with that same fuzziness attaching, again, to x or to conceptions of x.) So once it is given that y is x, it must be that y has the property of being absolutely and determinately the same as x. Their identity is not a matter of degree. Similarly we have the permanence of identity:

If x is the same thing as y then x is always the same thing as y.

Proof: x is always the same thing as x. So y, which is the same as x, has x's property of being always the same thing as x.

4

What flows from these findings?

Downwind from the necessity of identity we have the thought that, if x is the same thing as y, then their identity will hold regardless of how matters stand with other things. The identity of x with y will not then involve or depend upon anything that is different from or independent of x or y. The identity of x and y may of course be discovered in all sorts of ways that involve reference to other things, but constitutively the identity of x and y involves only x and y.[10]

Downwind from the Indiscernibility principle, we have an Adequacy requirement: whatever grounds the identity of x with y must by that same token, ground the indiscernibility of x and y.[11] This implies that, in the presence of an adequate reason to think that x is the same as y, there is adequate reason to think that, for

---

[9] See S&SR, pp. 188-92. The argument that follows relates to the metaphysical and matter-of-fact determinacy of the identity relation. Where the relation holds, it holds determinately. This is not yet to say that all identity questions are decidable or cannot be contestable. Nor can the fact that the identity relation is determinate, absolute, and not a matter of degree prevent questions of enough, good enough, or not good enough from arising *within the construction of the case* for accepting an identity. If the case is not conclusive, the outcome can be 'probably'. It cannot be 'nearly'. We return to determinacy at section 4, note 12, and then at the end of section 16.

[10] In S&SR, chapter 3, section 4, I tried to extend this near-truism into a principle D(x), the much controverted *Only a and b* rule. In replacing that rule by the Adequacy principle given in the next paragraph, I hope to confirm in another way some of the results I sought to achieve through that rule.

[11] The grounds for a claim of identity need not amount to a deduction.

all *z*, however *x* is to *z*, so too will *y* be to *z*. The importance of this requirement will appear—along with the sortalist way of meeting it—when one confronts questions of splitting or fusion. Our claim will be that nothing can count as a ground of identity unless it arises from a conception of a kind or sort of thing which *x* and *y* each exemplify *and* this same conception vindicates the unqualified or *ceteris paribus* presumable transitivity of the identity relation. See section 10.

Consider next the permanence of identity. The identity of an object or a person is altogether unlike a hat or garment that one can take off or put on. In the literal sense there is no such thing as something's or someone's getting a new identity. The one way in which a thing that persists *cannot* change, so long as it maintains whatever steady and particular state of rapid flux is essential to it, is in respect of being the changeable thing, the cow, horse, human being...that it is. There are not two relations among substances, namely simple identity and identity over time or through change—no more than there are varieties of sameness (unless mere similarity, not strict identity, is the relation at issue). Identity over time or through change is the simple or ordinary identity of things that last over time or through change. It is the identity relation as restricted to things that change.

The absoluteness and determinacy of the identity relation will discourage us from trying to make sense of identities or of objects that are vague or indeterminate,[12] but it cannot exclude vague or indeterminate *conceptions* of this or that object itself or of the sortal concept it falls under—or of both. Section 16 *ad fin.* returns to this matter.[13]

From the determinacy of identity we may advance further perhaps. Where identity is concerned, it seems impossible to make sense of 'almost'. Why? Well, *x* is neither almost *x* nor almost not *x*. So, if *y* is *x*, then *y* is neither almost *x* nor almost not *x*.[14] That flows from indiscernibility. Given also the principle of

---

[12] If the necessity of difference is added to the necessity of identity (see note 8) and we treat 'determinately' as relevantly similar to 'necessarily', then through the same argument (reported in note 8) we obtain the determinacy of difference in addition to the determinacy of identity. See again Williamson, 'Necessity', countering my 'On Singling Out an Object Determinately', in Philip Pettit and John McDowell (eds), *Subject, Thought, and Context* (Oxford: Clarendon Press, 1986). See section 16, where both the need and the means are shown for accepting this conclusion that, if *x* and *y* are different, then they are determinately different. Their difference is not a matter of degree.

[13] For the Lockean term 'sortal' and its continuing usefulness, see P. F. Strawson, *Individuals: An Essay in Descriptive Metaphysics* (London: Methuen, 1959), Part Two.

[14] There is more about 'almost' at the end of section 16. I adjourn for another day most of the questions that will arise about compound quasi-sortal concepts such as *heap of coal, bar of soap, lump of clay,* and the tolerance of the 'indeterminate particulars' that fall under them of diminution, replacement, exchange of their constituents, vel sim. See *S&S*, pp. 205–6; *S&SR*, pp. 94, 37–40.

Such particulars may seem, however, to furnish counterexamples to the claims I have made about 'almost'. In this regard, see David Lewis, 'Many, but almost one', in Keith Campbell, John Bacon, and

permanence, one then arrives at the thought that y not only isn't almost x but never was almost x. Nor then can it ever have been a close run thing for y to have been the same thing as x. By contrast, consider growing tall enough to be a guardsman or strong enough to lift 50 kilograms. One can describe what more it would take or would have taken to do that. Where identity is concerned, however, it appears that there is no describing anything like that. If y is not x, what chance could y ever have had of being the same as x?

If identity is all or nothing and leaves no room for nearly or almost, doesn't that rule out saying of someone that he just missed being the King of Sweden or was almost the first to discover oxygen? No. Once one thinks for a moment what is being said here, it is clear that in neither of these cases is there anybody whom he is being said to be almost identical with. All that is being said is that the person in question came close to being crowned King of Sweden or almost discovered oxygen before anyone else discovered oxygen.

5

So far we have been following through the necessary conditions of identity. But what are the sufficient conditions?

Here philosophers often deploy a principle of Leibniz's, the Identity of Indiscernibles:

If x and y have all their properties in common then x is y.

Lloyd Reinhardt (eds), *Ontology, Causality and Mind: Essays on the philosophy of D. M. Armstrong* (Cambridge: Cambridge University Press, 1993), pp. 23–37. Think here of a lump of clay and a part of it which excludes one molecule. On this I shall offer a single observation. But first let us distinguish (i) *the same lump of clay* from (ii) *the same clay*; and, under (ii), let us distinguish (iia) *the same kind of clay* (irrelevant) from (iib) the very same parcel or portion of clay.

In case (i), we normally tolerate diminution—almost to the point of the lump's total disappearance. Such tolerance is controlled by the use to which we put the lump. Think of a bar of soap, which continues through its diminutions as one and the same bar. It is a sort of artefact. Our thoughts here are precisely not mereological. Nor do we need 'almost' to qualify any of the claims of identity that we find reasons to affirm concerning the piece of soap.

In case (iib) our concern is with the clay in question. We care about its continued presence without addition or subtraction. Here our concern *is* mereological. In the terms proposed by Helen Morris Cartwright in 'Quantities', *Philosophical Review*, 79 (1970), pp. 25–42, one may say that our concern is with a *quantity*. Where identity of quantities is at issue, exactitude is everything. If we say that quantity q_1 is almost the same as quantity q_2, then all that that can be understood as meaning is that q_1 comprises almost the same amount of clay as q_2 contains. But an amount is a *measure* of quantity, not a quantity. And where measures are concerned, approximation is not well described as near-*identity*.

8   IDENTITY, INDIVIDUATION, AND SUBSTANCE

If we admit properties such as being the same person as Caesar or being the same building as the Pantheon, this principle is undeniable but useless. What we need here is a sufficient condition which does not presuppose identity.

One could try to follow Leibniz a little more closely. Claiming on the basis of his Principle of Sufficient Reason that there could never be two individuals indiscernible from one another, Leibniz sometimes appears to have believed that relations, including relations that appear to us as temporal and spatial, all supervened or depended in some special way on the totality of the successive states of the true substances of the world. In this spirit, one could interpret the Identity of Indiscernibles in a way that presupposed that all real properties were monadic.[15] But, even where every substance is unique, the Identity of Indiscernibles is still a questionable basis for any *general* definition or explication of identity.[16] It is worth noting, moreover, that in the world as we know it the Principle must be wrong, because one cannot exclude the possibility of an extended object that is perfectly symmetrical about all planes which bisect it. In the terms prescribed, how could one distinguish one half of the thing from its other half?

6

Let us put the monadic interpretation to one side and try another approach. Let us admit relational properties but purify them of all reference to particular objects already identified. Now however—as is well known—the Identity of Indiscernibles encounters another problem, concerning symmetry. Consider square 22 and square 43 on the chess board (Figure 1.1) that Strawson gives on page 123 of his book *Individuals*.

Strawson writes:

Think of a chess board. The universe we are to consider is bounded by its edges. The universe consists therefore of a limited arrangement of black and white squares... The problem is to provide individuating descriptions of each square, and to do so in terms of the view of the rest of the board obtained from each square... The problem cannot be solved even if the view from each square is allowed to comprehend the whole board. It is still impossible to differentiate square 43 from square 22. The view from each over the

---

[15] For discussion of Leibniz's doctrine here, see *S&SR*, p. 62.

[16] I note that *this* point is available to Leibniz himself—just in so far as it approximates to the claim that identity is a primitive and indefinable notion. See G. W. Leibniz, *New Essays on Human Understanding*, trans. and ed. Peter Remnant and Jonathan Bennett (Cambridge: Cambridge University Press, 1981), Book I, Chapter 3: 'The ideas of *being, possible* and *same* are so thoroughly innate that they enter into all our thoughts and reasoning, and I regard them as essential to our mind'.

Figure 1.1

whole board is the same: each has two white squares going away from it in one diagonal direction and five in the other...

In other words, one who considers the universe Strawson describes and who has none of the normal resources of demonstrative thinking and *nothing else to go by* except the principle of the Identity of Indiscernibles will be bound to identify the distinct squares 43 and 22.

At this point friends of the Identity of Indiscernibles[17] will object against Strawson that, even if squares 22 and 43 cannot be separated by reference to properties provided for in Strawson's set-up, these squares are 'relatively discernible'; 43 is to the left of 22, for instance. Nor is it true, they will say, that whatever square directly adjoins 22 directly adjoins 43. But where does such a defence leave us? With constructions or thought-experiments such as Strawson's, do the said friends want us to be concerned with inhabitants of the chessboard-world or with those who think about it without inhabiting it? If the first, then the objectors are taking advantage of the inhabitants' presumed mastery of demonstrative thinking within the layout of their chessboard world. But if the second then are not the objectors taking for granted the mastery of demonstrative thought and the grasp of left and right that enable Strawson and the rest of us who theorize about identity to distinguish the qualitatively identical halves of the chessboard? Can a grasp of Leibniz's Identity of Indiscernibles be all there is to demonstrative thinking? How can the understanding of the Identity of

---

[17] See, for instance, John Hawthorne, *Metaphysical Essays* (Oxford: Oxford University Press, 2006), pp. 8–11; compare also Willard Van Orman Quine, *Word and Object* (Cambridge, MA: MIT Press, 1960), pp. 230–1.

Indiscernibles be sufficient by itself for all the purposes of reference or the assignment of names?

7

Why am I so sure that there must be some other way of thinking about same and other that is independent of the Identity of Indiscernibles? Well, we do arrive at judgements of identity. We do so almost effortlessly in many ordinary cases. Yet imagine the process of trying to do so by enumerating all the properties of x and comparing them with all the properties of y. Without yet knowing any identities concerning x—without knowing properties of x other than those which are manifest at the moment of attempting the comparison—how could one assemble all the properties of x itself in order to check them against all the properties of y? There must be some other way—a way accessible in principle to someone who looks out at an object for the first time, keeps track of it and learns in due course to recognize it when coming upon it again. At this point the metaphysics of identity has no alternative, I suggest, but to reconstruct the thoughts that organize the epistemology of the relation and to reconstruct what thinkers actually do when they single out an object in experience, at once observing the thing's behaviour, speculating what it does when out of view and searching for the distinguishing marks (if any) by which this particular object may be distinguished from other members of its kind and (however fallibly) reidentified as one and the same.

8

According to the sortalist conception of identity which I have tried over the years to propound and defend, the question that organizes the efforts of one who seeks to track an object continuously through the changes that it undergoes is this: 'What kind of a thing is this object before me? What is it? How does such a thing behave?' At this point, having been driven hither by the search for a workable sufficient condition of identity—driven by nothing less than the logic of the matter—we ought to attend to Aristotle. For the *what is it?* question is Aristotle's question. According to him, substantives such as *man, apple tree, horse*...not only signal the appearances of the things we single out under these denominations but imply also a *phusis* or nature. The *phusis* of a thing is its mode of being. It is the principle of activity (activity or passivity, perhaps one should say, or behaviour or functioning) characteristic of a kind whose members share and possess in themselves a distinctive source of development and change by reference to which the persistence of a thing that has that nature can be determined and things of that kind identified and reidentified. Compare *Metaphysics* 1015a11, *Physics* 192b21.

The problem we had with a sufficient condition of identity was that we could not find any general condition. But the reason why we couldn't—or so it now appears—is that there is no such general or unitary condition to discover. When we ask whether *a* is the same as *b*, we must be ready to ask what *a* is and what *b* is, to consider what it would have taken to track each of them, to reconstruct the paths each one takes or has taken, looking at the same time for any marks that distinguish *a* or distinguish *b* among other instances of its kind. Despite divers analogies and structural resemblances, the *phuseis* (natures) of things are many and various.

Here I offer a Leibnizian supplement to Aristotle. What guides our individual and collective efforts to make sense of the world, to track things, and to reconstruct or imagine that which befalls them in the course of their traverse from one place to another outside our view, is a rough and ready but developing conception of what (sort of thing) a man, an apple tree, a horse... is. Leibniz would say it is a *clear indistinct idea*, an applicable and practically effective conception of such a thing, but a conception ready and waiting to be supplanted by what Leibniz would call a *more distinct idea* of it—an idea or conception that is better informed and more analytical or articulated.[18] As we enquire into the nature of that which confronts us, we subsume it provisionally and tentatively under more and more specific conceptions of the *phusis* which it instantiates, simultaneously inquiring into that *phusis* and correcting or refining our ideas about the *phuseis* of a host of other kinds that we encounter. (Compare Aristotle, *Posterior Analytics*, II, 19.) Our aptitude for this kind of work is all of a piece with our practical capacity to grasp the meanings of the substantives for thing-kinds which we learn not from verbal definitions but from examples that we encounter or that are shown to us. What helps to validate the work itself is that it must treat the conclusions it arrives at as answerable in the end to the formal properties of identity and to the Adequacy Requirement.

9

Here let us expect an objection. There is simply no difficulty, it may be said, in keeping a thing under continuous observation without making reference to any

---

[18] Cf. *S&SR*, pp. 80–5 and my 'Three Moments in the Theory of Definition or Analysis: its Possibility, its Aim or Aims and its Limit or Terminus', *Proceedings of the Aristotelian Society*, 107 (2006-7), section 8. Do not be surprised that Leibniz should appear on more than one side of this argument. That is the prerogative of a mind open to anything or everything.

sort or kind. Indeed it simply has to be possible to do this. Otherwise we could never fix upon a thing in order to ask *what is it?*

I reply by reverting to Leibniz's distinction between clear (workable/operationally applicable) ideas or conceptions of a thing-kind and more distinct (more analytical or scientifically and otherwise spelled out) ideas or conceptions. In this connection Leibniz would point out that, if we did not bring to experience something not itself of experience, we should be unable to make anything of experience. Innate within us there has to be not only an eagerness to look for continuities and a willingness to associate one presentation with some earlier presentation, but a predisposition also to search out certain particular kinds of thing. Different animals have evolved no doubt to search out different kinds. But everywhere the instinctual and pre-experiential idea which is implicit in our strivings and presides over them, has, I claim, to be an instinctual or innate grasp of the idea *object or substance of some sort f.* More precisely we need the conception: *object or substance endowed with its principle of activity/ functioning.*[19] It is not the bare idea of an object or the idea of a bare object to which might then be superadded just any nature or way of being and behaving. That is not the idea we work from. But suppose that, rather than work, as I think we do, from some, however provisional, determination of the idea of an object or substance of some particular sort endowed with its own discoverable principle of activity or functioning, we did operate with the bare idea of an object (or the idea of a bare object). Then what thoughts would that idea prompt us to have, and what questions to ask, when we witnessed the metamorphosis of the caterpillar into a chrysalis and the chrysalis into a moth or butterfly? What thoughts would we have in watching a warehouse fire in which a bronze statue is reduced to a molten lump of metal? Everyone will agree no doubt that the statue is now a molten lump of metal. But what does it mean to say that? A simple continuity criterion of identity requires that this verdict be taken to be a verdict of identity. But that reading is at fault.[20] The notion of identity it invokes cannot subject itself to the requirements we have derived from the logic of the relation. Apply Leibniz's Law (the Indiscernibility of Identicals, not the

---

[19] That is to say that implicit in these instinctual strivings is the inarticulate grasp of a *formal concept*. Such a formal concept is a determinable whose determinations are more and more specific kinds of thing. See Chapter 11, which bears upon the rest of the complaint made by the objector who figures in the first paragraph of this section (9). The formal concept here in question is of course a first-level concept.

[20] The true meaning must be that the statue was made up from the material which is now a molten lump. See *S&SR*, pp. 39–43, revising similar passages in *ISTC*.

Further to the examples given in the text against any simple continuity criterion, consider the human zygote, to be treated in the next section. See note 25.

Identity of Indiscernibles). The lump of metal has survived the fire. The statue has not survived it. The statue was made by Rodin (say); this mass of metal was not. And now consider transitivity. In the subsequent adventures of the lump, what else will the bare continuity theorist be forced to say the statue is identical with? What else will he end up identifying the statue with? Bare continuity supplies no principle, no rhyme or reason.[21] Moreover, in bypassing the *what is it?* question and neglecting to ask how a thing of the kind in question comes into being, persists or passes away, the bare continuity theory will not compel us to ask what it is we have in front of us. Is it a proper continuant? Or is it something rather different? Suppose that we confront at a given moment an amoeba, a thing which perpetuates its lineage by dividing. The amoeba we confront cannot be traced through its divisions as one and the same substance. The lineage is a particular lineage but scarcely a particular substance. The lineage is something realized and instantiated by short-lived particulars. It is a sort of universal.

10

Until we reached the question of a sufficient condition, the logic of identity seemed simple and austere. The ragged or discursive character of everything that I have been claiming since we began upon the question of sufficiency has none of that simplicity or austerity. So it needs to be shown how the sortal conception of identity can satisfy the formal requirements we began with.

Let us begin here with the best case, namely where we have a natural kind whose members, the *g*s, share in a *phusis* which brings with it an empirically discoverable real principle of activity or nature which underlies and undergirds— in ways that Putnam and Kripke (and in his own way Leibniz) have each described—the application of certain ordinary substantives or sortal predicates. Where the workings of such a nature serve to demarcate a kind of organism with a settled single-track pattern of coming to be, maturation and passing away, and where that nature enters into our conception of the concept under which we single out members of the kind,[22] the judgements of same and other which we

---

[21] Compare Leibniz: 'La continuité toute seule ne constitue pas la substance non plus que la multitude ou le nombre la constitue...Il faut quelque chose qui soit numeroté ou répété ou continué', Gerhardt, II, p. 170. The demand that an object or substance be 'unitary' invites a similar comment: one *what*?

[22] This is to say that that nature informs any sortal conception or idea that is good enough to enable one who possesses that conception to single out members of the extension of the concept. See Chapter 8. In my neo-Fregean usage, the concept lies at the level of reference (Bedeutung) and the conception or idea lies at the level of sense. Among conceptions of a concept some are conceptions of

arrive at on the basis of our conception of that nature will determine a relation that shadows or recapitulates the way in which properties come to qualify particular organisms of this type. We have here everything we need to meet the Adequacy Requirement which was explained in section 4, third paragraph. The transitivity of the relation we are invoking in making these judgements flows from something inherent to the kind of thing we are concerned with.[23] These judgements arise from our capacity to track a thing of that kind and in their collectivity they reconstruct a sequence of states or phases that are states or phases of a kind of thing that is possessed of the whole complex of dispositions and other properties which underlie such a thing's mode of behaviour or activity.[24]

Even here though there are complications. Consider a conspicuous paradigm of substance-hood such as the human being. Where twins will be born and the zygote divides, the formal properties of identity will fall into jeopardy unless we conceive of the organism as starting upon its own proper existence or life from a point—some fourteen days after fertilization—after which division is embryologically impossible. In so far as this shaping of our idea of the life span of the creature is applied to all the organisms in question (is not reserved for cases where the zygote does in fact divide), it fills out the idea of that kind of continuant or substance and enlarges our understanding of its moral and metaphysical import. It is that idea thus refined and delimited by empirical enquiry that furnishes a ground of identity that meets the standard set by the Adequacy Requirement.[25] (See section 4, third paragraph.)

---

a sortal concept and thus conceptions (inter alia) of how a thing has to be and what it has to be in order to belong to the extension of the concept. For a diagram illustrative of these dispositions, see Chapters 4 and 8. See also Introduction, section 4.

[23] This assurance is not to be confused with an assurance against all error in the identification of things with that nature, or against other misconceptions of that nature itself. There is never such an assurance.

[24] Compare the passage from Leibniz's preface to *New Essays*, quoted in *S&SR*, p. 84.

[25] It may be asked why, in the cases where no division takes place, we shouldn't identify the zygote with the embryo—even as we shall identify the embryo with the future foetus and the foetus with the future baby. But in the case of the zygote which may divide that would be a failure to follow through the conception of human being that was motivated by the logic of identity. That logic demands that any true ground of identity should satisfy a requirement which is only the corollary of the Indiscernibility Principle. (See note 11 and Section 4 thereabouts.) Contrast with such respect for the Adequacy Requirement a kind-conception which has the organism begin as a zygote—or as an egg, or a gamete (why not?)—allowing at the same time that some zygotes do and some zygotes do not end up as single whole embryos.

11

Where the nature of a thing is not nomologically grounded in the way just described—as also in cases which involve interference in the normal workings of an object's principle of activity—it is only to be expected that our theories of identity and individuation will encounter numerous difficulties. That will trouble us soon enough. (See sections 16 and 17.) First though I want to review the defences of the conception which we have been taking for granted, the conception I mean of the world of changeable, enduring objects that are extended in space and persist through time.

Parmenides, asking how something that is could possibly come to be from what is not, gave logical arguments to show that that which truly is—the real reality—must be changeless, imperishable, one, unique, boundless on all sides, 'motionless in the limits of mighty bonds', continuous and without spatial or temporal differentiation. His argument was effectively disarmed when Aristotle showed that the challenge Parmenides had set out could be divided and then answered piecemeal. It was disarmed completely. But it seems the question of change never goes away. The most recent challenge comes from a new picture and a new argument. If we are to understand change, it is urged, we must replace our everyday or *endurantist* conception of substances by a less familiar so-called *perdurantist*—or, as I might prefer to say, *stroboscopic*—conception. The things we take to be enduring (it is argued) are really successions of changeless, distinct and instantaneous temporal parts.

12

David Lewis writes:

Sometimes you sit and then you are bent; sometimes you stand or lie, and then you are straight. How can one and the same thing have two contrary intrinsic properties? How does it help to say [as the endurantists say] that it has them at different times?[26]

Lewis's explanation of 'intrinsic' may be given as follows:

We distinguish *intrinsic* properties, which things have in virtue of the way they themselves are, from extrinsic properties, which they have in virtue of their relations or lack of relations to other things.[27]

---

[26] David Lewis, 'Tensing the Copula', *Mind*, 111 (2002), pp. 1–14.
[27] David Lewis, *On the Plurality of Worlds* (Oxford: Blackwell, 1986). p. 61.

Lewis is right to insist that being straight and being bent are not extrinsic properties. These are not relational properties. But does the fact that I was (at t_1) sitting and was later (at t_2) standing really render such properties relational?[28]

If I am seated now, today, in front of a wooden table, does the involvement here of the wooden table, the time, and the place make my being seated into a relational state? How can that involvement have that effect? In so far as there is a relation in the offing here, I protest, it surely holds between (1) a non-relational and faultlessly intrinsic state, my state of having sat down or being seated, the state itself resulting from the action/event that initiated the state; and (2) the scene (at that table/that time/that place) where that action or event of sitting down took place. What can prevent what is *already* an intrinsic state from having a relation to a time or place? All we need to do is to render the reference to an intrinsic state explicit.

For formal purposes there may be a reason to represent 'David was seated at table t during the period p...' by R(d,t,p...). But this notation was never designed to reveal the whole nature of the verb/predicate R nor even the plurality and diversity of everything that might be supplied to places held open within the brackets.[29] We learn nothing from the notation itself about the philosophically serious idea of a relation that David Lewis needs to call in evidence if he seeks to insist upon the non-relational intrinsic character of being bent, straight... sitting, standing....

13

With Lewis's argument in front of us concerning what he calls 'temporary intrinsic' properties, a word now about the proposal that Lewis draws from it, namely to transfer onto a succession of nouns the temporal indication that seems to qualify the verb. Thus the sentence 'David sits at t', usually understood as saying that the enduring continuant David sits at time t, has to be recast as saying of the momentary thing, David-at-t, that it/he sits.

---

[28] See Bede Rundle, *Time, Space, and Metaphysics* (Oxford: Oxford University Press, 2009), pp. 84–8.

[29] Compare the way in which Donald Davidson has made explicit the dependence of the language of actions upon events. See his *Essays on Actions and Events* (Oxford: Clarendon Press, 1980), pp. 105–96, and James Higginbotham, 'Adverbs', *Routledge Encyclopaedia of Philosophy* (London: 1998), <https://www.rep.routledge.com/articles/adverbs/v-1/> and 'Sense and Syntax: an inaugural lecture delivered before the University of Oxford' (Oxford: Clarendon Press, 1995). For collateral considerations and arguments, see my 'Verbs and Adverbs and some other Modes of Grammatical Combination', *Proceedings of the Aristotelian Society* 86 (1985–6), pp. 273–304.

My first comment is this. It is one thing for a physicist to seek to displace the world-view of substances and their alterations—and to displace it entirely—by an altogether different one, as in the spirit of Ernst Mach's assertion:

bodies are bundles of reactions connected by law... that which is constant is always the connection of reactions according to law and this alone. This is the critically purified concept of substance which scientifically ought to replace the vulgar one.[30]

It is another thing to seek to replace ordinary objects by successions of thing-moments—this-horse-at-t, that-river-at-t, or David-Lewis-at-t. At one and the same time, how can we deny ordinary substances their status as proper continuants, insist that ordinary substances are really *constructs*, yet lean shamelessly upon the ordinary understanding of substances when we come to specify that from which these constructs are to be seen as constructed or assembled? (Within a straightforward advocacy of Mach's proposal one would not even attempt such a thing. One has left all that behind.) Are thing-moments such as this-horse-at-t to be introduced or explained not in a way that presupposes horses and times but directly and simply by creative definition or by bare postulation?[31] Even as one considers that sort of question, moreover, it is necessary to ask one more: could one bestow upon a thing-moment so defined—durationless, it seems, given the argument on which the whole construction depends[32]—all the properties of shape, disposition, and attitude upon which the perdurantist will have to found the intrinsic properties of sitting, standing... bent, straight... and the like on which the original argument depended?

14

It is not an option for philosophy to reject the four-dimensional conception of the world urged upon us by philosophers and metaphysicians of science. But, in accepting that, one is not committed—or so I suggest—to see things, people and organisms in perdurantist fashion as made up of instantaneous temporal parts. The four-dimensional conception need not favour either side in the logico-metaphysical dispute in which we have been engaged. We can think of a 'three-dimensional' substance in the ordinary endurantist way, then think of the

---

[30] See Roberto Torretti, *The Philosophy of Physics* (Cambridge: Cambridge University Press, 1999), p. 237.
[31] For the power of creative definition—as of postulation—to create paradox or perplexity, see *S&SR*, pp. 173-6, a discussion inter alia of Geach's Tib/Tibbles example. On creative definition, see also Patrick Suppes, *Introduction to Logic* (New York: Van Nostrand, 1957), chapter 8.
[32] Compare Rundle, *Time, Space, and Metaphysics*, p. 87.

space-time region the substance passes through during its lifetime, then construct the space-time correlate of the substance as a time-series of pairs consisting of the substance and the places the substance occupies at successive times. For any frame of reference, the places in question will be what Carnap calls instantaneous cross-sections of the whole space-time region through which the substance passes.[33] Proceeding in this way, one can advance philosophically unimpeded and with an open mind to the question of the relation between substances and space-time.

We distinguish effortlessly between Socrates and the succession of events that makes up Socrates' life history. Can we not make a philosophical distinction then between Socrates himself and a succession of events in four-dimensional space-time? At any moment in Socrates' life we can answer the question which person Socrates is. But, we cannot say which particular succession of events Socrates is 'identical' with until Socrates has departed this life and the series of events in space-time that make up his life is complete. We can say of Socrates that he could have adopted a different defence at his trial at Athens in 399 BC. But of a completed series of events in space-time we can hardly say that that very series might have comprised different occurrences. (A set-theoretical object such as a series can only be defined by reference to its members. And something similar must hold of a mereological sum or fusion of temporal parts. See Chapter 11.) We can of course say that, in the place of this or that succession or series of events or thing-moments, a different succession or series might have existed, comprising perhaps a similar initial section and a different defence at the trial later. But if we want to take it fully seriously that the Athenian citizen Socrates, the real Socrates, might have mounted a different defence, it won't be enough to say that sort of thing. To speak simply of a different succession of events from the succession of actual events of Socrates' life and point out that it includes an alternative defence does not show that there is room for *Socrates himself* to mount an alternative defence. Let us distinguish then between the person Socrates who might have defended himself in a different way and a succession of thing-moments or slices.

---

[33] Compare Rudolf Carnap, *Introduction to Symbolic Logic and its Applications* (New York: Dover, 1958), pp. 157–8: 'a *thing* occupies a definite region of space at a definite instant of time, and a temporal series of spatial regions during the whole history of its existence. I.e. a thing occupies a region in the four-dimensional space-time continuum. A given thing at a given instant of time is, so to speak, a cross-section of the whole space-time region occupied by the thing. It is called a *slice* of the thing (or a thing-moment). We conceive a thing as the temporal series of its slices. The entire space-time region occupied by the thing is a class of particular space-time points which we speak of as "the space-time points of the thing".' In the text I have departed at one point from Carnap because a cross-section of a space-time region is surely a *place* not a slice of a thing.

There is room for both substances and thing-moments. But let us be ready to predicate different properties of them.

Should then such ordinary thoughts and attributions as ours be dispensed with altogether? Or should we seek for some compromise that hunts down four-dimensional surrogates for the properties of the ordinary substances? It is better still, I think, for us to hold onto the proper recipients of such attributions, leave the attributions undisturbed, and rest content with the fact that the enduring substances we normally think and speak of register perfectly satisfactorily within the four-dimensional continuum. See again Carnap, as quoted in note 33. It is true that the three-dimensional things that have these histories—the things that Carnap indispensably begins with in his explanation of the physicists' scheme of things—are not singled out under concepts that are fundamental to space-time physics or cosmology. But that will scarcely exempt such things from the laws of nature that govern the material world.

15

To the philosophical four-dimensionalist who likes to think of substances as possessing temporal parts as well as spatial parts, the category differences just dwelt upon may appear pedantic and inconsiderable. But these differences point towards something of profound interest to us, namely the constraints upon any conception of body or substance which can be open to an organism or person that acts, deliberates, or enquires. A conscious being cannot (in action) think of itself—or of the persons, organisms, or physical objects that it encounters—as having the shape of a succession of events that is present only in part at the moment of action or deliberation. Nor can it think of itself as an event or a succession of events in the making. To act and think as it does—to conceive of itself as a creature with limbs by which it has some purchase on however small a portion of reality—a conscious being must think of its whole self as present at the moment of reflection, perception or action and poised to persist in that way into the future. It must think of itself at t as extending in space wherever its parts—its head and limbs—are at t. It must conceive its past as consisting of the earlier phases or stages of the life of the whole being which it itself is.[34]

---

[34] It is neither necessary nor sensible to try to set out these points in terms of a *generic* notion subsuming both an object's existence at a time or its persisting through time *and* its occupation of space or space-time. See Kit Fine, 'In Defence of Three-Dimensionalism', *Journal of Philosophy* 103 (2006), pp. 699–714, esp. 700–1.

To hold out for the category differentiation that underlies these contentions is anti-scientific, if you will. But it is in no way at odds with the scientific worldview itself. Indeed it vindicates modes of description that are natural, habitual, and seemingly indispensable—physics apart—to almost all branches of science itself.[35]

16

Back now to identity and change. Suppose that we extend the ideas set out in section 9 from the individuation of natural substances to the individuation of artefacts. Taking artefacts as things fashioned in such a way as to subserve some designated purpose or purposes—purposes which may be enlarged or extended and more and more closely specified as the artefact endures through time—one might say that, just as a natural thing has a principle of activity, so an artefact has its mode of operation or functioning. How close or illuminating is that parallelism? In the limiting case, where almost changeless near-passivity does duty for activity, there is no particular problem. Think of a cast-iron one pound weight or the scales-balance whereon it enables us to weigh things. But there are 101 more challenging cases.

Following the narrative of Plutarch's Life of Theseus, consider Theseus' ship as preserved through the centuries by the Athenians for its annual voyage from Piraeus to the shrine of Apollo on the island of Delos. Suppose in the spirit of Thomas Hobbes' use of the example (see S&SR, pp. 92-3) that, even as the ship was refitted year by year with new planks or spars, a long line of cunning fathers and sons or daughters salvaged every plank or spar that its repairers cast aside. Suppose that a moment came when the family discovered they had collected everything that was needed to reassemble the original components of Theseus' whole ship. Never mind the constantly renewed ship plying its annual course to Delos, they might say. If you want to see the real thing, you will have to come to our dry dock in Piraeus and see the ship itself. Indeed, even before collecting absolutely everything, members of the family might claim that they had a large enough aggregation of planks and spars to count themselves the new owners of Theseus' original ship.

---

[35] Think what damage would result from expunging the fundamental distinction between substance and process/narrative/event from most ordinary scientific exposition. Indeed consider in that connection all the descriptions that figure in the citation given at the beginning of section 2. Consider biology. And see Chapter 12.

In cases where we had the *phusis* of a natural substance following its own course, situations of this kind were excluded. For an artefact, however, there is no norm of development that can rule out such happenings. Nor can the whole matter be delegated to a scientist who will delve deeper and deeper into the principle of activity 'natural' to a ship or to that sort of ship. There is no such principle. An artefact is its makers' thing. What is needed is not for us to interrogate nature but to spell out the conception that animated the making of the artefact and determined the specific kind that it was fashioned to instantiate.

On one sortalist conception of what it is, the ship of Theseus must be the ship that was constantly repaired and renewed. But if one says that, then one must seek to discredit the reconstruction in the dry dock in the Piraeus.[36] In defence of that reconstruction, a mereologist-philosopher may say that, strictly speaking, the ship ceased to exist so soon as it lost a part (see Chapter 10 on mereological essentialism and note 9 there, on what David Lewis calls the Principle of Unique Composition), but propose that the reconstruction be seen as the *reinstatement* of Theseus' very own ship from temporary abeyance. Setting out a third and less implausible view, another sortalist may say that the technical-cum-practical interest that users have in the purpose that is served by an artefact must be balanced by the concern that users of a cult-object must have with the import of the thing's original condition and materials, its history, and its link with its maker or makers. Looking for a conception of the ship that mediates between all those considerations, and thinking of the sort or kind that it determines conformably with that, one might insist that it is for priests and mariners to trace the ship through repairs and renewals over the years, yet insist also that the process of renewal and material replacement cannot be carried indefinitely far without the loss of the very ship that Theseus dedicated to Apollo.[37]

---

[36] If one wants to discredit it—for this or any other reason—one should perhaps say that the aggregation of spars and planks in Piraeus *was once* Theseus' ship (note the tense), meaning by this only that at the outset that aggregation once constituted the ship. On the 'is' of constitution, see S&SR, pp. 39–43. Concerning this *was once* and the non-temporal character of genuine identity, see the last part of section 3 above, on 'always'.

[37] Hereabouts disquieting questions will appear. What happens at the point in time when some minor renewal or replacement, but the last ruled admissible, disqualifies the ship in the water from being Theseus' ship? If, at the point where the ship at sea came to comprise fewer original materials than the reconstruction in Piraeus then comprised, where was Theseus' ship? Had it gone into abeyance? Or was it back in Piraeus? If you insist on the latter view, then do not ask at what speed it returned there! But rather than expose the third approach to such questions it will be better surely for one who prefers this option to insist, against Hobbes and the possible coexistence of two instances of Theseus' ship, that, as with any ship, some parts of it—keel, kelson, stern... are simply essential to that very ship. Evidently, the artefactual conception that all such speculations would require would have to be spelled out in some way which will allow for disassemblage and

Rather than plunge immediately into the ins and outs of more specific conceptions of the particular concept that Theseus' ship is to fall under—rather than do this from the state of uncertainty that is inseparable from a more or less imaginary example deprived of any whole context—it may be wise to turn first to something entirely general and much more important than any particular example. It is this. If the identity of a substance (or the like) is to be a matter genuinely at issue, then (1) the dialectic of same and other within which questions of persistence or non-persistence are resolved must cohere with some sufficiently specific conception of the sort of thing that the particular item in question exemplifies; and (2) the conception of what that item most fundamentally is and of the sort or kind in which it belongs must furnish in its specificity an essential part of the basis for adjudications of same and other; and (3) these adjudications must be answerable *in context and in their collectivity* to all the formal requirements that were set out in section 2. Finally (4) the conception and the adjudications that it makes possible must cohere well enough with cognate conceptions of cognate kinds of thing and the adjudications that those conception enable. (Compare the sort of coherence that equitable legal judgment needs to have with the previous judgments and comparable precedents of the Common Law.) Only where verdicts and grounds are answerable to such a standard will there be a secure framework for the determination of genuine identity.

In a plea for tolerance, it may now be protested that these requirements set much too stringent a standard for the resolution of problems such as the one Hobbes has proposed. After all, it may be said, Theseus' original ship was at once 'the thirty-oar ship' (see Aristotle, *Consitution of Athens*, 56) with all the archaic features implicit in that description and also, by virtue of its constant use, a working ship. After extensive repairs and modifications to the ship, can it not be insisted that the *ship at sea* is still the same *working-ship* as the ship launched by Theseus, even though it is no longer exactly a thirty-oar ship? And can it not be said also that the *ship in the dry dock* is one and the *same thirty-oar ship* as the ship launched by Theseus, even though it is not the same working-ship as the ship at sea? I reply No. Such tolerance will give real trouble. If we give the concept *working ship* the same sort of fundamental status as we give the *thirty-oar ship* concept and we allow *working ship* to be no less conclusory for the identity of Theseus' ship than is *thirty-oar ship*, then we shall have a contradiction. For, combining Leibniz's Law with the *working ship* concept and then with the *thirty-oar ship* concept, we shall find that Theseus' ship is at sea and find also that it is in

---

reassemblage at different locations, as well as providing for an object that undergoes such processes to enjoy temporary suspension from concrete existence.

the dry dock. (See *S&SR*, pp. 53-4 and *S&S* and *ISTC* Chapter One *passim*.) The objector cannot approve both concepts as individuatively fundamental. Nor can he request tolerance for both of them in that capacity.[38] Given one particular artefact, just one concept must (on pain of contradiction) be fundamental, and that status must flow from the however special and specific account of its thing-kind that informs the creation and the preservation of that particular artefact.

How good are the philosophical prospects for such a view? Disobliging persons will ask what sort of matter of fact it can be that Theseus' ship lasted well into the fourth century BC if that means no more than that year by year the Athenians decided that it had. But that is a sadly truncated report of our account. Our account was that, continuing the cult of Apollo that Theseus had initiated, the Athenian priests and mariners saw themselves, perfectly justifiably, as Theseus' particular inheritors in this matter. Their office was to continue the cult that he had begun. As regards the ship, they had to repair it, but to do so in an appropriate and seemly fashion. What counted as appropriate and seemly was a question delegated to them. But there is nothing wrong with that if artefacts owe their existence to the way in which human beings conceive them, fabricate them, and maintain them or bequeath them to others to maintain. It is for human beings to play their part carefully and responsibly in settling what will become the facts of the matter.

Is that good enough? It may be objected that I have long since committed our enquiry to the matter-of-factual-cum-metaphysical absoluteness and determinacy of identity (cf. section 3, at the end and section 4, notes 8, 9, and 12), yet admitted also that our conceptions of substances, artefacts, and almost every other kind of thing are incompletely determinate. I reply that this difficulty, if it is a difficulty, is not peculiar to artefacts. Nor is it a problem. It is often pointed out in a similar cause that our thoughts about mountains leave massive indeterminacy about their exact extent. This point has often figured as a part of the case for the possibility of indeterminacy of identity. But indeterminacy of exact extent is irrelevant, I say, to questions about the identity or difference among mountains. It is true that, if mountains were simply aggregates of earth and rock, then the indeterminacy of their extent would be fatal to the determinacy of their sameness

---

[38] Unless we think we can find in the place where Theseus' ship was in (say) 650 BC two different things, *both* a thirty-oar ship and a working ship. Compare the way in which it may seem possible for two different things to be in the same place at the same time—the ship for instance and the aggregation or mereological sum of its parts (see Chapter 2). But how can that kind of thought be available here? Theseus' thirty-oar ship was not a mere aggregate. Moreover, Theseus' thirty-oar ship of 650 BC and Theseus' working ship of 650 BC were one and the same ship. On this point see also the end of the commentary that I have appended in Chapter 2 to the paper (1968) 'On being in the same place at the same time'.

or difference. But mountains are not simply aggregates, and their sameness or difference is not mereologically determined. Similarly, even though the concepts of ship and ship of Theseus are in certain respects indeterminate, *that* sort of indeterminacy was no impediment to the matter-of-fact determinacy of the truth that the thirty-oar ship which set out for Delos in 399 BC was identical—and determinately identical—with the ship that returned slightly late in that year, delaying in this way the execution of Socrates (Plato, *Phaedo* 58).

That reply will not satisfy the objector. At this point perhaps he will ask us to consider the ship of Theseus at a point around 315 BC or thereabout when doubts arose whether the priests and mariners were still in possession of Theseus' very own ship. Here the question of determinacy will seem to require much closer attention. If identity is absolute and determinate, then so is persistence. Will the mariners' and priests' conception of the thirty-oar ship really suffice for them to say which addition or subtraction of plank or spar marks the ship's very last moment? I am committed to say yes. The question might have angered the relevant authorities. They might have objected to being put on their metttle to answer it. But the idea that it lay within their competence to give a ruling on the matter amounts to little more than we agreed to when, having already embraced the proof of the determinacy of identity, we embraced a quasi-constructivist model of artefact-individuation. Priests and mariners could make a mistake about the moment when the ship ceased to exist, but such a mistake could only be demonstrated (I suggest) by reference to *their* conception or some going improvement of that.

So much for identity, but what about difference? If persistence is excluded beyond the final or crucial addition or subtraction of plank or spar, and the ship we have arbitrarily soon after this event is not determinately identical with what was there before, then is what remains *ipso facto* determinately and definitely different from what there was before? Again I shall say yes. After the decisive addition or subtraction I think we must say 'This is what is left of Theseus' ship', 'Here is all that remains of that ship' or 'This is a sad remnant of the ship of Theseus'.[39] The remnants of a thing are not the same as the thing itself. (It is a mereological exercise to say more.)

Are these latter ways of speaking mandatory? I say they are mandatory because I claim that difference is no more a matter of degree than is identity. That is a further claim beyond the determinacy of identity. Why make it? Well, if we

---

[39] We might also say 'This *was* Theseus' ship'. Museum directors will prefer to speak in that way perhaps. But let it be clear that a tensed identity *need* not count as a genuine identity. (See section 3, at the end.)

contrapose the principle 'if x is the same as y then x is determinately the same as y' (secured to us by the indiscernibility of identicals), and we then recruit the so-called Brouwersche principle in the form (hard to deny) 'if not p then determinately not determinately p', then Prior, Kripke, and Williamson have all they need to prove that, if x is not the same as y, then x is determinately not the same as y.[40] Rather than seek to disturb this result, or try harder to make room for degrees of identity or difference, it is better to explore the ways to dispense with all thought of degrees of difference, and to seek to understand the things that the proof can show to us.

First, though, let it be clear what the proof does not show. It does not show that considerations of degree, good enough or not good enough, close enough or too far away from the origin, can form no part of the case for affirming or for denying an identity. (Cf. note 9 of section 3.) The definiteness I claim for identity and the definiteness I claim for difference relate to the conclusion towards which the case points, namely the final verdict: 'identical', or 'not identical', or 'identity not proven'.

Secondly, let us revisit our finding (in sections 3 and 4) how little room there is, where identity and difference are concerned, for 'almost' or 'nearly'. An object a is not almost the same as the object a. Nor yet is a almost different from a. We cannot say of a either that it is almost the same as a or that it is almost not the same as a. So, if a is the same as b, we cannot say either of these things of b.[41] Why does 'almost' cohere so badly with identity? The reason, I hazard, is that our thoughts of what nearly happened or almost came to pass presuppose that, whatever was going to happen or just miss happening, the objects that participated in the events to be described can be identified independently of those events. That is the way we think—and we think that way (or so it seems) because no other way will cohere with the way in which we have to single out continuant substances.

The outcome of this section is as follows. If artefacts are substances, they represent a fairly special case. But it is not impossible to provide an account of their individuation. Let us not demand more than we need from the sortal conceptions by which we have to make our way in the empirical world. Let us

---

[40] For the details, see note 8 (section 3) and note 12 (section 4), see S&SR, p. 117, and see Williamson, 'Necessity'. I note that the contraposition which begins the proof is in the form which intuitionists find no fault with. I emphasize also that the proof relates to factual/metaphysical determinacy, not epistemic.

[41] Can we say, with a different scope for 'not', 'either a is almost the same as a or else a is not almost the same as a'? No. For a is *exactly* the same as a. There is no question of 'almost'. If, using a special emphasis, we do find ourselves saying 'a is not *almost* the same as a' then the 'not' signals a sort of cancellation of the very form 'a is almost the same as a'. It is quasi-metalinguistic.

learn to live with the logical determinacy of identity and of difference and let us inquire as necessary and as the relevant conception demands into the empirical facts that we need so badly whenever we are moved positively either to assert or to deny identity—whether in relation to artefacts or in relation to other kinds of substance.

17

So much for cases where the thing-kind—the *what a given object or substance* is— is not nomologically grounded. And so much for artefacts and the problems they present. Now let us revert to the kinds where there is a nomologically well-grounded principle of activity of a natural thing, but focus attention upon the case where there is radical interference in the normal workings or output of that principle. In philosophy as it now is, the most conspicuous case is that of the person.[42]

Beginning with the usual example in its original presentation and prescinding from variations and complications that have been proposed, I refer to the case where Brown and Robinson each undergo an operation which involves the removal of the brain from the skull. Through a surgical blunder Brown's brain is placed in Robinson's skull. The resulting person, whom Sydney Shoemaker, the inventor of this example, calls Brownson, has Brown's brain and Robinson's body.[43] Suppose that his psychological states, including apparent memories, are those that one would expect Brown to have. Is Brownson then Brown?

The question created some excitement inside philosophy and even outside. It prompted the thought that all that counts in matters having to do with the identity of persons is psychological continuity, a relation which some have claimed to disentangle from all involvement with identity. Others reached for their response along other routes. Here is the sortalist approach. Brown is a person. How are we to think of a person? As an ego or self? As a self among a multitude of other selves? In the absence of anything more, that is not so much a false as a useless starting point. (On its own, *self* is not an autonomous sortal or individuative concept. At best, it is simply a determinable whose more specific

---

[42] Unless the most conspicuous case is still that of an earthworm which can be cut in half and be succeeded by two perfectly viable earthworms. Or so one is told. Subject to there being no scientific facts favouring one half over the other, the case appears in just one respect analogous—so far as the logic of identity is concerned—to that of the amoeba, on which see *S&SR*, pp. 72–3, 83–4. See also the end of section 9. But there is also a vital difference. In the case of the amoeba, division is part of the regular life cycle. Not so in the case of the worm.

[43] See Sydney Shoemaker, *Self-Knowledge and Self-Identity* (Ithaca, NY: Cornell University Press, 1963).

determinations will be more properly individuative.) How then to understand *person*? Well, in practice and in our everyday thoughts, our paradigm for a person is a human being, a bodily substance, a creature whose overwhelming interest for us is that we have to *make sense* of it and be ready to treat with it. A person is not just any sentient or conscious being. A person is one of us, a human being.[44] As such a substance develops from a foetus, grows up, lives and matures, the principle of activity of the substance becomes progressively more complex and its modes of agency, cognition and feeling, its powers and capacities, its fund of information, experience and memory all become more copious and more and more specific.

On these terms, shall one say that Brownson and Brown are the same human being? Have the events that Shoemaker describes resulted in Brownson's participating in Brown's very own principle of activity and holding on to Brown's very own life?

18

Prominent within Brown's store of information, experience, expectation, and intention, some of it highly particular, is his experiential memory. Let memory be hostage for all the rest. Suppose that Brown, when he was 13 years old and playing in a parent–pupil cricket match on a school speech day, bowled out his father. Brown said he would never forget doing this. But what about Brownson? Well, Brownson says that he bowled out Brown Senior. But does Brownson really *remember* doing so? The only reason why he says he remembers (it might be said) is that he has been given Brown's brain. Mustn't we still ask whether Brownson was there at the cricket match? Was it Brownson himself who, when he was 13, bowled out Brown Senior on that occasion?

In reply to that question, some will respond by saying: 'Never mind identity. Concentrate rather upon psychological continuity, where that embraces identity but does not definitionally require it. And, as regards memory, "quasi-memory" will suffice.' But this is an unfortunate response and gratuitously destructive of our understanding of what we need to be able to mean by what we say. I say this for three reasons.

First, in so far as the proposed relation of psychological continuity is not answerable to the Adequacy requirement, and in so far as psychological continuity does not create even a presumption against the division of the brain into

---

[44] An indexicality not lightly to be dispensed with. Cf. *S&SR*, p. 198 and my 'Reply to Paul Snowdon' in Lovibond and Williams (eds), *Identity, Truth and Value*, pp. 244–8. See also Chapter 5.

halves and the splitting of a (so-called) 'stream of consciousness' among multiple Brownsons,[45] Brownson may have no clear title to be anything more than a propagule (or a 'layered offshoot') of Brown. In so far as we use psychological continuity as a surrogate for identity and no more is claimed than psychological continuity, we must be prepared for the possibility that a survivor of brain surgery done upon Brown may represent not the *substance* Brown but the clone (the clone-type) to which a possible plurality of Brownsons belong, where the clone is a universal instantiated in separate or separable consciousnesses. At the outset, we began with a question of the identity of an individual subject, but now a radical change of subject is in prospect—in both senses of the word 'subject'. Given the terms of discussion now proposed and the replacement of identity by 'psychological connectedness', Brown must span somehow (however incoherently) the metaphysical categories of particular and universal. Once that divide is spanned, Brown is no longer an individual person but a corporate being, a being with an open-ended plurality of representatives. If the particular Brown in front of you says that he both understands your interests and intends also to protect them, be careful. It may seem that he speaks for Brown. But another representative—another propagule from Brown—may be ignorant or indifferent in relation to your interests. The Brown who faces you may be (or 'represent') a corporate being.

The second point is cognate with the first and no less important. Once we reconceive direct memory to the point where we cease to require of such memory that the rememberer should have him/herself been present at the event supposedly directly remembered, we remove direct memory itself from a role that is integral to our understanding of direct memory. Why do I say that? I say it in the interests of a proper understanding of what is meant by 'remember'. Within the fabric of human knowledge, not everything can depend on testimony. At some points somewhere, there have to be eye-witnesses possessed of direct or experiential memory. Without experiential memory as normally conceived, the idea of witness must go to waste (and with it received ideas of empirical knowledge). When it is understood in the received way as identity-involving, experiential memory can be asked to vouch for the claim that an event occurred and was thus and so. It can submit itself to cross-examination. The subject who really remembers in the normal sense of 'remember' is in a position to try to place a remembered event within the course of his or her life and to take responsibility for his or her account of what happened, of what s/he saw or heard and of how that was. But if the idea of memory is torn from this web of ideas where it belongs

---

[45] See *ISTC*, Part Four.

and normal requirements are excised, shall we know what we understand by experiential memory? Can one really scrub out a key part of what 'remember' means and the expectations that it arouses yet expect all the rest to stand?[46] These are not the terms on which we can understand the creation and accumulation and recertification and renewal of knowledge. It would be far better, if we want to insist that Brownson is Brown, to abandon the attempt to dilute identity into psychological continuity and see whether we may insist that Brownson *was* present at the cricket match.

Thirdly, so far as Shoemaker's version of Brown and Brownson is concerned, it seems unnecessary to do the proposed violence to the idea of experiential memory. Let us stay rather with the question as originally posed concerning the original thought-experiment (where the question of a division of Brown's consciousness does not arise). If our way with the Brown–Brownson question is to seek to determine whether Brownson participates in Brown's principle of activity or inherits Brown's very own life, then we may begin by asking whether Brownson can recall some sufficiency of the other details concerning the cricket match, place it as an event in the narrative of a single life which was Brown's, report the event in the manner of a participant and so on... Once we are satisfied (if we ever are) under that head and satisfied *mutatis mutandis* with regard to other aspects of awareness, it will be time to pass to the neurological-cum-characterological-cum-physiognomical aspect of things. Brownson's body is Robinson's body. But the character, mien, and typical responses of Brown depended in part on his physiognomy—indeed on his whole bodily physiognomy (if I may stretch the meaning of the word so). The functioning of a human being, the capacity to express oneself in act, gesture, and attitude, all depend on a mutual accord or co-adaptation, at once personal and lifelong, between the brain and the rest of the nervous system. (This is not on any sane understanding a mere contingency.) Not only that. These things depend also upon the settled co-adaptation (another non-contingency), achieved over the passing of time and constantly adjusted, between the nervous system and the limbs—something

---

[46] Cf. *S&SR*, pp. 218–19. There is one account of experiential memory—of quasi-memory so-called—which does not attempt an impossible subtraction from the given meaning of 'remember' (a meaning held in place not by a definition but by a whole pattern of thinking and speaking), but seeks to define quasi-memory from scratch. See Derek Parfit, *Reasons and Persons* (Oxford: Clarendon Press, 1984), p. 221. For criticisms of that definition, see *S&SR*, pp. 213–30. One of the more important of these criticisms is that what Parfit offers is a definition of 'accurately-quasi-remember' which it is impossible (or so I believe I have shown) to turn into a definition of plain 'quasi-remember'. Strictly speaking, *that* term is unexplained. Perhaps 'quasi-remember' had better mean 'it is for x as if he remembers' but *that* explanation depends on the *unamended* sense of 'remember' that we are advised to abandon.

again personal and lifelong. How could Brown-in-Brownson enjoy all of that? Nor must one omit to mention specifically the face. Brownson has the wrong face (as well as the wrong voice). It is true that a person we know may be wounded or disabled or paralysed or disfigured, even given a new face or voice. This may represent a truly terrible subtraction from a going concern, but human life can allow for it. The trouble about Brownson is that his condition does not represent a stage in *any* going concern from which we can allow for such subtraction.

19

It is very hard then to see the events so far described as representing the unfolding through time of the principle of activity of a conscious substance. But imagine now (it may be objected) that, soon after the surgical interventions upon Brown that we have enumerated, Brownson were to appear to resume a conversation that we had begun once with Brown. Suppose that Brownson deploys intonations which seem to be all of a piece with what we should have expected if Brown hadn't (as a philosopher convert might say) been transplanted to a new body. To imagine such a happening is to imagine that all the right muscular connections and adaptations are established between Brown's cerebrum and Robinson's voice-box. To imagine this sort of thing in sufficient detail might perhaps establish its *logical* possibility. All that logical possibility can establish, however, is the absence of a contradiction indictable by logic alone. Beyond that, what we really need to know is whether, biologically, neurologically, surgically... speaking, the principle of activity of a person allows or excludes the kind of event that we have imagined. And then we still have to ask whether constitutively speaking even this is impressive enough to count as the persistence of *Brown himself*. Where the kind of possibility in question is correlative with medical and scientific actualities, what is the closest approximation that it is possible for a brain transplant from Brown to achieve to the characteristic activity of that human person?

There is an ineluctable temptation for those who are convinced by Shoemaker's thought-experiment to proceed as if on the principle that, if Brown can do without this or that (his own legs or face or voice...), then this or that (whatever it is) is not an essential part of what it is to be the human being Brown. In the end, it will seem, the only thing that will count as essential to the human person is the brain or cerebrum. But *that* conclusion is profoundly at variance with our metaphysics, with our philosophy of living and being, and with our understanding of what we mean by our words. There is something wrong—and something less and less persuasive *at each point*—with the way of thinking that leads step by step to that conclusion. The conclusion to which we are driven, however gradually, shows there is something wrong. It is not a way of thinking of human beings—or of persons.

Why has this way of thinking seemed so irresistible? Maybe because, when we speculate that Brownson utters the words 'I am Brown', this engages our human impulse, the interpretive impulse, to make sense of anything that presents itself as human utterance by another and to find out there 'one of us' (whether friend or enemy). Maybe it seems irresistible because, given the glimmer of life, there seems to be no alternative. But we know already that there *has* to be an alternative. (An atom-by-atom copy of Brown would say 'I am Brown'. But the copy can't be the original.) So we must find a way to say something or other about what sort of thing Brownson would have to be. We might call him a *shadow* or *umbra* or *relic*...of Brown. There is no need to deny that events such as Shoemaker describes—if ever they occurred—would demand at the very least *some* such response. There is no need to advocate harsh treatment of these beings. But the thing that events such as Shoemaker describes *cannot* demand is that we reconstruct—as if from scratch—the notions by which we live and treat with one another, or our ideas of the full range of capacities proper to a human being, a human being *not* reconceived as a sort of artefact.

20

The thing that matters much more than the Brown–Brownson question is the larger problem it illustrates, not for the first time. We have described it already. Where there is a claim of identity, what does it involve for the answer to match the question? There has to be more to the finding of identity between x and y than the discovery that y has moved smoothly into the place of x as the closest continuer for x, the successor to x, the inheritor of x, or the perpetuator of the same clone- or person-type as x. The object y must arrive where x was in a way that manifests the unfolding of a nature inhering in a thing with the history of an individual substance—or else in a way which somehow converges upon that. On the sortalist view, it is that thought or some adaptation of that thought which must shape the whole dialectic within which we must try to decide questions of same and other.

21

The sortalist theory of identity and individuation may appear wide open to the accusation of anthropocentrism. But there is nothing anthropocentric about insisting that the judgement of same or other should have a content and be answerable by virtue of that content to the logic of identity. There is nothing anthropocentric about insisting that, as we learn more and think more, we should always be ready, at the level of sense, to adjust our ideas or conceptions of the thing-kinds under which organisms, other natural things, artefacts... are singled out. Only through fallacy (I have claimed) can the partiality, incompleteness or indeterminacy of our conceptions be transmitted automatically from the level of sense to the level of reference, either to substances themselves or to their kinds.

It is of course a sort of anthropocentrism for us to focus our attention so intently upon the kinds of kind (ship, horse, etc.) that impinge on human life and human awareness. But (except in so far as it may be claimed that there is something special about scientific instruments and the like) such a focus does not amount to a claim of cosmic importance.

Sortalism is no sort of theory about the ultimate constituents of the universe. It is a theory about finding identities. But like any other would-be respectable piece of philosophy, it *leaves room* for the idea of a completed theory of ultimate constituents. That complete theory would surely dispense altogether with the continuants we know, their kinds and their qualities. (Radical developments of that sort are prefigured in the citation from Mach in section 13.) Why though should those who will propound the completed theory want to deny the existence of the levels or categories of being that the ultimate constituents of reality subvene/sustain/make possible?

The sortalism I have defended must be content to see itself as one rather special and particular component of a more general theory of identity and individuation, a theory embracing all sorts of other categories of being beside substance— categories of event, process, state, disposition, field, and heaven knows what else. Such a general account will of course confront questions and difficulties which I have not attempted or foreseen, concerning what it will take to assign their proper logical content to claims of identity that lie outside the category of substance.[47]

---

[47] For comments received on the occasion of a lecture in Amsterdam which I put together from an earlier version of this text (David Wiggins, 'Identity, Individuation and Substance', *European Journal of Philosophy*, 20 (2012), pp. 1–25) I am indebted to the Editor and the Editorial Committee of the *European Journal of Philosophy*. I am indebted to Timothy Williamson both for that which I have applied from his *Vagueness* (London: Routledge, 1995) and for the specific comments that he gave me on my earlier text. In revising that text, treated as a draft for the final paper given here, I benefited from extended improvements proposed by Gareth Jenkins, not least at section 14.

2

On Being in the Same Place at the Same Time

1. It is a truism frequently called in evidence and confidently relied upon in philosophy that two things cannot be in the same place at the same time. Plainly this principle, which I shall call S, ought really to say that two things cannot *completely* occupy exactly the same place or exactly the same volume (or exactly the same subvolumes within exactly the same volume) for exactly the same period of time. No man is the same as his forearm. But there is a volume such that a man can wholly occupy it and such that both man and forearm are in it at exactly the same time. But this does not count.

2. More interestingly, think of a sponge and the water that makes it a wet sponge. That need not count against principle S if we can press into service the physico-chemical theory of molecules to distinguish subvolumes or sub-subvolumes of the total volume occupied by the sponge from those occupied by the water. But it is difficult to believe that this determination of ours to allow nothing to count against S gets us to the bottom of the matter. What is the a priori or metaphysical compulsion to think in our present way about these questions? Or is there no such compulsion? What if in defiance of fact and the actual laws of chemistry and physics the water and the sponge were so utterly mixed up that spatial distinction seemed impossible, not only at the molecular level but also at the atomic and at the subatomic? And what if even then you had only to squeeze to get water and sponge apart again? Surely they would be the same sponge and the same (consignment of) water afterward. Would they have been in exactly the same place at the same time?

3. Before going any further, we need to consider another kind of case. A tree T stands (leafless, suppose) at a certain spot at time t_1 and occupies a certain volume v_1 at this time t_1. All and only v_1 is also occupied by the aggregate W of the cellulose molecules which at t_1 compose the tree. Indeed it is their occupation of v_1 which precisely determines that the volume which the tree occupies is volume v_1. The tree T and the cellulose molecules W are thus in

exactly the same place at exactly the same time. Are they identical? This is what S implies. But $T = W$ only if whatever is true of T is true of W (Leibniz's Law). It follows that $T = W$ only if T and W have exactly the same conditions of persistence and survival through change. But self-evidently they do not. That suggests that S is false. But can we qualify or restrict it? And can we not try to understand better about the tree and its wood?

4. Suppose T is chopped down and then dismembered and cut up in such a way that every cellulose molecule survives. It seems that W then survives. And there is just as much wood in the world as there was before. But T, the tree, cannot survive such treatment. Conversely, suppose the tree is pruned and the clippings are burned, or that it undergoes an organic change which destroys some of the original wood cells. Then the tree T survives but W, the aggregate defined as the aggregate of such and such particular cellulose molecules, does not survive. On the other hand, you could define another notion of aggregate and give detailed conditions for suitable co-option and expulsion of the members (wood-cells, etc.) of such an aggregate. Perhaps you could get these conditions for gradual organic variation of membership exactly right and produce an entity W' with exactly the same principle of individuation as T. But that would be a boring trick. You would have defined a *tree*—and not wholly in terms of molecules or wood cells. You would have contrived an identity-connection between something in the category of stuff and something in the category of substance but only by introducing the concept of something organized and substance-like—that is, something foreign to the category—into the category of stuff.[1]

5. At this point, it springs to the eye that the non-identity of T and W shows nothing against John's Locke's statement 'We never finding, nor conceiving it possible, that two things of the same kind should exist in the same place at the same time, we rightly conclude that, whatever exists anywhere at any time excludes all of the same kind, and is there itself alone...[otherwise]...the

---

[1] There is much more to be said both about identity and about mereological treatments of the notion of aggregate. I have tried to say a little of it in *ISTC*, pp. 11–13, 67–8, 72.

The argument seems to apply equally to artefacts. Mrs Jones at t_2 unpicks her husband's old sweater and winds the wool into a ball. Equating matter and object, we shall have to say the wool is the sweater. But suppose she then at t_3 crochets a pair of bed-socks with the wool. Then by transitivity the sweater is the pair of bed-socks. But the bed-socks were crocheted at t_3 out of a ball of wool which was before t_2 [made into] a sweater, and the sweater was not at t_3 crocheted out of a ball of wool which was before t_2 a sweater. We must refuse to equate matter and object, and refuse to think of this as a paradoxical refusal. It is not. Crocheting, like knitting or weaving, is a way of *making* bed-socks. The material must pre-exist the making, and survive it. But *what* is made cannot pre-exist its fabrication.

notions and names of identity and diversity would be in vain, and there could be no such distinctions of substances or anything else from one another' (*Essay Concerning Human Understanding*, II, xxvii, 1.) We shall return to that claim at paragraph 9. Meanwhile three more paragraphs about '$T \neq W$'.

6. Does the non-identity of T with W show that T is something *over and above* W? On one interpretation of this phrase [but see *Postscript and Commentary*] it precisely is not. The tree is *made of* (or *constituted of* or *consists of*) W. What 'A is something over and above B' denies is 'A is (wholly composed of) B' or 'A is merely (or merely consists of) B.' If A is something over and above B, then of course $A \neq B$. But, on the proposed interpretation of the phrase, the proper point of saying 'over and above' is to make the denial that B fully exhausts the matter of A. But W does fully exhaust T and so, in the sense stipulated, T is not something over and above W. If we want to study T, of course we must study (inter alia) W.

7. If it is a materialistic thesis that $T = W$, then my denial that $T = W$ is a form of denial of materialism. It is interesting though how uninteresting an obstacle these Leibnizian considerations—real though they are—put in the way of the reduction some have contemplated of botany and all its primitive terms to organic chemistry or to physics. (If it does not follow from $T \neq W$ that trees are something over and above their matter, how much the less can it follow that they are immanent or transcendent or supervenient or immaterial beings. This is obviously absurd for trees. A Leibnizian disproof of strict identity could never be enough to show something so intriguing or obscure.) I should expect there to be equally valid, and almost equally unexciting, difficulties in the reduction of persons to flesh and bones,[2] in psychophysical event-materialism, and in the materialisms which one might formulate in other categories (such as the Aristotelian categories *property* and *state* or the categories *situation* and *fact*). *Over and above* is one question, *identity* is another. But of course the only stuff there is is stuff.

8. What I have tried to show about wood and tree has some affinity with a philosophical thesis which it has become a commonplace of philosophy to defend in terms of different *logical types* to which different sorts of object must belong.[3] I prefer to put the matter in my way because it makes a smaller claim, because (in contrast with informal explanations of type-theory that offend against that theory

---

[2] See *ISTC*, p. 57.
[3] See Russell's *Lectures on Logical Atomism*, VII, reprinted in Bertrand Russell, *Logic and Knowledge: Essays 1901-1950*, ed. Robert Charles Marsh (London: Allen and Unwin, 1956), pp. 254 ff., and G. Ryle, 'Categories', *Proceedings of the Aristotelian Society*, 38 (1937-8), pp. 189-206.

itself) it leaves room for self-consistent statement in the object language of a perfectly intelligible connection between trees and cellulose molecules, and because of the high degree of intelligibility enjoyed by the following Leibnizian principle for predicative (as opposed to constitutive) 'is': if and only if A is an f (or is φ) then A is identical with an f (or with one of the φ things); and if and only if A is one of the fs (or φ things) then it must share all its properties with that f (or φ thing).[4]

9. It is time to return to S revised. The tree and its molecules and wood cells do not disprove what was originally intended by principle S. What has been shown is only that we must reformulate S to read, with John Locke,

> S^*: No two things *of the same kind* can occupy exactly the same volume at exactly the same time.

[Or, better still, should we say that two substances cannot be in the same place at the same time?] This aspires to be some sort of necessary truth. Under that aspect it may appear to have at least three sources of support. [But see *Postscript and Commentary*.]

(*i*) Space can be mapped only by reference to its occupants, and spatial facts are conceptually dependent on the existence of facts about particulars and the identities of particulars. If space is to be mapped by reference to persisting particulars, then the non-identity of particulars A and B, both of kind f, must be sufficient to establish that the place of A at $t_1 \neq$ the place of B at t_1.

(*ii*) A criterion of identity for material objects will have to be something like this:

> I_m: A is identical with B if there is some substance concept f such that A *coincides* with B under f (where f is a substance concept under which an object can be traced, individuated, and distinguished from other fs, and where *coincides under f* satisfactorily defines an equivalence relation all of whose members <x, y> also satisfy the Leibnizian schema $F x \equiv F y$).[5]

Now I_m logically implies S^*. So if I_m is an a priori truth, then so is S^*. Finding that A and B coincide under f settles the question whether $A = B$. There is nothing more to decide. [See the criticisms of this argument given in *Postscript and Commentary*.]

---

[4] See *ISTC*, pp. 10–11, 61.
[5] See my 'The Individuation of Things and Places', *Proceedings of the Aristotelian Society*, suppl. 37 (1963), pp. 177–202. See also *ISTC*, pp. 34–6, 72.

(*iii*) It may appear that there is a conceptual basis for another truth: namely,

S**: *A* and a proper part or constituent *B* of a third thing *C*, where $A \neq C$ and $A \neq B$, and where no part or constituent of *A* is identical with any part or constituent of *B* or of *C*, cannot completely occupy exactly the same volume at exactly the same time.

The basis for this truth elucidates its import. Suppose *A* and *B* were distinct and in the same place at the same time. Then they could not have been distinguished by place. But in that case they would have had to be distinguished by their properties. But no volume or area of space can be qualified simultaneously by distinct predicates in any range (colour, shape, texture, and so forth). [See *Postscript and Commentary*.]

10. Perhaps (*i*), (*ii*), and (*iii*) afford some conceptual basis for the truth that material things have to compete for room in the world, and that they must displace one another. But they will scarcely throw light upon the question of the water and the sponge, or questions about chemical compounds and alloys [see *Postscript and Commentary*].

11. By way of conclusion, let us consider a puzzle contrived by Geach out of a discussion in William of Sherwood and intended by Geach to qualify any perfectly general acceptance of Leibniz's Law. A cat called Tibbles loses his tail at time t_2. But at t_2 somebody had picked out, identified, and distinguished from Tibbles a different and rather peculiar animate entity—namely, Tibbles *minus* Tibbles's tail. Let us suppose that he decided to call this entity 'Tib'. Suppose Tibbles was on the mat at time t_1. Then both Tib and Tibbles were on the mat at t_1. This does not violate *S** or *S***. But consider the position from t_3 onward when, something the worse for wear, the cat is sitting on the mat without a tail. Is there one cat or are there two cats there? Tib is certainly sitting there. In a way nothing happened to Tib at all. But so is Tibbles. For Tibbles lost his tail, survived this experience, and then at t_3 was sitting on the mat. And we agreed that Tib $\neq$ Tibbles. If we stick by that decision at t_3 we must allow that at t_3 there are two cats on the mat in exactly the same place at exactly the same time. But my putative adherence to *S** obliges me to reject this. So, I am obliged to find something independently wrong with the way in which the puzzle was set up. It was set up in such a way that before t_2 Tibbles had a tail as a part and Tib allegedly did *not* have a tail as a part. If one dislikes this feature (as I do), then one has to ask, 'Can one identify and name a part of a cat, insist one is naming just that, *and* insist that what one is naming is a cat?' This is my argument against the supposition that one can: at t_1 does Tib have a tail or not? I mean the question in

the ordinary sense of 'have,' not in any peculiar sense 'have as a part'. For in a way it is precisely the propriety of some other concept of *having as a part* which is in question. Surely Tib adjoins and is connected to a tail in the standard way in which cats who have tails are connected with their tails. There is no peculiarity in this case. Otherwise Tibbles himself might not have a tail. Surely any animal which has a tail loses a member or part of itself if its tail is cut off. But then there is no such cat as the cat who at t_1 has no tail as a part of himself. Certainly there was a cat-part which anybody could call 'Tib' if they wished. But one cannot define into existence a *cat* called Tib who had no tail as part of himself at t_1 if there was no such cat at t_1.[6]

Postscript and Commentary

Returning to this piece forty-seven years after it was written, I found the published version hard to understand at some points and hard even to read. The paper has been cited, criticized, or referred to far too often, however, for it to be omitted or be substantially rewritten. The mistakes and oversights must all remain in the text—to be pointed out (where I know them) in this *Postscript*. At the purely editorial level, however, it has seemed imperative to intervene at a number of points simply to discern and clarify the paper's direction and to signal its route to its conclusion. Editorial matters apart, proper acknowledgement is made now to John Locke's priority in seeing the need to qualify somehow the principle that two things cannot be in the same place at the same time.

For purposes of cross-reference between text and commentary every paragraph of the text has been numbered.

Paragraphs 6 and 7. The expression 'something over and above' usually leads to confusion. Paragraphs 6 and 7 are no exception. Slightly less confusedly or obscurely, someone might want to raise the question whether the non-identity of T and W stands in the way of saying that '*T is nothing but W*'. I reply that the non-identity ought indeed to discourage *that* particular claim. Maybe it would be better to say 'There is more to a tree than its stuff' and then say (more or less as before) that neither the non-identity of T and W nor the fact of there being 'more to' T than there is to W can show that physics, chemistry, and other sciences of matter fail to apply equally to T and to W. The non-identity '$T \neq W$' does however serve to point to a substantive, further and distinct question, namely

---

[6] Professor Geach kindly permitted me to allude to his formulation of this puzzle, but he has no responsibility for the purpose to which it is put here.

whether the sciences of botany, forestry, dendrology... can in the serious sense be *reduced* to physics and chemistry. That is a very different question from that of these sciences' *applicability* to T. (See S&SR, p. 156 n. 18.)

Paragraph 9. The reader will not find here a good argument to show why two things or two things of the same kind (or kind of kind) cannot be in the same place at the same time, nor yet an argument to show why two substances cannot be in the same place at the same time.

Consideration (i). It is true that there might be some difficulty in telling one f from another after both land in exactly the same spot at exactly the same time. When they move on, how are we to know which one is which? But, even where there would be that difficulty, how much can that show? If there is an argument here it is inconclusive.

Consideration (ii) is without force. It is simply untrue that I_m implies Locke's principle. The idea that it does rests on a culpable equivocation upon 'coincide'. In the context of I_m, 'coincides' is the relation (alias 'the same f as') by reference to which a substance A may be tracked and be identified as one and the same as A', and A' be tracked and identified as one and the same as A''... These identifications have to be adjudged on much else beside mere position. (See I_m.) Where they pass muster, there is a finding of proper identity. But being in the same place at the same time is coincidence in a less demanding sense than this and may be insufficient in itself for identity.

Once we undo this muddle and put my use of 'coincides' away as confusing, we are in a position to appreciate, following Peter Simons, that there are at least three relations in question here. First, there is identity. Second, there is the relation that Tib+tail and Tibbles have, namely that of having all their parts in common. (He reserves the verb 'coincide' for this relation.) And third there is the relation of superposition or being in the same place at the same time.

Suppose we follow A, A', A"... all the way to place p at time t. What prevents the separate tracking of a different substance X, X', X"... from leading all the way to the very same place p at time t? If that were to happen then the A (A', A"...) substance and the X (X', X"...) substance would be *superposed* one upon the other. (I borrow this useful term from Peter Simons.) But would they be bound to be identical? That question remains. I_m does not entail anything like Locke's principle.

Consideration (iii) is equally unavailing. As charitably salvaged and simplified by Simons—let us move across to his version and forget mine—it can be reduced to the claim that, if x and y are superposed then they must have their parts in common. Simons shows that this claim is dubious in itself. He shows also that, even if the claim were true, superposition would still—alas—not entail identity.[7] The doubtfulness of that entailment was already evident from the examples of *T* and *W* and of [Tib+Tail] and Tibbles. They have all their parts in common and they are in the same place at the same time, but not everything true of the one is true of the other. (See paragraph 11 of the original essay.) The moral I draw is that [Tib+Tail] is a mere aggregate and Tibbles is a substance. Compare the case with *T* and *W* of paragraphs 3 to 7 of the 1968 paper.

The question that now remains is whether two *substances* can be in the same place at the same time. Simons offers an example to show that they can. It relates to the ship of Theseus:

> ... a form-constant ship is a material continuant which has the form of a ship and has this form at all times at which it exists and without interruption. It is of no account whether it is always made of the same matter ... so long as the capacity for performing the function is maintained ... A matter-constant ship, on the other hand, is a material continuant which has the form of a ship but which ceases to exist if any matter is added or taken away.

By means of this example Simons seeks to illustrate the possibility of the superposition of two substances, both ships, without identity—the possibility, that is, of substances, distinct by virtue of having different identity-conditions, being at this or that time in the very same place. But it matters whether all is well with the form-constant and matter-constant conceptions of a ship—and it matters whether all is well with holding to *both* conceptions at once. Neither of the conceptions that Simons suggests is very convincing as a conception of a *ship*. In Chapter 1, section 1.16, I argue against the very *cotenability* of competing conceptions of Theseus' ship. It is a question though whether what I say there will generalize to all the possible examples of the superposition of distinct substances that Simons might produce.

Finally, however inconclusively, let me express my would-be agreement with Ayers's thought that, if two substances were in the same place at the same time, they would place conflicting demands upon the disposition of the matter supposedly common to them. See my discussion of Ayers at Introduction §6 (end). But I am not sure that I should know how to demonstrate that in every imaginable case two distinct substances would have to place conflicting demands.

In 1968 my chief thought was that an *aggregate* and a substance in the same place at the same time do not place such competing demands. So much still seems certain.

---

[7] Peter Simons, *Parts: A Study in Ontology* (Oxford: Clarendon Press, 1987), pp. 216–17, 220, 237, and more generally chapter 6.

3

Substance

1 Introduction

The notion of a substance—of a persisting and somehow basic object of reference that is there to be discovered in perception and thought, an object whose claim to be recognized as a real entity is a claim on our aspirations to understand the world—has been host at various times to countless internecine battles, not all of them very well understood by the protagonists of the warring doctrinal persuasions.[1] Aristotle began with the Greek word for being, which had an established life outside philosophy; and he deployed the variety of its forms to offer definitions of substance. We shall look at one of these definitions in a moment. But Aristotle was never in a position to fix his topic of discussion once and for all, because his conception of what ought to be achieved by a discussion of *ousia* constantly outgrew his definitions. Things did not improve when Aristotle's successors decided to treat it as more or less clear what topic it was that he had introduced—as if the only problem were to improve or complete or correct or supersede his investigation of it or else to add to the list of ancillary notions that Aristotle had already introduced for its further elucidation, such as form, essence, entelechy, actuality and potentiality. But when Aristotelians or rationalists insisted upon the notion of a substance and empiricists like Hume or Russell claimed to reject it, were they really talking about the same thing? It is hard here to disentangle topic from thesis.

---

[1] That is often the fate of technical notions. In order for philosophy to avoid wars about words such as those that 'substance' has occasioned (contrast just wars about the identity or nature of that which is denoted by a word with an established use), the best thing would be to insist upon an explicit definition for every term of art, given in language that had an established everyday life outside philosophy. The effort of making definitions would identify the presuppositions of the author—which he or she could then avow. In cases of doubt, technical terms would be defined over and over again by each author who was prepared to use them. Unluckily 'substance' (variously *ousia*, *on*, *hupokeimenon*, *substantia*, *ens*) was never introduced in this way—and now it never could be.

2 An Objection and a Preliminary Defence

Shortly we must try to disentangle just some of these things. But there is a real point in facing immediately the empiricist rejection of substance—if only because it will promote the effort to attend better to what Aristotle and the rationalists meant by substance (and/or a substance).

Among representative statements of the empiricist rejection, it may be best to consider Hume, *A Treatise of Human Nature*, I. i. 16:

> We have no idea of substance distinct from that of a collection of particular qualities.... The idea of a substance as well as that of a mode is nothing but a collection of simple ideas that are united by the imagination and have a particular name assigned them, by which we are able to recall... either to ourselves or others that collection.

Compare *Treatise*, I. iv. 4:

> The imagination is apt to feign something unknown and invisible which it supposes to continue the same under all these variations: and this intelligible something it calls a substance, or original and first matter.

Compare also I. iv. 5:

> If any one should [say] that the definition of a substance is *something which may exist by itself*... I should observe that this definition agrees to everything that can possibly be conceived.

These are hostile characterizations by one who deliberately made no use of the idea of substance or a substance. Inheriting the situation we now inherit—anxious not to be mesmerized by the history of the subject yet unable to turn our back on that history lest we repeat old errors or neglect old insights—we can only gain a fresh or authentic grasp upon the ideas that Hume was rejecting by referring back to the questions that prompted Aristotle to introduce them and his inheritors to take their stand upon them. Grasping the sense of 'substance' from these philosophical uses, we must look for a unitary or central idea of substance. But we have to be ready for the possibility that the idea is sustained by a diversity of theoretical interests—unless, of course, we prefer now to abandon it. But to abandon it is less easy than Hume has made it appear.

Look back at Hume's characterizations. How else can a set of qualities cohere together than by being properties of one and the same subject? Or, abandoning that line of defence as question-begging, let us ask what sort of a collection it was that Hume had in mind. How is it to be specified? Either the kind of collection Hume speaks of is specified by reference to some subject of the properties, or else it is specified enumeratively by reference to the properties that are members of the collection. In the first case, Hume does not escape the questions that come with the idea of the subject of the properties. In the second case, every new property and every old property deleted must result in a new collection of the kind Hume proposes. But then there will be no question of doing justice to the thought, which we do not know how to do without, that we can gradually amass and correct a larger and larger amount of information about one and the same thing, the same subject, and can come to understand better and better in this way how these properties intelligibly cohere or why they arise together. Nor is there any question of doing justice to the thought that this last is what we *have* to do if we are to make sense of the world at all. Salient among things that we have to recognize if we are to make sense of the world are the substances. That at least will be the claim of those who lie within the sphere of influence of Aristotle.

3 Aristotle's First Account of Substance

3.1

The idea of a substance begins its serious philosophical life in Aristotle's *Categories*. A substance—or, in the terms of that work of Aristotle's, a first or primary substance—is something that is neither in anything else nor predicable of anything else. That is a definition of a sort. It is Aristotle's earliest definition of a substance. But it needs to be unpacked.

Begin with the idea of a subject of discourse, or anything at all that you can talk about, whether abstract or concrete. Then arrive at substances by disentangling them from other subjects of discourse. Among these other items you can talk about, some are *in* others in the way in which colours and their determinate shades are in things. Put them aside. Some are *in* things in the way in which knowledge in general or some specific and particular knowledge (e.g. that 'Socrates' is spelled with the letter sigma in Greek) is *in* things. Put them aside too. (Henceforth let us continue to italicize these sorts of *in*.) To the extent that anything is not *in* other things in these ways, it enjoys a certain autonomy. Something that has this autonomy may be causally dependent on other things in the way in which the infant depends on the mother; but, that does not matter. Ontologically speaking, the infant is still independent—at least to the extent so far explained. (Note also that according to this conception, before it is made radically stricter in the way in which it was at the hands of Leibniz, ontological autonomy of the kind we are concerned with is prima facie consistent with one substance's being a *part* of another substance.)

On Aristotle's view of matters, when items are excluded that are *in* other items, the items that are left over to be ontologically more fundamental will either be sorts of thing (animal-kinds such as horse or man, for instance) or else particular concrete things such as Arkle or Victor or Socrates. But now, if we stipulate that a primary substance should be not only ontologically autonomous (not *in* anything in the manner previously explained) but also *not predicable of anything else*, then animal, horse, or man—secondary substances, as Aristotle calls these, or kinds of primary substance—can be set aside as less fundamental than particular concrete things. A particular concrete thing, Socrates or Arkle, is the sort of thing that *is* other things (e.g. is a man, is an animal, is a horse) and can be *qualified* by other things (e.g. colour or knowledge). But the particular thing is not itself true of other things. It does not qualify other things. Rather, a concrete substance, a this such-and-such, is the sort of thing to support and to make possible *other* subjects of discourse. It is not itself predicated.

Suppose that is all right so far. Then, if the question is asked, 'What makes up the world?', one kind of answer can be found in the claim that the primary substances are the basic constituents of the world. Everything else that is (everything beside the primary substances) is by virtue of being either one *kind* of primary substance (that is, by virtue of being some secondary substance), or else by virtue of being some *qualification* of primary substance, or *in* a primary substance. Moreover, primary substances are the subjects of change. 'It seems most distinctive of substance that what is numerically one and the same is able to receive contraries' (*Categories* 4a10).

3.2

Entering into philosophy on these terms—furnishing an answer to displace or improve upon certain sorts of Pre-Socratic answer to the question of what there is, the Milesian or Eleatic answers, for instance—the notion of a substance is of course attuned from the outset to an ontology of things that are salient and privileged within the world-view of a human inquirer, the inquirer who reasons, argues, draws conclusions, asks questions about the world, and inquires there for an answer to these questions. Such an inquirer thinks of primary substances as *continuants* (a non-Aristotelian but useful word), and he thinks of himself as one continuant among many, etc. Such an inquirer has from the nature of the case to be ready or eager to make new discoveries about the primary substances that he encounters. He is ill prepared for the suggestion that the world of primary substances is a mere by-product of his natural and epistemological situation; that all that there is is flux or atoms or electrons or packets of energy; or that the world we inhabit is one where the persistence of any entity through time is seriously problematic. Indeed an Aristotelian is better prepared for the opposite suggestion (scarcely open to us) that the entities invoked by scientific theories are constructions or abstractions from the familiar world of primary substances.

3.3

What else is there to say in general about substances so conceived, in advance of any particular study of particular kinds of them? Well, working freely from the suggestions that Aristotle furnishes in the first five chapters of *Categories* and exploiting the connections between primary and secondary substances, one may take off from the point that, given any object that is putatively a primary substance, one can ask the question 'What is this thing?' and expect there to be a certain sort of answer to the question—a secondary substance answer. This answer will neither presuppose another answer in the way in which 'it runs' or 'it is white' do (these are answers in the Aristotelian predication-kinds corresponding to the question *what is it doing?* and *what is it like?*, predication-kinds which presuppose the first predication-kind answering the question *what is it?*) nor presuppose another answer in the way in which 'tinker', 'tailor', 'soldier', 'sailor' do. (A soldier is a *man* who is engaged to fight for a given army, a sailor is a *man* in some way engaged in navigation, etc.) Rather, the answer must carry us to a certain sort of conclusion, as 'man', 'horse', or 'olive tree' do. Where no such conclusory answer is provided to the question 'What is it?', it will be indeterminate what we are thinking about. (If it is indeterminate what we are thinking about, the situation is not to be redescribed as there being some indeterminate thing that we are thinking about.) The search for such answers is all of a piece with the expectation that a primary substance will belong to some secondary substance whose members *survive* certain sorts of change, *come into being* in a certain specifiable way, *tend to be qualified* in certain specifiable ways, *tend to behave* in certain specifiable ways, and *tend to cease to be* in certain specifiable ways.

We need an example. One might identify the thing one finds under a treestump by saying 'See that maggot!' Identifying it as a maggot—rather than as a 'bug' or 'creepy crawly', which is where the identifier might start—commits the identifier to think of it as a creature with specifiable tendencies of movement and behaviour (e.g. flight from light or interference) of which a great deal more might be discovered, as a creature with a certain life-cycle of which much more might be discovered, as a creature with a certain way of appearing, and so on. If that is right, then to pick something out as a maggot is to take a certain epistemological risk (which is how it should be) and to subsume it under a conception that the modern entomologist's conception supplements, sorts out, and situates in a larger descriptive and explanatory framework. This is the place to remark that the entomologist's work will reveal that the said maggot is the larva of the fly commonly called the bluebottle. That will show that (unlike 'bluebottle') 'maggot' is not the ultimate or unproblematically conclusory answer that it seemed for the question 'What is it?'. An entomologist will study in depth the actual nature of the relevant species of insect. By these efforts, he will focus the question—make it clearer what the issue turns on—and he will also reveal the further facts by which the question might be settled whether an arbitrary something appearing later is or is not the same thing (the same insect) as that maggot.

4 Kinds and Activity

Consolidating all this, we may say that primary substances belong to kinds (fall under secondary substances) whose members (instances) are something or other in the category of substance and are qualified in the further categories of *quality*, for instance, or of *quantity* or of *doing* or of *being affected* or ... They persist, not through any and every change but through changes that arise from their ways of being and acting—from their mode of activity, as one might say. This last, the principle of activity, will be founded in their shared nature, which Aristotle characterized at a later moment in his philosophical development (but compatibly enough with *Categories* in respect of the point we are concerned with here) as follows:

The primary and proper sense of nature/*phusis* is the *ousia* [being, way of being] of those things which contain in themselves as such a source of change [or principle of activity]. Matter is called nature/*phusis* in so far as it is capable of receiving this nature/*phusis*, and the processes of generation and growth are called nature/*phusis* because they are processes derived from this nature/*phusis*. Nature/*phusis* in this sense is the source of change in natural objects [that is substances] which is somehow inherent in them, either potentially or actually. (*Metaphysics*, book 5, 1015a11)

If substances are things that have a source of change or principle of activity within them, then it is to be expected that a thinker who has the conception of a particular kind of substance k endowed with its corresponding particular nature and who grasps, by means of that conception, the concept of horse or olive-tree or man or bluebottle (or whatever k it is) will be able (under conditions favourable enough) to single out k things as k things, tell ks from other things and tell one k from another. Understanding well enough the principle of activity of things of the kind k, he knows what it takes to trace a particular one of them through space and time. For cases of doubt or difficulty (arising from change, for instance) we look to him or others no less familiar with these creatures to suggest what else needs to be found out.

5 Further Developments of the Aristotelian Idea

Substances are what the world is articulated into when the segmentation of kinds corresponds to the real divisions in reality. In Aristotle's picture, the world will be articulated into primary substances without distinct secondary substance-concepts ever cross-classifying anything. One and the same entity will not turn up in the extension of distinct specific kinds of substance.[2]

How if at all can a modern philosophy enlarge upon Aristotle's foundational conception of substances? One's first thought might be that when the world is divided into the kinds or sorts $f, g, h, j, k\ldots$ that divide it into true primary substances, there will be, for each such f, indefinitely many true generalizations in the form

for every x such that x belongs to f, x is φ,

where being φ is a property well chosen for f. That is to say that an Aristotelian secondary substance f that articulates genuine primary substances will make possible the extrapolation across all f things of a host of manifest or discoverable properties. In further development of this, one notices that this is the place to accommodate an insight that originates, I think, with Bertrand Russell. Suppose we go down to the beach and for the first time in our life we encounter a seal; and suppose that we hear the seal bark. Then, if we venture the guess that all seals bark, nature will reward our daring. Barking (unlike being wounded or ill, say) is a property that is well made for extrapolation across the whole class of seals. When we divide the world into the kinds that divide it into true substances, we find indefinitely many kind–property pairs $<f, \varphi>$ that are well made for scientific generalization and the other purposes of description and explanation. What is more, we know what it is for this condition to fail. If we were to treat the complement of each secondary substance or substance-kind as itself a secondary substance or substance-kind—something that Aristotle cautions us against at *Categories* 3b26—we should find no such kind–property pairs. (The complement

---

[2] Adjoining a non-Aristotelian preoccupation to Aristotle's concerns, one finds oneself saying that if that doctrine is right then if we wanted to say that there are persons among cetacea as well as among hominids, then the concept of person would not be a substance-concept. Nothing can fall under two discrepant principles of individuation. (For the hazards of acquiescing in such cross-classification see *S&SR*, chapter 1.)

of a kind would comprise absolutely everything that did not belong to that kind.) If, despite our not falling into this absurd error, the kinds we choose to divide the world into yield miserably few kind–property pairs that are well made for scientific and explanatory generalization, then the chances are that we must look for a better articulation of substances. Or that is the picture.

There is at least one more way in which the philosophy of substance bears upon the idea of reality. We begin with the point that, if we have an entity x that belongs to the genuine secondary substance or substance-kind of fs, then x is not more or less of an f than other things that belong to that kind... (Nor, incidentally, is it more or less of a substance than some object y that falls under a distinct substance sort or secondary substance k.) The Aristotelian claim is that, given a true secondary substance g, either the object x is a g and fully a g or x is not a g at all. ('Substance, it seems, does not admit of a more or a less...any given substance is not called more or less that which it is' (*Categories* 3b34–6).) So far with Aristotle, but this claim can be fortified.

Suppose that an entity a is the same as the entity b. If so, then whatever is true of a is also true of b and vice versa. (This principle is often called Leibniz's law, because it is entailed or presupposed by Leibniz's stronger two-way claim: *eadem sunt quorum unum alteri substitui potest salva veritate*: 'the same are those things that can be substituted the one for the other without detriment to truth'.) But every object is entirely determinately the object it is. So, for every object a, a is determinately the same as a. But then, by Leibniz's law, if a is indeed b, b is entirely determinately the same as the object a. (For further discussion see Chapter 1, sections 16–17.) The only doubt this deduction can leave is not the question of validity or Leibniz's Law but the question of how the system of primary and secondary substances can sustain the application to the world of so strict and unrelenting a conception of the individuation of substances as the deduction shows the concept of identity to demand.

That question is pursued in Chapter 1, but in the present chapter, let us revert to the claim that not just any grammatically suitable characterization can count as the adequate or explicitly conclusory answer to the question *what is this thing?* We can pick out someone as a poet. But one person *can* be more or less of a poet than another. 'Poet' is not a conclusory answer to the question 'What is it that is singled out here?' (Byron was born in 1788. But the baby who was born in 1788 was not the same poet as the poet who published *Childe Harold* I–II in 1812. For the baby was not a poet. The baby was, however, a human being and the same human being as Byron, the poet. It is in the light of an understanding of what a human being is and does that the identity of baby and the author of *Childe Harold* has to be determined. It is in the light of the corresponding principle of activity that the biography of the human being who became the poet is to be understood.)

What follows? It follows that any system of secondary substances with a claim to separate reality into its genuine primary components must arise from a set of principles of activity on the basis of which identity questions can be glossed as questions about the holding or non-holding of a completely determinate relation. This is not to say that everything that is needed can be written down or said in a finite space. It is only to say that the system of real secondary substances must have a density and depth that provides for it to be expanded to the point where any identity question that actually arises can be glossed or elucidated as a question about the all-or-nothing relation that we have seen identity to be.

6 Legacy of the Aristotelian Conception

These are exigent requirements. Moreover, because of the close coherence that is coming to light between the formal logic of identity, Aristotelian metaphysics, and Aristotelian philosophy of nature, the philosophy of substance may seem to be in danger of committing us to positions that the progress of science since Aristotle makes it harder and harder to sustain. As a zoologist he still ranks among the great scientists and interpreters of nature, but it is no longer plausible to look for philosophical support for the scientific ultimacy of a biology and a physical science pitched at the particular level of insight that Aristotle himself found so compelling and at which he expected to be able to describe the operation of the final causes that govern the cosmos. We shall touch on this again (see section 13), only remarking here that the theory of substance becomes yet more complex in Aristotle's writings subsequent to the *Categories*. It also becomes more confusing, in ways to which we shall recur. (See section 11.2.) In the interim, however, we must mine further the conceptual riches that come to us with the simple neo-Aristotelian conception.

The idea we now have of a primary substance is evidently not—let it be clear—the idea of a 'we know not what'. Nor is it the idea of substance that we find in Kant, when, under the influence of Hume, he writes: 'People have long since observed that in all substances, the real subject, that which remains after the abstraction of all accidents (as predicates), remains unknown' (*Prolegomenon to Any Future Metaphysics*, sect. 46). The real subject, Socrates or Arkle, is one and the same as the palpable, perceptible substance Socrates or Arkle. This is nothing inherently unknown. It is something we know much about, albeit imperfectly. And, however difficult the empiricists were destined to find the Aristotelian idea of a substance—we have already seen Hume's hostile account of these things—this is the notion of substance we find has been communicated by the Scholastics to modern philosophy as it was before Kant or Hume, and as it was when Descartes claimed that a substance is something that exists in and through itself and can exist without dependence on anything else (*Fourth Replies*, in *Oeuvres*, ed. C. Adam and P. Tannery, vii 226) or when Spinoza stipulated:

> By a substance I mean that which is in itself and is conceived through itself: in other words, that the concept of which does not need the concept of another thing from which it has to be formed. (*Ethics Demonstrated in Geometrical Order*, first part, definition iii)

It was this same notion that Leibniz was drawing out further when he wrote in his correspondence with De Volder, the Dutch physicist,

> Nothing is permanent in a substance except the law itself which determines the continuous succession of its states and accords within the individual substance with the laws of nature that govern the whole world.
>
> Simple partless substances are nothing more than sources and subjects of the whole unfolding series of perceptions. These series of perceptions all express with the greatest and most fitting variety the same world of phenomena. By these means the supreme substance communicates its own perfection so far as it is possible to many substances which depend upon it. Each of these many substances must be conceived as a microcosm or concentration of the whole world and (some less so, some more so) as, so to speak, an assemblage of the attributes of divinity. Nor do I think that any other rationale for the way of things can be understood. Everything had to be this way if it was to be at all. (Gerhardt, II, p. 263)

Aristotle had not of course said in *Categories* that substances were partless or the sources and subjects of the whole unfolding series of perceptions. The world-view of the rationalists was not that of Aristotelian science. In several ways, it was anti-Aristotelian. But the rationalists continued to conceive of intelligible ultimate reality in terms of substances that make up the world. Both formally and in respect of explanatory role, they conceived of substances much as Aristotle had. Leibniz's search for that which underlies all the rest of reality had begun with the Aristotelian conception of a subject of predications (*hupokeimenon*) conceived as that which is self-sufficient and in no need of other things. Then he was led to doubt that any true substance could stand in a part–whole relation to any other substance, or be other than causally autonomous. So his disagreement with Aristotle issued in a disagreement about the extension of the notion. But (even at the furthest point, where Leibniz concluded that only souls or soul-like things could be substances) this was still a reinterpretation of the original idea of substance in Aristotle, whose influence we can see directly at work in such passages as this:

Aristotle has called nature the principle of motion and of rest.... [The] divine law once established has truly conferred upon substances some created impression which endures within them or... an internal law from which their actions and passions follow... there is a certain efficacy residing in things, a form or force such as we usually designate by the name of nature, from which the series of phenomena follows. (*On Nature itself or on the Inherent Force and Actions of Created Things*, Gerhardt, IV, p. 505)

7 The Collision of Rationalist and Empiricist Claims

The moment has come to ask why the idea of a subject that is an individual substance represented such a difficulty for the empiricists.

Perhaps the best place in which to witness the clash between empiricism and the philosophy of substance is Leibniz's *New Essays on the Human Understanding*. This work represents an imaginary conversation between Locke, whose part Leibniz compiles scrupulously from Locke's *Essay On Human Understanding* and assigns to a character he calls Philalethes, and Leibniz himself, whom he calls for these purposes Theophilus. The most important exchange on this matter is at II. 23. In Remnant and Bennett's translation of chapter 23 ('Of our Complex Ideas of Substances') we have:

> PHILALETHES. §1. The mind takes notice that a certain number of 'simple ideas go constantly together: which being presumed to belong to one thing... are called so united in one subject by one name; which through heedlessness we are apt afterward to talk of... as one simple idea, which indeed is a complication of many ideas together'.
>
> THEOPHILUS. I see nothing in the ordinary ways of talking which deserves to be accused of 'heedlessness'. We do take it that there is one subject, and one idea, but not that there is one simple idea. (p. 217)

What gloss have we committed ourselves to make (see section 2) on this exchange? The idea of the sun cannot be a conjunction of Lockean ideas (or properties), we have claimed, because that would mean that, whenever we learned a new property of the sun, we should have got ourselves a new 'complication' and a new idea of the sun. Every enrichment or impoverishment would have to determine a new complication—and a new subject of discourse. For the identity of a complication has to be determined by reference to its components. Does Locke recognize this? He continues:

> PHIL. Not imagining how these simple ideas can subsist by themselves, we accustom ourselves to suppose some *substratum*—something which supports them—wherein they do subsist, and from which they do result, which therefore we call substance.

THEO. I believe that this way of thinking is correct. And we have no need to 'accustom' ourselves to it, or to 'suppose' it; for from the beginning we conceive several predicates in a single subject, and that is all there is to these metaphorical words 'support' and 'substratum'. So I do not see why it is made out to involve a problem. On the contrary, what comes into our mind is the *concretum* conceived as wise, warm, shining, rather than *abstractions* or qualities such as wisdom, warmth, light, etc., which are much harder to grasp. (I say qualities, for what the substantial object contains are qualities not ideas.) It can even be doubted whether these accidents are genuine entities at all, and indeed many of them are only relations. We know, too, that it is abstractions which cause the most problems when one tries to get to the bottom of them. Anyone knows this who is conversant with the intricacies of scholastic thought: their thorniest brambles disappear in a flash if one is willing to banish abstract entities, to resolve that in speaking one will ordinarily use only concrete terms and will allow no terms into learned demonstrations except ones which stand for substantial subjects. So to treat qualities or other abstract terms as though they were the least problematic, and concrete ones as very troublesome, is to 'look for a knot in a bullrush' [Plautus], if you will allow me the phrase, and to put things back to front. (p. 217)

According to Leibniz, the way in which Locke really needed to see the complication of ideas (or qualities as other philosophers say) that make up our idea of the sun was as a substance/substratum (something Locke says we do not know) which shines on us *and* warms us *and* rises *and* sets *and*... According to Leibniz, Locke does not see the difference between that and what Locke does say. Nowadays some scholars claim that this is an unsympathetic reading of Locke.[3] But few if any of his philosophical successors were able to understand Lockean

---

[3] In his 'The Ideas of Power and Substance in Locke's Philosophy', *Philosophical Quarterly*, 25 (1975), revised for I. C. Tipton (ed.), *Locke on Human Understanding: Selected Essays* (Oxford: Oxford University Press, 1977), Michael Ayers argues in a way sympathetic to Locke that what Locke means is indeed that our idea of the sun is the idea of a substratum which shines on us *and* warms us *and* rises *and* sets... —that our ignorance of the substratum is our ignorance of the real essence or nature of a given kind of thing. It is this ignorance of the real essence or nature that shapes Locke's whole treatment.

> In order to mark the presumption of... a natural unity among [the powers, dispositions, properties that] we include under one complex idea on the basis of their observed coexistence [in a given kind of thing], we add [sic] the idea of 'some substratum wherein they do subsist and from which they do result'. The concept of substance, 'substratum' or 'thing (having such and such properties)' is thus a concept by means of which we refer to what is unobserved and unknown—or known only through its effects and relatively to the level of observation. In other words *substance* is a dummy concept and Locke's derision is directed against those who suppose it is something more.

'complications' of ideas otherwise than as implying that the idea of the sun is a complication of the idea of shining and/with the idea of warming and/with the idea of rising and/with the idea of setting *and/with* the idea of substance, which is the idea of we know not what support or substratum. (Note the entirely different role of 'and' in this reading from its role in the sympathetic reading, as I began by stating that. In that sympathetic statement 'and' conjoined sentential clauses. In a traditional reading of Locke it means, more or less, 'conjoined with'.)

Leibniz is only one of many who have read Locke, however wrongly, in this way. If Hume had read Locke otherwise than in this way, he would have had much more difficulty in taking substance to be as superfluous as it was (according to Locke) inscrutable.

8 Subject and Properties

Here let us continue the exchange between Philalethes and Theophilus.

> PHIL. §2. A person's only notion of pure substance in general is that of I know not what subject of which he knows nothing at all but which he supposes to be the support of qualities. We talk like children; who, being questioned, what such a thing is, which they know not, readily give this [to them] satisfactory answer, that it is something; which in truth signifies... when so used... that they know not what it is.
>
> THEO. If you distinguish two things in a substance—the attributes or predicates, and their common subject—it is no wonder that you cannot conceive anything special in this subject. That is inevitable, because you have already set aside all the attributes through which details could be conceived. Thus, to require of this 'pure subject in general' anything beyond what is needed for the conception of 'the same thing'—e.g. it is the same thing which understands and wills, which imagines and reasons—is to demand the impossible; and it also contravenes the assumption which was made in performing the abstraction and separating the subject from all its qualities or accidents. (p. 218)

At risk of painting the lily and repeating things the reader understands already, let us distinguish within Theophilus' diagnosis two distinct objections.

This is persuasive, yet, even as it persuades, it helps us to understand why Leibniz and countless others read Locke otherwise. For, if the idea of the sun is the idea of a substance/substratum which shines on us *and* warms *and* rises, there cannot be any possibility to 'add' the idea of substratum. The substratum is there already—in the grammar of the sympathetic reading. It is not optional. It cannot be *added*.

First objection. The Lockean idea of an *I know not what*, the bare idea of a substratum, is only the product of the separation of the subject from all its properties.

How was such a separation possible? It would have been helpful, and it would have discouraged Philalethes from giving a most implausible formulation to his thesis about the limitations of human understanding of material objects and our ignorance of their real essence, if at this point Theophilus had borne in mind Aristotle's distinction between the categories of substance and quality—the contrast between answers to the question '*What is* this thing?' and answers to the question 'What is this thing *like*?' Perhaps the empiricist knows as well as anybody else that the process of abstracting all the properties from a subject and amassing them as a conjunction or complication of qualities will in the end cause the subject itself to disappear. But the real palpable subject becomes invisible even more quickly than the empiricist realizes. It becomes invisible so soon as one seeks to abstract from the subject, a dog, a horse, a man, a tree or whatever, the property of being a dog or a horse or a man or a tree and to thrust that 'property' into the category of quality. What is an individual tree taken in abstraction from its being a tree? What is a dog when one prescinds from its being a dog? Under this abstraction, how are these things even to be conceived of? The subject is that which *has* the qualities, but why suppose that we can reach this subject by not thinking of it as having *any* qualities, not even the qualities that are essential to its being singled out as that very subject? (Or even worse by thinking of it as *not having* any qualities.)

The bare idea of a subject is one thing. To have such an idea is to conceive of an ordinary subject while leaving it entirely open what the subject is. One can certainly approximate to that sort of conceiving. (When we seek to imagine how things might have been for a certain thing x, we can hold constant what x is, what palpable substance x is, and explore all the variations in how it might have been.) The idea of a *bare subject* is an altogether different thing. No reader of Aristotle's *Categories* will ever agree to make sense of it. By subject (*hupokeimenon*) Aristotle had meant the visible, palpable subject that has qualities—not a substratum that is in itself quality-less, and *has* no qualities. The fact that 'substratum' began as a Latin translation of Aristotle's ordinary word for 'subject', namely 'hupokeimenon', but then came to be understood as denoting something hidden as if 'underneath', then as denoting an absurdity, only signals how old and how persistent the temptations are to commit the confusions with which Theophilus here charges Philalethes, never mind whether justly or unjustly. (For Aristotle's own albeit modest contribution to this confusion, see section 11.2.)

Second objection to what Philalethes does. Locke insisted that, in speaking of substance as a we know not what, he in no way intended to deny the existence of substances, i.e. the kinds of things that answer to what he calls in the heading for his chapter II. 23 'our complex ideas of substances'. But, even in that context, Locke's doctrine still leaves us inquiring for the better understanding that is needed to overcome the division Locke so recklessly insists upon—and that any Aristotelian must reject—when he writes that 'all the idea of substance of anything is is an obscure idea of what it *does* and not any idea of what it *is*'. (Cf. *Essay*, II. xiii. 19-20.)

9 Clear Ideas and Ignorance

9.1

Just once more let us revert to Philalethes' and Theophilus' conversation:

> PHIL. §4. We have 'no clear idea of substance in general'...
> THEO. My own view is that this opinion about what we don't know springs from a demand for a way of knowing which the object does not admit of. The true signs of a clear and distinct notion is one's having means for giving a priori proofs of many truths about it. I showed this in a paper 'Meditations on Knowledge, Truth and Ideas' (p. 219)

The point becomes clearer in the light of the paper of Leibniz's that Theophilus cites. (See Gerhardt, IV, pp. 422-6.) Clear and distinct knowledge—knowledge that not only supports recognition and promotes action (clearness) but provides also for the exhaustive enumeration and analysis of the marks of a kind (provides for distinctness, that is)—is too much to ask in an area where, from the nature of the case, there is no question, for finite minds such as ours, of a priori proofs. No readily imaginable extension of our scientific understanding could give those. But Leibniz insists that there is something else that is a possibility for us, namely *clear indistinct* knowledge, and this is knowledge too. Such is the ordinary knowledge and the ordinary clarity of idea that we have of what a man or a horse is; and such is the knowledge we have of Socrates or Arkle. I would add that the possibility of such grasp becomes philosophically intelligible when we reconstruct it, however artificially, as follows. Suppose we do not know what 'horse' means. Then someone can say to us, pointing to a horse:

> That is a horse. A horse is anything that resembles that thing in the right sort of way. If you want to know what the right sort of way is, well, simply on the basis of how much you *need* to know, look hard at that thing, take note of what it does and how it behaves and how it interacts with other things. When you arrive at a reliable recognitional capacity of the kind—and this will come very swiftly indeed if your efforts are subject to correction by others—then, even if you stop there, you will know, however minimally, what a horse is. You will know enough to understand 'horse'.

In our own times, the principal champion of one version of some such Leibnizian conception of the semantics of natural kind substantives has been the American philosopher Hilary Putnam.[4] We must note, however, that the reconstruction just offered does not guarantee that speakers will always grasp the sense of names of new kinds of substance. Nor does it guarantee that all the substantives that people try to introduce in the manner described will have senses that are well-founded. Nothing ought to guarantee either of these things. The reconstruction simply explains the one thing that needs explaining, namely how, where a substantive does have a well-founded sense, a grasp of the sense and an ordinary knowledge of ordinary substances is possible.

9.2

The combination of ideas that we have drawn from Aristotle and Leibniz is a powerful prescription against most of the vexations by which empiricists from Hume onwards—J. S. Mill, Ernst Mach, Bertrand Russell, and A. J. Ayer, for instance—have attempted to undermine the concept of substance (or in Mill's case, to reduce it to that of mere body). What now stands in the way of the proper reinstatement of the concept? Three things perhaps. First there are certain unintended effects of the symbolism of modern logic which prompt us to see relations where there are only states or properties. (See section 10.) In the second place, there are the further accretions to the doctrine of substance for which Aristotle himself and his admirers have been responsible. (See section 11.2.) Thirdly, there is some continuing obscurity about the need, if any, for an idea of substance that is more than an idea of body. (See section 13.1.)

10 Recent Further Misconceptions of Substance and Property

We have seen how important it is in any account of substance such as Aristotle's to mark the distinction between basic predications that answer the question *what is x?* (sortal predications, as they are often called in present-day philosophy) and predications that answer questions such as *what is x like?*, *how big is x?*, etc. The symbolism of modern first-order logic, employing the notation 'φx', 'ψx' for all

---

[4] Hilary Putnam, 'Is Semantics Possible?', *Metaphilosophy*, 3 (1970), pp. 187–201.

such answers, does not mark this distinction. Indeed it has discouraged many twentieth-century philosophers from attending to it.[5]

In opposition to those who emphasize that distinction, understood as Aristotle understood it (cf. *Metaphysics* 1028a31–1028b2), a difficulty has recently been urged against the very idea of continuants that endure through time. It has been urged by philosophers eager to replace the ontology of enduring, changing substances with a supposedly more fundamental ontology of things-at-moments or things-in-phases. These philosophers are constructionalists, one might say, with respect to substances. They expect to be able to treat questions such as whether x is the same man as y by deploying some equivalence of the following general kind: x is the same man as y if and only if the thing-at-a-moment x (thing-in-a-phase x) bears to the thing-at-a-moment y (thing-in-a-phase y) the ancestral of that relation R (whatever R may be) which holds between arbitrarily nearly simultaneously existing men-at-a-moment or arbitrarily temporally close men-in-a-phase. (Explanation of 'ancestral': x bears to y the ancestral of the relation R just if either x bears R to y or x bears R to some w that bears R to y, or x bears R to some w that bears R to some z that bears R to some z that bears R to y or ...)

It is a real question whether such treatments of identity could ever be made intelligible independently of the scheme that they are supposed to supplant. (Can one characterize the relation R altogether independently of one's diachronic understanding of what a man is, independently, that is, of one's understanding of the relevant principle of activity and so on?) It seems strange that so many philosophers should be happy simply to walk into this difficulty. But the first question is what reason is given for us to do so.

David Lewis, the most distinguished among active champions of the constructionalist view, writes:

The principal and decisive objection against endurance as an account of the persistence of ordinary things such as people ... is the problem of intrinsic [properties].

Lewis and his followers wish to distinguish intrinsic properties, which things have in virtue of the way they themselves are, from extrinsic properties, which things have in virtue of their relations or lack of relations to other things. He continues:

Persisting things change their intrinsic properties, for instance shape: when I sit, I have a bent shape; when I stand, I have a straightened shape. Both shapes are intrinsic properties: I have them only some of the time. How is such change possible? First solution: contrary

---

[5] Not all. See P. F. Strawson, *Individuals: An Essay in Descriptive Metaphysics* (London: Methuen, 1959), Part 2; Willard Van Orman Quine, *Word and Object* (Cambridge, MA: MIT Press, 1960), sect. 15.

to what we might think, shapes are not genuine properties. They are disguised relations which an enduring thing may bear to times. One and the same enduring thing may bear the bent-shape relation to some times and the straight-shape relation to other times. And likewise for all other temporary intrinsic [properties]; all of them must be reinterpreted as relations that something with an absolutely unchanging intrinsic nature bears to different times... This is simply incredible if we are speaking of the persistence of ordinary things... If we know what shape is, we know that it is a property, not a relation.[6]

As we have seen, the conclusion at which Lewis himself arrives on the basis of this difficulty is that people and other continuants do not endure but 'perdure': they are made up of temporal parts, which parts *can* have intrinsic properties such as a bent shape or a straight shape but do not last through changes in intrinsic properties. The question of identity through change is transformed into the question whether distinct but putatively related items belong to one and the same unitary but more complex thing, a certain complex or sum of temporal parts.

Lewis takes the problem of temporary intrinsic properties exceedingly seriously then. What would Aristotle have said about it? He might have said (cf. *De Interpretatione*, chapter 3 at 16a6-10) that it was all very well to represent these supposedly troublesome claims in the fashion of modern logicians as

Bent, t_1 (David).
Straight, t_2 (David).
Sit, t_1 (David).
Stand, t_2 (David);

but what these renderings overlook is that in the natural language sentences that they codify there is a copula (represented in logic by simple concatenation) or there are inflections of verbs. Separately from the properties and acts indicated by predicates, the copula (*be* or *do*) or the verb inflection brings with it time-indication, modality, negation, etc. Once we remember that, in the sentence 'Bent, t_1 (David)', the 't_1' goes with an 'is' that the notation suppresses and in 'Stand, t_2 (David)', the verb has an 's'-inflection that is elided by the notation, we can see that being bent is indeed a *property* that a person *has at a time* and standing is something that a person *does* at a time. (See Chapter 1, sections 12-13.) Being bent is not then a relation between a person and a time.[7]

---

[6] David Lewis, *The Plurality of Worlds* (Oxford: Basil Blackwell, 1986), pp. 203-4.
[7] On these and related matters, the reader may wish to read the paper by Mark Johnston, 'Is there a Problem about Persistence?', *Proceedings of the Aristotelian Society*, suppl. 61 (1987), pp. 107-55. Aristotle's position anticipates Johnston's. But see also Chapter 1, section 12.

11 Aristotle's Further Thoughts

11.1

In *Categories*, Aristotle provided most or all of what we really need in order not to misunderstand our own thoughts about change and to escape the idea that change stands in need of philosophical reconstruction. But in his subsequent writings he aspired to do more than this. He wanted to give a positive answer to Parmenides' doubts about change and to build upon this answer a more ambitious philosophical account of substance and of substances. This is the so-called hylomorphic account initiated in the *Physics*. Within this account, the ordinary substances of *Categories* come to be seen as compounds of matter and form and then, in further development of that account, a new tendency appears, as in the *Metaphysics*, for the title of true substance to be taken from ordinary things such as Socrates (seen now as a compound) and transferred to forms actualized in matter (entelechies), where the *form* of Socrates either is—or is correlative with— his *essence*. (In the technical language of the *Metaphysics*, the essence of Socrates is 'what being is for Socrates'.) In this new development—too large a matter to be treated fully here or at the length that that would require but too notorious to be passed over in complete silence—it is the form that makes Socrates the *this something* that he is. Or in another remarkable turn of Aristotelian philosophical speech, the form is the *substance* of Socrates (compare *Metaphysics* 1017b22, 1038b10) and it is the form which remains constant throughout all the changes which Socrates undergoes.

These developments have given endless trouble to Aristotle's commentators both ancient and modern. We shall paint into the picture so far presented some of these later Aristotelian details, struggle for a moment with the difficulties to which they seem to give rise, and defend the *Categories* conception of substance as well fitted to cohere with the best insights that can flow from the fresh understanding of Books 7–12 of the *Metaphysics* now set in train by modern scholarship.[8]

11.2

Advancing into the philosophy of nature from what he called dialectic (and we might call the philosophy of logic or language), advancing that is from the philosophical pursuits of the *Categories* and other logical writings, Aristotle was

---

[8] In a survey such as this it is not possible to do justice to a mass of new work but let me single out for mention Myles Burnyeat, *A Map of Metaphysics Zeta* (Pittsburgh, PA: Mathesis, 2001).

eager to confront the Eleatic denial of change. He summed up the Parmenidean attack upon change in the question 'How can what is come to be from what is not?' His response in book 1 of the *Physics* (chapters 7–8) comes down to this: in the course of a normal or non-substantial change, a change such as the becoming sunburnt of a white man, for instance, or the becoming educated of an ignorant one, we do not have the coming to be of something from nothing. We have the coming to be sunburnt of something that is there throughout, namely that which was first white and then sunburnt. Aristotle claimed that all change (all non-substantial change, rather) involved a change between two contrary attributes and involved a subject, the subject being that which first has the one attribute and then has the other. *Pace* Parmenides, this is not something's coming from nothing.

So far so good. In this case the *hupokeimenon* or underlying thing is simply the subject or substance itself. There is no special need for a full-scale hylomorphic theory in order to acknowledge the materiality and stability of ordinary substances. But what about the other case of change, namely substantial change, the kind of change where something new comes into existence—as happens with the generation of an animal or a plant? Here too, Aristotle had wanted to insist in his argument with Parmenides that this was not a case of something's coming to be from nothing, but a case of something's coming to be from something that is always underlying, namely matter, the matter first lacking and then acquiring a certain structure or form. 'By matter I mean the first *hupokeimenon* (subject/substratum) of each thing, that from whose presence something arises non-accidentally' (192a30–3).

Aristotle's only reason for using the word 'hupokeimenon' in such a place—hitherto meaning 'subject', something that submits to predication, rather than anything covertly underlying, but now suggesting something as if hidden or below—was the analogy between non-substantial and substantial change that Parmenides' denial of change had forced him to postulate. That analogy is surely both strained and troublesome, however. It is not just that the way in which Socrates pre-exists and persists through sunburning is very unlike the way in which a seed—plus that which the germinating of that seed sucks up from the environment—pre-exists and persists (in so far as it does) through generation. The argumentative strategy seems misguided.

All that Aristotle needs to say to Parmenides (as Aristotle reads him) is this: you deny change by asking how anything can come to be from nothing. Most change, where something comes to be φ having previously been not φ, carries no semblance at all of involving this. But even in the case where a change is a coming into being of something that previously did not exist, the only thing that could pose any real difficulty would be such an event's coming to pass inexplicably—or without there being any cause or reason why it did. What ground is there to think that the coming into being of a new thing is *inherently* inexplicable?

11.3

So much for the role that Aristotle gave to matter in his theory of substance. The next speculative leap is briefly recorded in Aristotle's philosophical lexicon, namely *Metaphysics*, book 5(Δ), where he anticipates the conclusions of books 7(Z) and 8(H) about what a substance is by saying that substance, *ousia*, can mean 'either [compare *Categories*] (1) the final subject/substratum (hupokeimenon) which is not predicated of other things or else (2) that which is a 'this' and separable: of this nature is the shape [*morphē*] of anything or the form [*eidos*, the same word as Plato had used for Platonic Form and Aristotle himself had used for species]' (1017b23–5). As we have said already in section 11.1, the second understanding of *ousia* that Aristotle mentions here scarcely differentiates the substance of a thing from the essence of a thing. 'The essence, the formula of which is a definition, is also called the substance of each thing' (1017b21; cf. 1028b15–18). But this is a conclusion that gives trouble to Aristotle and endless trouble to his interpreters. (See *Metaphysics* Z, chapter 13.) Such an essence seems too much akin to a universal, too much akin to something multiply instantiable, that is, for it to be this or that particular substance.

11.4

Another remarkable thing we shall find in Aristotle's use of the matter/form paradigm is that he should have been led by it to promote form not only over matter, but also over the compound of matter and form. It will be good to try to come to terms with all these developments. (In so far as the reader is disinclined to enter into them, let the reader skip to section 13.1.) Let us focus first on the initiatory moves by which Aristotle advances in the direction of his conclusion that substance is form and his idea that there is something that is the substance of *x*, which is its 'shape' or its form or 'the plan of the form'.

In *Metaphysics* Z.3 he writes as follows.

The word 'substance' is applied, if not in more senses, still at least to four main objects; for both the essence and the universal and the genus are thought to be the substance of each thing, and fourthly the substratum. Now the substratum is that of which other things are predicated, while it is itself not predicated of anything else. [Compare *Categories*, where it is the mark of a primary substance such as an individual man Kallias not to be predicated of anything.] And so we must first determine the nature of this [the substratum, subject, hupokeimenon]. For that which underlies a thing is thought to be in the true sense its substance. And in one sense matter is said to be of the nature of substratum, in another shape, and in a third sense the compound of these. By the matter I mean, for instance, the bronze, by the shape the plan of its form and by the compound of these (the concrete thing) the statue. Therefore, if the form is prior to the matter and more real, it will be prior to the compound also for the same reason. (1028b37–1029a7, trans. Ross and Barnes)

Before giving the rest of the passage to be quoted, I break off for a moment to reassure the reader that Aristotle has not simply let go of the items that were called in *Categories* primary substances.[9] However redescribed, these will have their central place in the full theory if the full theory does what it is meant to do; but the introduction of the new scheme of matter and form and the new status of compounds assigned to things previously accounted primary substances will have the effect of complicating their previously undisputed title to simple primacy. Back now to the rest of the passage:

We have now outlined the nature of substance, showing that it is that which is not predicated of a subject but of which all else is predicated. But we must not merely state the matter; for this is not enough. The statement itself is obscure, and further, on this view *matter* becomes substance. For, if matter is not substance, it is beyond us to say what else it is. [For] when all else is taken away [that might be predicated] evidently nothing but matter remains [to be that of which all else is predicated]. For of the other elements some are affections, products and capacities of bodies, while length, breadth and depth are quantities and not substances [either first or second substances]. For a quality is not a substance; but the substance is rather that to which these belong primarily. But when length and breadth and depth are taken away, we see nothing left except what is bounded by these, whatever it be; so that to those who consider the question thus, matter alone must seem to be substance. (1029a8–1029a19, trans. Ross and Barnes)

This is a conclusion Aristotle is going to say that he finds absurd and impossible, on the grounds (1029a27–29) that matter—as matter appears in the effort to find substance in that of which attributes are predicated—cannot be singled out as 'this' and 'it is accepted that separability and being a "this" belong especially to substance'. It is this kind of difficulty that opens the way, as we have said, to the candidature of form. It is from this point onwards that Aristotle sees form or sees essence as offering better prospects for separability and being a this, and starts to treat separability and being 'this' as better indicators of substancehood than not being predicable. But in the *Metaphysics* as we have it, and before he completes

---

[9] See for instance *Metaphysics* XII (Λ): 'There are three kinds of substance—the matter which is a this by being perceived..., secondly the nature, a "this" and a state that it moves towards; and again, thirdly, the particular substance which is comprised of these two, e.g. Socrates or Kallias.' (1070a9–13)

his case against the candidature of matter, a passage comes that has given much trouble over the ages:

By matter I mean [here, at this point in our enquiry] that which in itself is neither some particular thing nor of certain quantity nor assigned to any other of the categories by which being is determined. For there is something of which each of these is predicated, so that its being [the being of matter] is different from that of the predicates; for the predicates other than substance are predicated of substance, while substance is predicated of matter. Therefore the ultimate substratum is of itself neither a particular thing nor of a particular quantity nor otherwise positively characterized; nor yet negatively [characterized], for negations also will belong to it only by accident. (1029a20–6, trans. Ross and Barnes)

Coming where it does in Aristotle's discussion, this passage will probably remind the reader of the something-we-know-not-what account of substance and lead him to question the stand we have taken here to distance Aristotelian substance from the caricatural we-know-not-what. But, even if something almost equally questionable is in train, what is going on here is importantly different.

Note first that what we find in this passage is not so much Aristotle's own account of matter or of substance as an account of matter as it appears when considered as a candidate to be substance and as submitted to Aristotle's predication test. Nor is matter here matter as Aristotle normally thinks of matter. Nor yet is matter in this passage matter as Aristotle defined it in the *Physics*: 'By matter I mean the first subject/substrate from whose presence something arises non-accidentally', already quoted. (For nothing at all could answer to this sort of description if it had no properties that made it the right matter for that which arose from it.)

If the *Metaphysics* Z.3 conception of matter is special in these ways, why is it special? It is special because it arises from suppositions that are local to the dialectical context—most conspicuously, the assumption (1) (to be tested here outside the *Categories* framework and supposedly to destruction) that substance-hood is equivalent to ultimate non-predicability; the supposition (2) that only what is predicated of substance substantially can identify it as a subject—a supposition that can be relied upon to give amazing results where the putative subject is something like matter and matter is thought not to admit any real (or what-it-is type) predications; a supposition (3), which hylomorphism seems confusingly to import into the *Categories* framework, that if the man Kallias is a compound (a compound of flesh-and-bones and the form of man), then [being a] man [and/or being Kallias] must be predicated of the flesh and bones.

This and the whole dialectical context explains why the Z.3 account of matter is so strange. But what is one to think of the steps by which Aristotle reaches this

his conclusion? Well, there is no point in denying that supposition (2) may have arisen from a trend of thought slightly similar to that which leads into the seductive but absurd idea of the bare subject that we examined in the penultimate paragraph of section 8. But no less important than that mistake—a dead end leading to no Aristotelian conclusion not otherwise available—is the fact that supposition (3) is false. To see why it is false, consider ordinary predication. If Kallias is a man (if man is predicated of Kallias), then there is a man whom Kallias is identical with and with whom he shares all properties. This is an entirely general point about predication, not to be confused with the silly aspiration to reduce all predications to identities. (To test it, try another kind of predication. If Kallias is white, then Kallias is identical with some white thing and he shares all his properties with that.) Now suppose we try saying that, since man [or being Kallias] is to be predicated of matter (e.g. flesh-and-bones), flesh-and-bones is a man [or is Kallias]. On a proper understanding of what is being said, that had better not mean that a man [or Kallias] shares all properties with the flesh and bones. The flesh and bones does not sit or talk. 'Kallias/or man is the flesh-and-bones' is misleading. What it really means is that this flesh-and-bones makes up man or Kallias. What is *predicated* of the flesh and bones is not man or Kallias but the property of *constituting* Kallias or *constituting* a man.[10] If hylomorphism entails (3), then so much the worse for hylomorphism. Meanwhile there may nothing much wrong with (1), provided that we understand it in a manner better apprised of the falsity of (3).

12 Complaints about Aristotle's Further Thoughts

12.1

What follows? It follows that there was never any real danger of matter's counting (either in the ordinary sense or in the confused sense that was local to one context of argument) as ultimate subject. More importantly, any case there may have seemed to be against the *Categories* criterion of substancehood or against Aristotle's election in that work of entities such as Kallias, Arkle, Victor, etc. to be first substances simply collapses (cf. again *Metaphysics* 1070a9-13). It suggests also that there is no connection between ultimate subjecthood and the kind of ultimacy with which physics as we know it is concerned. Just to the extent that hylomorphism rests on a denial of the *Categories* doctrine—rather than

---

[10] In another place Aristotle recognizes what is effectively the very same point: see Book 9 (Θ) 1049a25 following.

hylomorphism's being an idea to be worked out in the progressive reconciliation with Aristotle's earlier views that one may hope to find in the later books of the *Metaphysics*—well, hylomorphism as so stated was simply a mistake.

But what mistake? Does it have to be a mistake? Let us go back now to the very idea, presumably definitive of hylomorphism, that a substance such as Kallias is a compound of matter and form. Kallias is 'this in that', Aristotle says—this sort of thing, namely man, in that sort of matter, namely flesh-and-bones. To understand such claims it is important to see that making them is utterly unlike saying that bronze is copper mixed with lead, and very unlike saying that a hammer is a stick of wood (the handle) attached to a piece of iron (the head). To say that Aristotelian form and matter are utterly different sorts of thing is not simply to say that they are very different *components*. As Aristotle says, the form is not a component at all. It is that which corresponds in the thing to a true account of its shape or the plan of its form.

These points are philosophical reminders for ourselves. They are not criticisms of Aristotle, who attained to a state of incomparably subtle awareness of these and kindred matters—not least the difficulty of characterizing the form of a perceptible substance independently of the requirements upon its realization in matter (how is one to say what a man is without reference to his embodiment?) and the difficulty of characterizing a substance's matter in a manner independent of all reference to the form that it is to realize. (Can we say how matter must be for it to realize man? Flesh and bones presuppose animal. What is more, not any old flesh and bones will suffice. We need the right sort of flesh and bones for a man in particular.) The question is how to follow these insights through into a simple or soundly based philosophy of substance that might still serve—even now—as a part of a sane philosophy.

At 1029a1 f., already quoted, Aristotle says 'If form is prior to matter and more real it will be prior to the compound also, for the same reason.' We have more or less allowed Aristotle his conclusion that matter is a poor candidate to furnish a substance or a this. But can we allow it to him that the form is prior to the compound of form and matter and therefore a better candidate than the compound for being a substance? The sense of priority that is to be understood here is a matter of debate among scholars. But it seems certain that, whatever its intended sense, it is a necessary condition of such a contention's being correct, and of Aristotle's being right to transpose his whole search for substance to the level of form, that hylomorphism should progress to the point where the form of Kallias should be specifiable independently or in advance of of the identification of the compound Kallias.

Can Aristotle meet this requirement? Can Aristotle advance beyond this claim:

Kallias = the form of man in such-and-such (this or that) matter?

By a pseudo-algebraic conversion, it might be suggested we can progress from this to

the form of (this) man = Kallias without (or in abstraction from) such-and-such matter.

But, even if this be held to make sense, Aristotle cannot 'solve' the equation for *form* until a value is supplied for 'such-and-such matter'. Indeed Aristotle's own high awareness of the points mooted in the paragraph before last would have forewarned him of the extraordinary difficulty of solving it (indeed of making sense of it). To recognize the materiality of the things that he had designated primary substances in *Categories* and to think of matter as he does at *Physics* 192b30-3 (already quoted) will not yet supply the equation with an independent fix upon 'such-and-such matter'. Where the specification of form is concerned, the would-be equation does not advance him much beyond what he knew about the secondary substances that he spoke of in *Categories* or beyond the species or *eidos* as Aristotle had first conceived of it. But this was something universal, multiply instantiable, and all the rest. Meanwhile, before the equation is solved for 'form', the matter of a thing can only be conceived of by abstraction from that very thing.

12.2

It is possible that, in defiance of Aristotle's teleological or final cause approach to biological questions, a molecular biologist might be asked to supply the extra information that would be required to solve (if not to explicate) the 'equation' recently considered.

Faced with such a specification of the matter, a philosopher of substance might seek to revive and renew hylomorphism, no longer as metaphysics but as a science of substances. Compare *Metaphysics* Z 17, where Aristotle claims that the substance of each thing is the primary cause or explanation of its being. (See for instance 1041b27-31.) The philosopher of substance would then have to seek to adjudicate in an open-minded way the collision between biology as Aristotle conceived it in top-down fashion and the pretensions (perhaps inflated, perhaps not inflated) of molecular biology to answer questions of organic development and the rest. It is unclear, however, that, transposing Aristotelian hylomorphism to this new key, a philosopher of substance ought to imitate Aristotle further in demoting 'compounds' such as Kallias or Arkle in favour of (what might tendentiously be called 'their own') forms or principles of biological organization.

For these forms or principles, however specific they are, will be in principle multiply instantiable.[11] Something similar must hold for essence.

The questions that still remain here are at least as obscure as the question that we have postponed so often, namely that of the philosophical significance of the idea of a substance. What point is there in having a notion of substance that is more than the notion of a material body—or more than the notion of matter at a moment?

13 What is at Issue when We Ask whether Something is a Substance?

13.1

Let us find our way back to questions of this sort by considering things that have often been treated as (at best) marginal candidates for the full status of substances—have even been treated as marginal by philosophers like Aristotle who made constant use of them as examples—namely artefacts. Should one doubt the proper substantiality of artefacts?

We claimed in section 4, section 5 (the last paragraph but one), and section 10 that the singling-out of a thing at a time *t* involves thinking that reaches backwards and forwards to points arbitrarily much earlier or later than *t*. In the case of artefacts we conceive of them and treat with them at once diachronically and by reference to the function that defines their kind. But how that function is to be conceived does not depend on something out there in nature that could further saturate our thoughts about clocks or chisels or houses or bicycles or fishing-rods. Nor again is it sensible to expect there to be any such thing as the natural development of a clock by which the question of identity and persistence might be judged. In the third place, even though artefacts are in no way exempt from the laws of nature (indeed artefacts represent the exploitation and application of those laws), it will be silly to expect the sorts *house*, *bicycle*, or *clock* to figure in rich open-ended sets of sort-property pairs that are well-made for inductive extrapolation across the whole kinds that they determine. Contrast what was said in section 5 about genuine substances. Indeed, being variously constructed out of various materials and working by various different mechanisms, clocks need have little

---

[11] As they are in the real-life case of twins, unless we distinguish the form of one twin from the form of the other twin by reference to the difference in the histories of the two twins. But then the primary substances or 'compounds', one twin and the other, play an indispensable part in the individuation of their forms, contrary to the claim that the forms are prior to the 'compounds'.

in common with one another—over and above being things designed to tell the time. Even if we subdivide clocks into subvarieties, it may be hard to see that the activity of any particular clock need amount to much more than its doing what it must do to tell the time. Little else can flow from the fact that it is this or that device, deliberately designed to tell the time. Finally, in certain cases where artefacts are natural substances as well as being artefacts, artefact kinds and natural kinds may seem to cross-classify substances in a manner contrary to Aristotle's desiderata. (See section 4, first paragraph and footnote.)

Such might be the grounds for the doubt concerning artefacts. The doubt rests on an undeniable difference between artefacts and the cases that we began with, where the sense of the sortal term under which we pick out an individual expands into the scientific account of things of that kind. (See sections 3.3, 4 (end), 5 (end) and 9.1.)

It follows that there is a temptation to maintain the purity of the original conception of substance, a temptation only strengthened by the relative intractability of some of the other questions in which artefacts involve us—not least questions of identity and difference and of the relative 'conclusoriness' of artefact terms which apply equally to one and the same thing. Yet the solidity, durability, and internal cohesiveness of a vast preponderance of our artefacts, some of them outlasting their makers (who certainly were substances) by millennia, would be a standing reproach to any would-be puristic ruling to the effect that artefacts stand at too great a distance from the natural continuants that furnished us with our original paradigm of substance. Indeed such a ruling would represent in at least one way an affront to the spirit of the original conception. For not only do artefacts submit to predication without being predicated, not only can they furnish us with a 'this' and furnish (in so far as we know what this means) something 'separable'. Their usefulness and effectiveness in the performance of their functions signals and celebrates the way in which artefacts contrive to exploit, by *interaction* with natural substances, that low-level, dependable, indispensable understanding in whose name we engage in the individuation and articulation of the natural substances that are Aristotle's original exemplars.

Here is the place where we have to acknowledge the chasm that lies between our outlook and the outlook of a philosopher like Aristotle, for whom the best insight into the whole nature of reality was that afforded by the final causality exemplified by living things, or the outlook of a philosopher like Leibniz, for whom the ultimate reality was a mental reality of simple partless soul-like substances on which the whole physical world depended or supervened (see Leibniz's letter to De Volder, quoted in section 6). For us the question of substances is not momentous in that way. Yet in so far as we take ordinary objects and ourselves to be substances (and continue to find a Humean rejection of the self as unsustainable in practice as Hume himself seems to have found it in his own ethical writing) the question is not one that simply disappears. It never disappears.

13.2

Artefacts are not the only objects that challenge reflection. In the chapter of *New Essays* succeeding the one from which we have quoted already, we find in Remnant and Bennett's translation of II. xxiv. 1:

> PHILALETHES. After simple substance, let us look at collective ideas. Is not the idea of such a collection of men as make an army as much one idea as the idea of a man?
> THEOPHILUS. It is right to say that this aggregate makes up a single idea, although strictly speaking such a collection of substance does not really constitute a true substance. It is something resultant, which is given its final touch of unity by the soul's thought and perception. However it can be said to be something substantial in a way, namely as containing substances.

Suppose a large body of men is moving across the countryside, billeting itself upon the inhabitants and commandeering their goods and services, advancing slowly but manifestly enough in some common direction. The best way of making sense of their activities may seem to be to see these men not just as individuals pursuing their own largely rapacious concerns but as men acting in ways answerable to the centralized authority of a commander. If the army the men belong to is an impressively cohesive and disciplined instrument of political will, then it may seem almost mandatory to one who observes the soldiers to 'give the final touch to the unity' of the aggregate entity that they collectively constitute. The observer may find it almost impossible not to see in the presence of the soldiers the presence of that to which they belong—at least until such time as indiscipline or the tendencies of individual soldiers to defect or disregard authority shatter (if they do) all sense of the presence of a larger thing with its own dependable principle of activity and its own way of conducting itself. Is an army then a substance?

Similar questions will arise with the ontological and explanatory claims of other corporate entities such as states, civic associations, clubs, companies, trusts, banks, and other 'legal persons', or with cabinets, committees, boards of management, and the rest, or with clans or nations or families. There are so many things that we want to say which seem to make ineliminable reference to such things. (Needless to say an altogether different set of questions arises if someone asks whether God is a substance.)

Let us distinguish here two questions. (1) Can we adequately describe reality without making mention of these things? (Can we find a recipe to translate every apparent indispensable truth about armies or nations or states into another truth that lacks such existential commitments? This will normally involve us in finding predicates coextensive with the predicates that have essential occurrence in the sentences to be reduced and then involve us in other potentially troublesome tasks not to be lightly undertaken.) (2) Are the entities in question sufficiently like our paradigms of substances to count as having any claim to substantiality? Do they tend to extrude one another from a given place or can two of them be in the same place at the same time? How important is that? Are there low-grade laws about how they behave? A negative answer under (2) will not commit the answerer to any particular answer to (1). But then, pending our retreat to some of the assumptions of earlier philosophical epochs, it will not be sensible to feel that we have to find permanently conclusive arguments here. Nor do we need to cling to those earlier assumptions in order to hold on to Aristotle's commonsensical and profound understanding of the relation between a subject and its various properties or qualities.

4

The Person as Object of Science, as Subject of Experience, and as Locus of Value

1. In this chapter* I ask how it is possible to hold in a single focus three different ideas:

(a) the idea of the human person as object of biological and anatomical inquiry, and the patient of divers medical interventions;
(b) the idea of the person as rational being and subject of consciousness; and
(c) the idea of the person as bearer of all sorts of moral attributes and the originary source or the conduit of intrinsic value.

2. We see people in all sorts of ways and under all sorts of aspects. But on the most fundamental level of singling out and individuation, what really is a person? Setting out upon this question, someone might say that, whatever truths there may be to discover about the relation of these ideas, the expression 'a person' obviously doesn't mean the same as the expression 'a human being'; and neither of these expressions means the same as 'a self'; so being a person or being a self isn't the same as being a human being. These are different concepts. And so, our interlocutor may say, moving now to the higher or more

---

* This is a reconstruction and revision of a paper given before a mixed lay, philosophical, and theological audience—an audience simply replete with immaterialist conceptions of the self—given at the behest of Dr Arthur Peacocke, Director of the Ian Ramsey Centre, Oxford, in a series dedicated to differing conceptions of the person and their legal and ethical implications.

For the purposes of the talk I drew, as was requested, upon S&S, especially chapter 6 and Longer Notes 6.14 and 6.36 (also the *Errata* to be found on the inside of the back cover of the 1981 paperback). Section 16 of the paper is the place where I started upon the thoughts taken further in my *ETL*, chapter 9. See note 19.

Substantial debts to John McDowell and Peter Winch are acknowledged at the relevant points, *ad loc.*

transcendent ground, 'a person x can be the same person as y without being the same human being as y, and a person w can be the same self as z without being the same human being as z.[1] And being a person need not even involve being a human being'.

These conclusions cannot follow from the lexical considerations the interlocutor brings in evidence. The speed with which we are carried to something so interestingly metaphysical suggests the necessity to make the distinction between sense and reference. Let us begin there.

3. Figure 4.1 gives a picture of the connections between sense and reference. It was drawn by Frege for Husserl in a letter dated 24 May 1891.

Given that 'person' is a concept-word—a predicative word—it will be the third column that chiefly concerns us. But since that column is constructed in partial analogy with the middle column, it will be best to begin with the relatively familiar case of a name or singular term. Here we find the name or singular term at the top, connected via its sense, on the middle line, to the thing that the term stands for, given at the bottom of the column. What then is the sense? To know the sense of the name 'Socrates' is to know what the name stands for. One who knows that knows who Socrates is—in the normal sense of the elusive but useful phrase 'knowing who Socrates is'. To know the sense of 'Socrates' is to have some however minimal idea or notion or conception of who or what Socrates is. Given a particular name, however, not just any way of saying what its reference is will impart or show equally well the sense of that

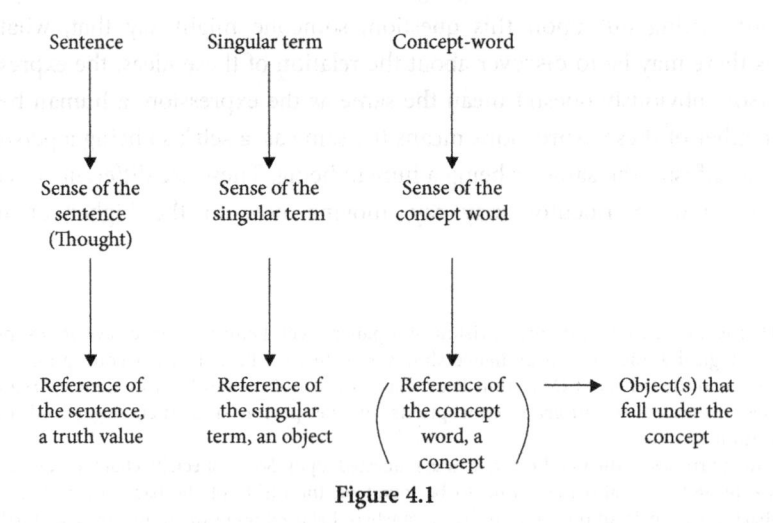

Sentence	Singular term	Concept-word	
↓	↓	↓	
Sense of the sentence (Thought)	Sense of the singular term	Sense of the concept word	
↓	↓	↓	
Reference of the sentence, a truth value	Reference of the singular term, an object	(Reference of the concept word, a concept)	→ Object(s) that fall under the concept

Figure 4.1

---

[1] For the logical difficulties that lurk here, see *ISTC*, pt. 1; *S&S*, ch. 1 and *S&SR*, ch.1 and pp. 53–4.

name.[2] For different names with the same reference may be annexed to different conceptions of that reference, to different ways of thinking about it, and to different ways of presenting it. Consider Venus and its two Greek names 'Hesperus' and 'Phosphorus', each name attaching to a different conception of the planet.

4. From the case of the singular terms we pass now to the case of predicative expressions and the right-hand column, which applies inter alia to verbs, to adjectives, and to substantives such as '[a] person' or '[a] human being'. According to Frege's scheme, these will be the kinds of expressions that stand for concepts—more or less (as we might naturally say) for properties. Here, just as to grasp the sense of a singular term and grasp its contribution to the meaning or truth conditions of a sentence is to grasp the term's mode of presentation of the object and thereby to know which object it stands for, so (analogously) to grasp the sense of a predicate, adjective or substantive, and grasp its contribution to the meaning or truth conditions of a sentence is to have grasped or 'cottoned onto' the predicate's mode of presentation of the concept that it stands for.[3]

Consider for instance the substantive (or concept-word) 'horse'. One way to explain the sense of '[is] a horse' and indicate the concept it stands for is to demonstrate a specimen of the kind of animal in question, by expanding *ad libitum* upon a body of descriptive information such as 'a horse is an animal that has a flowing mane and tail; its voice is a neigh; and in the domestic state it is used as a beast of burden and for riding upon'. Now consider, beside 'horse', the Linnaean predicate *Equus caballus*. It applies to the same creatures, and it stands for the same concept, but has a different sense. An explanation of this other sense might start from the zoological criteria for classification of animals as perissodactyl quadrupeds, locate the species horse within the genus *Equus* and the family *Equidae*, and then dwell upon the other anatomical and evolutionary marks of the species horse. This gives a different conception of one and the same species-concept. It imparts the conception that goes with the Linnaean predicate.

---

[2] Cf. John McDowell, 'On the Sense and Reference of a Proper Name', *Mind* (1977), pp. 159–85. For further Fregean testimony, see also Gareth Evans, *The Varieties of Reference*, ed. John McDowell (Oxford: Clarendon Press, 1982), ch. 1, and my *1976d*. The explanation of the sense of a name given in the text is framed to avoid treating the sense of a word as an independent entity or object in its own right.

[3] For an elaboration of this approach, which suggests a cautious repair to Frege's view of the predicative character of concepts, and for some further remarks about Frege's diagram, see my *1984* and *S&S*, p. 79 n, *S&SR*, p. 79 n.

Note that in the diagram Frege indicates the extension of the concept (property)—the things that answer to the expression in question—horizontally to the right of the concept, one step further from the sense than in the case of the proper name.

5. So much for 'horse' and *Equus caballus*. But might something similar apply in the case of 'human being', 'man', *'homo'*, *'anthropos'*? Here too there is a kind we encounter in the world of which we can frame a conception or frame various conceptions. Moreover, just as differing conceptions can steer the different substantives 'horse' and *Equus caballus* with their different senses onto one and the same concept, may it not be that the expressions 'person' and 'human being' are steered, by their different senses and differing conceptions of something that they stand for, onto the very same concept? That is not the only possibility. But if this possibility obtains, then the situation we have encountered could be pictured as in Figure 4.2.

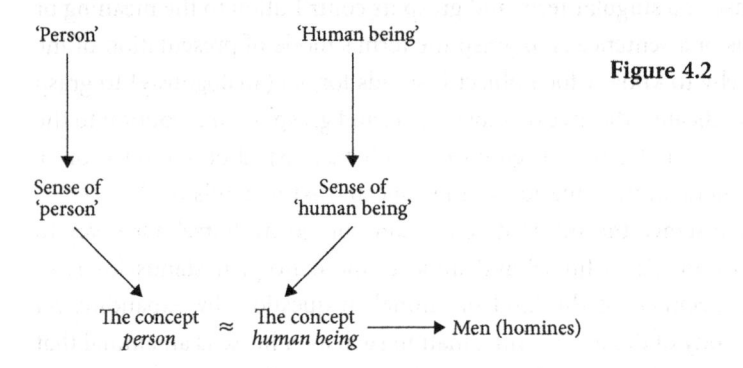

'Person'   'Human being'   **Figure 4.2**

↓   ↓

Sense of   Sense of
'person'   'human being'

         ↘   ↙
The concept ≈ The concept ⟶ Men (homines)
  person   human being

If matters stand as they do in Figure 4.2—if the references of 'person' and 'human being' are the same Fregean concept, or if they are linked indissolubly in ways yet to be described (see sections 15–18)—then it is consistent with all the differences that we hear between 'person' and 'human being' that it should be an illusion that there is a self-sufficient sense for the word 'person' that is independent of our conception of what a human being is.

6. The suggestion that the concept of what it is to be a human being and what it is to be a person cannot be sundered apart anticipates our eventual conclusion. But here, in advance of any attempt to say more about *person* or *human being*, I remark that there are two different ways in which a sense-sustaining conception can relate to the reference of a predicate.

Sometimes understanding a substantive or adjective correctly simply consists in conforming one's use of it to a publicly agreed stipulation or makeshift equivalence. An oculist is an eye-doctor; a house is a shelter against destruction by heat, rain, or wind (Aristotle). Similar definitions are no doubt possible— 'analytic' definitions, one might want to say—of 'vicar', 'train-driver', 'cavalryman', 'footplateman', 'surgeon', 'tenant', 'citizen', 'metic', 'minor', 'patrial'. Here, where an explicit verbal definition is possible, a correction can be necessitated only by the need to find a stipulation that consorts better with speakers' use of the word or by the need to respond to changes in social organization, technology, or law.

That is one case, the (more or less) analytical case. The other case is where there is no non-circular definition or explicit necessary and sufficient condition for the application of the term. In this sort of case the best thing that can be had is an explanation or elucidation that depends on the reference itself being made apparent—demonstratively or somehow otherwise—to one who needs the explanation. The understanding of the sort or property in question depends upon the enquirer's grasping the stereotype that supports or is supported by the recognition of the things/specimens/subjects that fall under the concept.[4] Here the conception is answerable to experience and corrected against experience. It is extension-involving, one may say. (See Chapter 8.)

7. That is the general case, where the concept *human being* belongs. But the focus shifts now to the word 'person' and the concept that it stands for. Beginning with the least controversial part of the case for the assimilation that I shall propose between *person* and *human being*, I begin by suggesting that our first grasp of the concept *person* can be no less extension-involving than our grasp of *human being*.[5] Secondly, I remark that 'person' is conspicuously unlike 'chairman', 'vicar', 'president'—titles that are conferred on something already singled out in another way. (Or so I think.) Moreover, the concept *person* had better not be like the concepts of various kinds of executant, or concepts that have to change (strictly, be replaced) in response to new legislation or to technological progress. Among such concepts one might count *cavalryman* or *footplateman*, or legal concepts that we may decide at any moment to modify (or, strictly speaking, replace), e.g. *tenant, citizen, metic, minor,* or legal concepts that

---

[4] See *S&S*, ch. 3, citing and modifying Hilary Putnam, 'Is Semantics Possible?', *Metaphilosophy*, 1 (1970). See also Chapter 8 here. I take a stereotype for the reference of 'f' to be a standardized or idealized set of *de re* beliefs about what it is to be an f or about fs (plural). This technical notion (Putnam's notion) of stereotype, being *de re*, also embraces the suggestion, where applicable, of picture or pictorial idea. For 'extension-involving', see further *S&S*, pp. 10–11, 79–86, 210–11; and *S&SR*, pp 79–80.

[5] Here though I shall not deny that there is need for a reconstruction of the way in which as infants we come in the end to think of ourselves as the same kind of creature as the human beings who attend us and care for us in our infancy and early childhood. 'All of us tend to think of ourselves as primarily mental creatures and of others as immediately physical realities' (Fernand Pessoa). How do we transcend this tendency? Except in so far as sections 8 and 13 following bear upon this matter, the question lies beyond the reach of this chapter.

we simply invent, such as *patrial*. Whenever x is one of these sorts of thing, we can look for a more fundamental answer to the question 'what is x?'. 'Person', on the other hand, has the appearance not of presupposing but of providing such an answer.[6]

8. In his book *Individuals*, P. F. Strawson claims that the concept *person* is primitive.[7] In order to understand this claim, we need to say what this primitiveness is relative to. I read Strawson as saying that, without the idea of a person from the start, you could never build up to it from any combination of ideas such as those of experience, body, causality... But the fact that you cannot build up in this way (and probably cannot build up in any other way from any other starting-point that doesn't already involve self, conscious subject, etc.) need not imply that nothing more can be said by way of elucidation of what a person is. The thing that the claim of primitiveness prepares the way for is rather this: that a person is, *par excellence* (and as a presupposition of most or all of the traditional questions that have given so much trouble in the philosophy and epistemology of mind), the bearer of *both* M-predicates *and* P-predicates, where M-predicates are predicates 'that we could also ascribe to material objects' and P-predicates are predicates which Strawson says we could not possibly ascribe to material objects. They comprise such things as actions, intentions, thoughts, feelings, perceptions, memories, and sensations: a person is 'a type of entity such that *both* predicates ascribing states of consciousness *and* predicates ascribing corporeal characteristics... are equally applicable to a single individual of that single type'. This is not a definition of 'person'. Rather, the claim has the status of an elucidation or a reminder, helpful to those who know already what a person is, of what it is that they know already.[8]

Strawson's proposal is persuasive. But to put it to further use, I need to make the case for an emendation. Strawson's explication of P-predicates as predicates that we could not possibly apply to material objects is not neutral with respect to

---

[6] What is more, any comparison of 'person' with these executant or functional terms seems to make a mess of what we mean by 'a good person'—a point familiar to readers of Aristotle, if not to Aristotle at *Nicomachean Ethics* I. 6. Goodness in persons is not a form of functional or executive or technical goodness.

[7] P. F. Strawson, *Individuals: An Essay in Descriptive Metaphysics* (London: Methuen, 1959), p. 101.

[8] Needless to say that, here and elsewhere in his chapter, Strawson has arguments and perceptions which I have not tried to reproduce. On elucidation, see *S&S*, p. 4, with Ludwig Wittgenstein, *Tractatus Logico-Philosophicus* 3. 263, 4. 026, 4. 112; Mark Helme, 'An Elucidation of *Tractatus* 3. 262', *Southern Journal of Philosophy*, 17 (1979), pp. 323–34.

the question 'Are persons material objects?'.[9] However it is interpreted, that question is a substantive one. Explications such as Strawson's ought not to presuppose that it is settled. To attend to this point, let us distinguish two ranges of predicate, separately and positively, as follows:

(i) M-predicates are predicates of persons that are matter-involving;
(ii) P-predicates are predicates of persons that are (directly or indirectly) consciousness-involving, in the way in which action, intention, thought, feeling, perception, memory, and sensation are mind/awareness/consciousness-involving.

And what happens now? There is no damage to Strawson's critical appraisal of the problem of other minds. But the question arises whether all P-concepts may turn out to be M-concepts. In its full generality, I should not know how to show that this must be so. For present purposes it will be enough to make it plausible by examples and to align the result with the questions I proposed at the outset, in section 1.

9. First consider the P-concept (or P-property) of remembering.[10] Suppose Henry plants a tree. For Henry to remember planting the tree, his subsequent recall of his planting must be related in the right sort of way to the incident. For, even though he did plant the tree, Henry's simple and correct conviction that he remembers planting it is not fully constitutive of his really remembering doing so. He may have forgotten the actual planting and someone may have told him about it later. Henry may have imagined the planting; and, even as he imagines it, he may have forgotten that he knows about the action only from another person's account. This is a real if remote possibility. What is required then, in addition to the right kind of agent-centred thought on Henry's part, is that there should be a certain direct and specific causal or explanatory relation between his planting the tree and his capacity to recall the planting. Nothing less than something of this sort has to hold for it to be true that Henry remembers. What is more controversial but seems almost equally certain, is that it is impossible to say what the right sort of causal connection is between an incident and the memory of it without having recourse to the idea that the incident leaves its mark upon the one

---

[9] For a cognate but potentially divergent criticism, see Bernard Williams, 'Strawson on Individuals', in *Problems of the Self* (Cambridge: Cambridge University Press, 1973).

[10] The argument following leans in part upon C. B. Martin and Max Deutscher's 'Remembering', *Philosophical Review*, 75 (1966), pp. 161–96; and it recapitulates S&S, Longer Note 6.14. For the ancestor of all these speculations, see H. P. Grice, 'The Causal Theory of Perception', *Proceedings of the Aristotelian Society*, 35 (1962).

who remembers it.[11] If this is right, then a purely conceptual (albeit not purely a priori) inquiry discovers to us that the P-property of remembering must also be a rather particular M-property. How could an incident leave its mark on an immaterial being? How on any other terms could there be personal or experiential remembering?

This argument has important parallels when we consider other faculties that are distinctive of persons. Consider the P-property of perceiving. For there to be a perception of x, it is not enough for the putative perceiver to report truly about how x looks or be able to draw or describe x just as x manifests itself there then. That is not sufficient. (And it is not even necessary; for the putative perceiver O may *mis*perceive x.) For there to be perception of x there must also be a place π from whence O apprehends x and x must affect O the perceiver in the way in which objects obtrude upon perceivers located at the place π. In the absence of some determination of such a place, no satisfactory distinction can be made between perception and misperception. And what else can fix the place where the perception is from but the body, head, and eyes of the perceiver? (It may be said that the place from whence the perceiving takes place can be deduced from the content of the perception itself. Hardly though where what is at issue involves the correctness or non-illusory character of the perception!) So again, a P-property, here the P-property of perceiving, turns out to be matter-involving. It is an M-property. On further investigation it will of course turn out to be a rather particular one, involving a visual system.

10. Suppose you are persuaded that, if you push a serious account of what each P-property is as far as it will go, you will always find something matter-involving.[12] That will not prevent us from distinguishing among M-predicates between predicates standing for ordinary corporeal properties such as weighing thirteen stone, lying still, running, stumbling, limping... and predicates that ascribe states of consciousness—predicates, that is, of action, intention, thought,

---

[11] Some call this mark a memory trace, where that may be conceived under the specification 'the normal neurophysiological connection whatever it is, between rememberings and the incidents of which they are rememberings'. This is not a circular procedure. But, even if it were circular, this would not matter for present purposes, which relate to the *necessary* conditions of remembering. Deutcher and Martin carefully explore a multiplicity of alternatives to the explicit memory-trace account of the causal connection between incident and experiential memory of incident. They show that none of these accounts can simultaneously allow for the possibility of prompting and define the particular sort of prompting we are looking for between incident and representation.

NB. It is no part of the argument I offer here that one who remembers, either he or his homunculus, *consults* or *goes by* the mark or trace that the event remembered leaves upon him.

[12] For the materials for a similar argument about pain, see Richard Wollheim, 'Expression and Expressionism', *Revue Internationale de Philosophie*, 68–9 (1964). More generally, see the discussion in my *1976e*, pp. 120–1.

feeling, perception, memory, sensation... Nor will it prevent us from disclaiming all aspirations to reduce personhood or its attributes to fundamental properties recognized by the sciences of matter.[13]

11. Modifying in this way but also reinforcing Strawson's claim of the primitiveness of the idea of person, let us pause for a moment and attend now to the first of the questions mooted at the outset, in section 1, namely the relation of the idea (a) of the human person as a subject of medical or biological investigation and experiment to the ideas set out there as (b) and (c). The ordinary idea of a person is not the idea of a body, or even of a living body. Nor can one build up to the idea of a person by combining these with other ideas. Or so we have claimed. But maybe one can move in exactly the opposite direction and say that the body of a person is that which realizes or constitutes the person while he or she is alive, and will be left over when, succumbing finally to entropy, the person dies.[14] On these terms the idea of body may appear as a kind of abstraction from the idea of person.[15] On the same terms it becomes possible to understand how (subject to certain prohibitions) the body may without insult or disrespect be subjected to surgery or even to dissection and its processes be subjected without criminality to 'impersonal' experiment and research. There is no way to enforce this way of looking at these questions. But it makes sense of the faith by which a great part of human life is now lived.

12. Even if the idea of person is primitive, more can and must be said more positively about it. In *Sameness and Substance*, where I wanted to show that experiential memory was at once essential to personhood and not constitutive of the identity of persons, I resumed Locke's account of personhood as follows:

x is a person if *x* is an animal falling within the extension of a kind whose typical members perceive, feel, remember, imagine, desire, make projects, move themselves at will, speak,

---

[13] There are at least two distinct senses in which the words 'physical' and 'material' are used inside and outside philosophy. The two senses seem to be:
   (1) *x* is material if and only if *x* falls under a sort whose proper characterization reveals its matter-involvingness;
   (2) *x* is material if and only if (a) *x* falls within the extension of a predicate φ that is *reducible* to predicates that pull their weight in some physical theory or science of matter, and (b) it is possible to say in terms of φ what *x* is.

On the exigency of reduction, see *S&S*, p. 169; also J. H. Woodger, *Biology and Language: An Introduction to the Methodology of the Biological Sciences including Medicine* (Cambridge: Cambridge University Press, 1952), pp. 267 n., 272, 336–8, as quoted in *S&S*, p. 148.

[14] See *S&S*, p. 164.

[15] Cf. Woodger, *Biology and Language*, p. 278: 'Neither can the method which uses the physical language exclusively deal with persons except by means of the *abstract* notion of body.' (Italics added.)

carry out projects, acquire a character as they age, are happy or miserable, are susceptible to concern for other members of their own or like species... conceive of themselves as perceiving, feeling, remembering, imagining, desiring, making projects, being susceptible of concern for others..., who have and conceive themselves as having a past accessible in experience—memory—and a future accessible in intention....

Surely this from Locke cannot be very badly wrong—so far as it goes. (Where though are games, or dancing, or making music?) But the thing we should notice here is the constant need for *aposiopesis*—the incompletability that is registered by the dots. This is not an analytical definition such as 'oculist = (df) eye-doctor'. Nor is it a stipulation answerable to nothing in experience except the decision by English speakers to abbreviate some yet longer formula by the word 'person'. What then is to be the guiding idea that sustains our mature conception of *person*? What keeps together the attributes that figure in the Lockean enumeration?

In the same chapter of *Sameness and Substance*, I offered what I hoped might better approximate to an organizing principle: '*x* is a person if and only if *x* is a living animal whom we have no option but to account as a subject of consciousness and as an object of interpretation and reciprocity'. But implicit in this proposal there is a relativity that was not made fully explicit in *Sameness and Substance* and had better now be signalled and clarified.[16] The relativity consists in the fact that it rests *with us, with human beings*, to take account of this creature as a being open to our comprehension and consideration—and sometimes demanding that. Another person is not simply another intelligence, but a being whom it is *for us* to treat with, to communicate with, and to interpret...

13. What is meant here in philosophy by interpreting? To interpret *x* is to make sense of *x*, where making sense of *x*'s speech is just one special case of something much more general.[17] I begin with an abstract description of what this involves—a description unrecognizable to ordinary lay subjects who make sense

---

[16] See *S&S*, p. 173. On relativity in this sense, with acknowledgements to an idea of Williams's, see my 'A Sensible Subjectivism?' in *NVT*, especially section 11 and Longer Note 24. I note that such relativity will not and cannot confer sense or significance upon the expression 'person for us'. On 'solidarity', see my *2008-9*.

[17] On interpretation, see e.g. Donald Davidson, 'Radical Interpretation', *Dialectica*, 27 (1973), pp. 313–28; Richard Grandy, 'Reference, Meaning, and Belief', *Journal of Philosophy*, 70 (1973), pp. 439–52; Gareth Evans's and John McDowell's Editorial Introduction to *Truth and Meaning: Essays in Semantics* (Oxford: Clarendon Press, 1976); and (above all else) section 1 of McDowell's article in that volume, 'Truth Conditions, Bivalence, and Verificationism' (pp. 44–5); *S&S*, at Longer Note 6.36.

of one another but calculated to bring out that which is so apparently astonishing in its however commonplace achievement by human beings.

One who interprets has at his/her disposal at least three kinds of predicate of conscious subjects and of the environment in which they exist:

(i) predicates of conscious subjects, such as 'x believes that...', 'x wants this', 'x strives to...', etc.;
(ii) predicates of the reality that impinges upon conscious subjects;
(iii) predicates by the application of which one conscious subject can attribute to others not only actions, not only policies and intentions and ends, but also things they mean by their intelligible speech.

One who would make sense of others draws upon this store of predicates of other subjects and of the objects and events that impinge upon them, and distributes such predicates over subjects of interpretation and the realities that impinge upon these subjects in such a way that (α) the propositional attitudes ascribed to subjects are intelligible singly and jointly in the light of the reality to which the subjects or their informants are taken to have been exposed; (β) the actions, policies, and ends ascribed to subjects are intelligible in the light of the propositional attitudes that are ascribed to subjects; and (γ) the things the subjects count as saying by their utterances either reflect or condition the ascriptions counted acceptable under the requirements (α) and (β).[18]

This is not an account of what persons set out to do when they try to make sense of one another. It is an account only of what—somehow, yet to be explained—they actually *achieve*. On the level of theory, the account can suggest what there is out there for human creatures to go by when they interact with one another in the same space and strive there for mutual comprehension. But, if this is the task, how must they begin upon it? What is the entry point for interpretation? And how is the mass of possible predications under (ii) to be narrowed down to those both available and of interest to the subjects who are to be made sense of? Until something is supplied under both these heads, what an utterly astonishing feat interpretation must still appear! What is achieved will not appear any less mysterious until we think what power will accrue to an interpreter so soon as he or she interacts with other human beings and under the *unthinking* but *correct* assumption that he or she and they share in a common nature, share in a common way of being and struggle to satisfy a host of similar needs. Working in that way, one who interprets proceeds as if others are attuned to the same

---

[18] On (α) and (β), see especially McDowell, 'Truth Conditions'.

reality as he is, assumes that others are impinged upon by the same features as he is and are struck by the same saliencies as he is, assumes that others try to make sense of him even as he tries to make sense of them, and assumes that other subjects not only have vital needs rather similar to his, the interpreter's, but are susceptible also to the very same sorts of practical consideration as he is. Such assumptions are as hazardous sometimes as they are indispensable, but they are not a matter for deliberation and decision. For there is no other way. Assumptions of these kinds can be modulated point by point, piecemeal, so soon as an interpreter far along in the process puzzles to account for apparent disagreements between himself and those he seeks to understand. The net can then be drawn tighter, and the theoretical requirements (α) and (β) can be read in a way that engages further with the requirement (γ). But unless human beings begin without reflection or hesitation in a way that amounts to something like this and each is prompted *by his own nature and formation* to proceed so—and unless each one does *in fact share in some fairly specific nature* with those he is trying to make sense of—it seems incomprehensible that any fine-grained mutual comprehension should be possible that approximates to our everyday experience of making sense of one another.

14. It may be objected that, in attributing such productivity and power to the assumption of shared human being-hood, I have overlooked or underrated the innate rationality of persons. But I reply that rationality as such—the pure disembodied rationality that the objector has in mind—specifies few if any *ends* or *concerns* or *preoccupations*. In the absence of a shared nature or mentality that will suggest ends or concerns or preoccupations that interpreters and subjects have a common care for, interpretation will border still upon the miraculous.

The idea of person (I conclude) needs the idea of a being with a specific nature. It needs that idea as badly as the moral life of ordinary human beings needs the thoughts we now express most easily in terms of personhood. As the meeting of these two notions becomes closer, and more and more of the marks of human-beinghood come to be taken for marks of personhood—and as the idea of *person* borrows what it needs from the individuative force of the idea of *human being*—it may not matter very much whether or to what extent the concepts finally coincide. One may or may not want to say that to be a person is the same as to be a human being. But in practice the *extensions* of these concepts will coincide, and it will be no accident that they do.[19]

---

[19] If we want to make room for concepts to differ even if their extensions coincide, we should of course need a richer object-language than Frege allows himself, one equipped with the expressive resources to represent necessity and possibility.

15. Presented with the human form, we immediately entertain a multitude of tentative expectations, unless something inhibits or perverts this response. That is how it has to be. But faced with a Martian or an automaton (unless this be a creature or creation synthesized by procedures that would somehow carbon-copy all the contingencies of human frame and human constitution) we should have to be mad to entertain any of these expectations. A person is a creature with whom human beings such as we are can get onto terms, or a creature that is of the same animal nature and psychophysical make-up as creatures with whom we can get onto terms, there being no clear limit to how far the process of getting onto terms can go. This is not how we seek to define 'person'. We cannot define it. But in the presence of a certain method of elucidation, we do not need to define it.

The idea of human being not only sustains the possibility of the interpretation of persons by persons. It not only provides for the individuation of creatures that are persons. By involving us (in ways already described) with ideas of making sense of the other, it also reveals moral possibilities for the human beings that we are, namely possibilities—I shall now argue—of reciprocity with the other and solidarity with the other. It reveals such possibilities even where it cannot command or enforce them.

16. At this point we reach the question of the relation of the ideas (b) and (c) that we set out in section 1. I begin upon this matter with the contrast between two philosophical texts, undeterred by the fact that the first recalls one of the most hackneyed of twentieth-century philosophical assertions or the fact that the aptness of the second was suggested to me by an article that was intended as a critique of the same opinions as I have been defending here.[20]

---

[20] Shortly after I had published *S&S*, my then colleague at London University, Peter Winch, presented a critique of chapter 6 of the book in his presidential address to the Aristotelian Society, October 1980. See 'Eine Einstellung zur Seele', *Proceedings of the Aristotelian Society* (1980-1). His critique was invaluable to me in making me see how far I had fallen short of saying what I ought to have said, and in making me appreciate how much there was that Winch and I were jointly opposed to, albeit in very different ways. Without Winch, moreover, I should not have thought to pursue the second of the two suggestions offered at this point in the argument by offering the quotation from Simone Weil. See *The Iliad, or the Poem of Force*, tr. M. McCarthy (Iowa City, IA; Stonewall Press, 1973). p. 6. For the first quotation, see Ludwig Wittgenstein, *Philosophical Investigations*, trans. G. E. M. Anscombe (2nd edn, Oxford: Blackwell, 1958), p. 223. In my *Ethics: Twelve Lectures on the Philosophy of Morality*, Chapter 9, the contentions here of section 17 are developed further, repeating some of the claims made in the present paper, as they are in my *2008-9*.

> If a lion could talk, we could not understand him.
> *Ludwig Wittgenstein*

> Anybody who is in our vicinity exercises a certain power over us by his very presence, and a power that belongs to him alone, that is the power of halting, repressing, modifying each movement that our body sketches out. If we step aside for a passer-by on the road, it is not the same thing as stepping aside to avoid a billboard: alone in our rooms we get up, walk about, sit down again quite differently from the way we do when we have a visitor.... But this indefinable influence that the presence of another human being has on us is not exercised by men [such as one's adversary in Homeric warfare] whom a moment of impatience can deprive of life, who can die before even a thought has a chance to pass sentence on them. In their presence people move about as if they were not there.
> *Simone Weil*

At one pole, what Wittgenstein seeks to dramatize is the interpretive divide between intelligences between whom there is no prospect of the agreement in responses that makes interpretation possible. At the opposite pole, the thing Weil describes is what it *is* to treat another being or fail to treat that being as a subject of consciousness and as potentially one of us—a subject of reciprocity, that is, and the possessor also of a will potentially at variance with our own. To be ready to take a person *as* a person, what I have to be ready to do is to explore that uncircumscribed possibility. To treat a person like a thing—to treat them like a billboard—what I have to be ready to do is to suspend all the impulses on which that uncircumscribed possibility precisely depended.

Consider wilful killing. Consider what we have to lay aside even to contemplate the actuality of this. Where there is danger from a mortal enemy, someone may kill the enemy intentionally and without a further thought. There may be no time to have a further thought. The to-and-fro of ordinary interpretive intercourse in which we are normally caught up has already been conspicuously suspended. For some people, it takes a great deal to put that into abeyance. How slow some are with a gun precisely shows how much it takes to make them do so—a fact clearly recognized in all systems for the basic training of military recruits, conscripts, or other trainees. But where nothing has put the to-and-fro of ordinary human intercourse into abeyance, consider how much, how many habits of mind and feeling, you have then to put aside coolly to contemplate simply cutting off or 'taking out' another person. Obviously, all these habits of mind can be laid aside. That they *can* be laid aside and often are does not show that such revulsions of mind and feeling are superficial to the human soul. By their force and persistence, such as it is, they remind us that the very first part of morality is what it forbids us to do. The point is not that they cannot be put aside, but the psychic and visceral cost—and the prima facie *unreason*—of doing so.[21]

17. If this were the right place, I should try now to measure how much of ordinary morality can be founded in the subjective responses ingrained in ordinary human beings by the ordinary mutual interactions through which we make sense of one another. I should try to show how morality so conceived could graduate to a level at which values emerged as objective as well as subjective,[22] and try also to show how the account that it suggests of moral concerns and moral qualms can vindicate the claims of these attitudes to be manifestations of a genuine however limited or constrained moral disinterestedness. More loosely, someone might say that these are manifestations of benevolence. But that is not quite right. Indeed it is mistaken. We need not positively wish a stranger well or care already about them in order to be shocked to the core by something terrible we see done to them. That abhorrence points to that which is metaphysical in the idea of person, something almost but not quite beyond words.

The time is come to conclude. The problem that we set ourselves in section 1 was how to hold in a single focus (a), (b), and (c)—that is the biological, the mental, and the moral aspects of personhood. We rendered the idea (a) tolerable by proposing that the idea of the body be seen as a sort of abstraction from the plenary idea (b) of a person. We reach (c) by understanding under (b) how badly our idea of person as subject of interpretation needs the idea of human being. That idea adds matter, substance, and the possibility of individuation

---

[21] In asserting the unreason of giving up these feelings I have it in mind that, where these are our actual feelings and we have no reason of our own to give them up—and where we have no idea of what will become of us without them—it will be simply gratuitous, indeed stupid and silly, to suggest that it is irrational for us not to try to wipe the slate clean in order to deliberate from a standing start of pure self-interest. Of course that is the suggestion implicit in the more rationalistic discussions of challenges to morality such as Glaukon and Adeimantus' tale of Gyges' ring in Plato, *Republic* II or the Prisoner's Dilemma 'paradox'. Such discussions begin from extreme situations that obscure what are real possibilities in less extreme situations and usually proceed as if the whole matter could be approached from a fresh starting-point reached without paying the cost mentioned in the text. They never acknowledge the intimate mutual involvements of the raw materials of morality—ordinary morality itself, not *ersatz* morality or far-sighted self-loving prudence—with everything that is presupposed to interpretation. For a discussion of some of these matters not open to any of these criticisms see pp. 119–20 of J. L. Mackie's *Ethics: Inventing Right and Wrong* (Harmondsworth: Penguin, 1977).

[22] 'Subjective' here makes reference, not to a metaethical category but to a source of the ethical and the concerns that are natural to normal human beings. See my 'A Sensible Subjectivism?' in my *NVT*. See also *ETL*, Chapter 9.

to our conception of persons.[23] Thus fortified, our conception of persons as subjects of consciousness and objects of reciprocity and interpretation is what directs and animates our search for the attributes of human beings in virtue of which we can see our engagement with them as the root of morality and the great conduit for its solidaristic concerns.

---

[23] It implies, for instance, that the history of a person stretches as far back as the human foetus. As so often—as almost always—we use the mature form of the organism to characterize the creature in question. Cf. *S&SR*, p. 64 (note 3 *ad fin.*) Nevertheless, in the interaction of the human being conception and the person conception, maybe *human being* is not quite always the dominant partner. It is under sway of the *person* conception perhaps that we seek to determine when we are to say that someone 'is no more'.

5

Sameness, Substance, and the Human Person

TPM: I gather that a new edition of *Sameness and Substance* will appear next year (2001)* under the Cambridge imprint. Have you changed your mind at all about personal identity?

DW: The chapter on that subject is completely new. But no. I still think, as I have said in further elaboration of *Sameness and Substance*, that the only way for us to make sense of the concept *person* is to think of persons (the persons we are, not divine persons) as subjects (or potential subjects) of fine-grained interpretation by us, as subjects for whom we are subjects of fine-grained interpretation and as creatures with whom we can have relations of reciprocity and solidarity. I still hold then that there is a concealed *indexicality* within the idea of a person. And I still hold that, once one follows through properly in thinking about what interpretation and reciprocity involve on the levels of reason and reasonable response and what it requires for one person to be 'on the same wavelength' as another ('on net' with another), one is forced to the conclusion that the only *stereotype* we can have of a person—and the only effective conception we can have of what a person is—is the conception of a human being, a fellow creature, *our* fellow creature. A person is a rational being with a distinctive and particular animal nature, origin and physiognomy,[1] namely ours. That is not a definition—there are no proper definitions to be had here—just a reminder of things you know already but which I seek to persuade you we should allow to impinge on philosophy.

---

* For the Autumn 2000 edition of *The Philosopher's Magazine* the editors requested an interview concerning *Sameness and Substance Renewed* (2001). The reprint makes some abridgements, incorporates clarifications of my original answers, and extends the interview by an exchange with two imaginary new readers of the magazine.

[1] I seek here to generalize the received notion of physiognomy to embrace not only the face but the whole bodily person.

The word 'stereotype', as it occurs in the previous sentence, is used in the sense that Putnam attaches to it. See Chapter 8.

Another claim I would enter is this: the idea that you or I or our colleagues could have been other than human beings—that we or they, these same people, could have been something else or could have had another nature—this is an illusion. Sometimes it is a delusion of Gygean omnipotence. In a fairy story, other 'possibilities' besides our being human beings can be comprehended (being a horse, being an insect, being disembodied, etc). But one can't really make complete sense of them.

In heraldry a martlet is a swift without any feet. For purposes of a heraldic device, martlets can even be painted or drawn. But can sense really be made of a *bird* that lacks feet? Perhaps. But not without some answer to the question how these creatures nest, then hatch and nurture their young. A martlet is meant to be a bird. It is not enough for martlets to mate on the wing. Understanding a story is one thing. Grasping a proper (more than merely logical) possibility is another.

TPM: You don't mean, do you, that every *conscious being* is a human being, that every being that can have reasons for what it does, etc, is a human being?

DW: That's right, I don't mean that. Indeed, think of animals. They are conscious and they do things for reasons. The predator waits at the foot of the tree because his prey will have in due course to come down. Isn't that his reason to wait? My claim is not about consciousness or having reasons to do things[2] but about what persons are. But it's not an idle stipulation—or even a stipulation. Look at the way in which the word 'person' (and its predecessors, 'prosopon' [face, character in a drama, etc.] and 'persona' [mask]) arrived in the language. Look at its sources in law and religion. I don't mean that the terms on which the idea of a person has reached us are such as to render it an analytic truth that persons are human beings. My claim is a more substantial and more controvertible one. It is founded in a contention arising from the business of interpretation, about what it takes for some being to be (actually or potentially) 'on the same wavelength' as we are (and vice versa). It is founded in a contention about shared norms of human reasonableness whose content stretches well beyond the logically a priori into the whole complex of specific responses that human beings can expect of other human beings, given the constitution that is ours by nature.

What about Martians? you ask. Well, concerning Martians I try always to exercise what Keats called negative capability. The positive thing I am saying matters much more than the denials by which I am urged sometimes to complete it. Rather than worry about my rash denials, listen instead to Marcel Mauss (in 1938):

---

[2] The thing that is special about human beings is not that they have reasons to do what they do or to behave as they do but the range and variety of reasons they can have for what they do.

Who knows what progress the Understanding will yet make on this matter [of the notion of person or self]... Who knows even whether this 'category', which all of us believe to be well founded, will always be recognized as such? It is formulated only for us, among us. Even its moral strength—the sacred character of the human 'person'—is questioned not only throughout the Orient... but even in the countries where this principle was discovered. We have great possessions to defend. With us the idea could disappear.[3]

At this point in his essay Mauss celebrated (as I read him) not so much the historic diversity of conceptions of personhood that he had begun by putting in front of his readers as the gradual emergence from these conceptions of a better conception.

TPM: In *Sameness and Substance Renewed* do you still emphasize the distinction between natural things such as human beings and artefacts? Do you still press the corresponding distinction between natural-kind concepts and artefact-kind concepts? Could you say something here about that distinction?

DW: Yes I do still emphasize this contrast and I hope I can explain it here. So let us bracket persons for a moment and focus on something outside the disputed area.

There are 101 ways to compare and contrast (say) a cat and a cooking stove, or a natural thing and an artefact. The cat is alive. That is important, but not the key to the whole distinction. For many natural things and substances are not alive, such as a glacier or a fossil or a formation such as the Chesil Bank. The stove is manufactured. I suppose that cats might some day be produced by synthesis in the laboratory and then manufactured. And some day some crazy boffin might set out to redesign the cat, not by cross-breeding (which subjects every intermediate variety to some ecological test that it might fail under natural conditions) but by gene-splicing. But such mixed cases must not upstage the clarification Hume brought to these matters: 'natural may be opposed either to what is *unusual, miraculous* or *artificial*' (*Enquiry Concerning the Principles of Morals,* Appendix III).

The chief distinction between natural things and artefacts that I think I know how to rescue here elaborates upon the third of Hume's categories. It turns upon the distinction between the way in which any particular cat relates to its thing-kind concept and the way in which any particular cooking stove relates to *its* thing-kind concept. It depends upon a difference between the two ways in which we make and understand these specifications. If I can recognize cats, track

---

[3] Marcel Mauss, Huxley Memorial Lecture 1938: 'Une Categorie de l'Esprit Humain: la Notion de Personne, celle de 'Moi'', *Journal of the Royal Anthropological Institute*, 68 (1938). Note the date. Without reference to Mauss, I have attempted to set out one relevant sense of 'sacred' in my *2008-9*.

particular ones, chronicle their doings, reidentify them, etc, I qualify as having an adequate conception—a clear (i.e. effective) if not fully articulate conception—of this thing-kind concept. Almost certainly I have no definition of 'cat'. Rather, it's as if at some point in my life I have been presented with specimens, *that* one and *that other* one, and I have caught on somehow to the idea that something was a cat *if and only if* it was relevantly like that first specimen and/or that other specimen. (This is only commentary not semantic analysis.) It's as if I have caught on to the idea that relevant non-superficial similarity between a new candidate and the specimen was a matter of the candidate's having a full-blown nature (an Aristotelian *phusis*) from which it followed that the candidate would come into being in a particular way, live in a certain general way, look a certain way, behave in a certain way. The new candidate must have (much) the same mode of activity as the specimens. When a cat is singled out by someone who has caught on in this manner, the cat is singled out as having a narrowly specifiable whole nature that is sustained (reliably enough, even if in a manner partly inscrutable) by the operation of certain lawlike (law*like*) norms of nature. The conception of the thing-kind concept that I need to become party to in order to understand 'cat' is at once *deictic*, dependent that is on exposure to real specimens of the kind, and *nomological*—better *quasi*-nomological—by virtue of its (the conception's) reference to the workings of a distinctive nature that is exemplified by the specimens and sustained by the larger more or less lawlike tendencies of the real world.[4]

Now for the thing-kind concept *stove*. I count as having an adequate conception of this, if I know that an object is a stove if and only if it is a fuel-burning or power-consuming device or apparatus for cooking or heating (say) food or water. (That is more or less a definition of cooking stove.) No very specific nature is required—still less any nature that is nomologically specific. 'Stove' is a functional term. Somehow—but this is all—somehow any device that is a stove must serve the designated function. Furthermore, there are few if any lawlike tendencies that are *specifically* required of stoves as such (or clocks, or pens, or mills or . . .) over and above their fulfilment of their particular function.

Such differences as these between natural thing and artefact are reflected further in what it takes for a particular animal to persist in being and what it takes for a particular stove to persist in being. Over time the animal may, by entirely natural processes, exchange most or all of its bodily constituents for others. That creates no problems for a sane philosophy of identity. But puzzle

---

[4] For 'cat' I have dwelt on the animate case. But *mutatis mutandis*, counterparts for most of these features can be discerned in the natural but inanimate case.

cases illustrate the difficulties that such exchanges can create for our thoughts about artefacts.

TPM: Why would it matter if persons came to be seen not as belonging to the natural kind *human being* but to some non-natural kind?

DW: It matters first because, for real, when it comes to the real, our experience as animate human substances is one of interacting with other human and non-human animate and non-animate substances. Despite all our differences from one another, our experience is that of creatures possessed of a specific common nature, a rather specific common mode of activity and a rather specific shared constitution or (stretching the word a little) a shared physiognomy.

That is how it is. But your question is about what is so important about its being thus. My reply is that our sharing in a given specific animal nature and a law-sustained mode of activity is integral to the close attunement of person to person in language and integral to the human sensibilities that make interpretation possible. Secondly, that sharing in a specific animal nature and mode of activity is a precondition of the human solidarity (where present) that excoriates the treatment of a human being—of *one of us*—as a mere thing or a mere tool. And, thirdly, that affinity in nature and activity is integral to our picture—a non-deterministic picture—of our capacity, singly and collectively, to determine, within a framework not of our own choosing and replete with meanings that are larger than we are, our direct and indirect ends. Within this framework we can find our place and exercise our capacities. We see ourselves not as things with a function—what on earth could a person, as a person, be *for?*—but as autonomous, self-moving, animate beings, beings who find themselves in the world and seek to leave their own mark upon it, make the best of what they find there, and look (if they are lucky) for something that each one of us can come to think of as his or her own proper work or calling.

That is how things are until the thought-experimentalists arrive—and hard on their heels the 'far-sighted' activists and futurologists of the medical and other sciences, eager to improve the human condition by improving not the thoughts or habits or health of human beings but the human being itself.

Among the intellectual exercises that the thought-experimentalists have proposed, some invite us to contemplate processes such as teletransportation (as in Derek Parfit's work) that break down the distinction between singular and universal, and between instances and that which they instantiate. (For if it were possible at all, nothing would prevent teletransportation from making multiple copies of the person who underwent it.) In so far as such a collision results from their proposals, the thought-experimentalists have changed the subject from persons and their persistence to something different. Their concern now is with a kind of concrete universal. But the life of the persons we are and concern ourselves with is the life of singular subjects, not plural or corporate things.

As for the second group (the futurologists, you might call them), the prospect they hold out includes among other things the constant repair of the human body by transplantation of organs and/or the fine-tuning of the human constitution by gene-therapy. Little or no harm yet. But for the longer term my fear is that the conception of a human person by which the clairvoyants for the enhancement of human faculties will seek to replace our present idea of a self-moving, animate living thing with a will and a destiny of its own, must become the conception of something that is there to be adapted, reinvented, reconceived, and reshaped (contrast healed or cared for or protected). Who will decide the point of purpose or aim of these 'improvements'? Who will estimate their success or look anxiously to their larger effects upon human existence?

In the here and now, at a point far short of this last prospect of reconceiving and retooling, there has of course been a huge increment of human well-being. In practice, moreover, the going conception of personhood is still, in the common sense and humanity of the medical professions, properly circumscribed by the recognition of the limitations of our human constitution and our animal nature. We can still hear and understand (in more peaceful parts of the world, at least) the warnings that sound against an instrumental or artefactual conception of the human and listen attentively to denunciations of the impulse to see people as things, as tools, as mere numerals, as fungibles or as cannon fodder. We are still proof, where there is time to reflect, against the idea that nothing that a human being might idly wish is out of the question or excluded by essentially human limitations. We can recognize our natures and the natural world as setting multiple limits upon the desires that we can take seriously. But suppose the idea falls away altogether that we have an animal nature that gives us specific capacities *and* specific limitations. Will a new disquiet assail our desires themselves, in a world no less denuded of meaning by the phantasm of omnipotence than ravaged by our already evident insatiability?

It is hard not to lapse here into rhetoric. (I have already.) It is hard to translate into exact philosophical declarations the unease that is prompted by the prospect of a shift of our conception of ourselves towards the conception of something non-natural. But the question I have just asked is not meant as rhetorical.

TPM: I hear your question. But I know that you do not want anyone to answer it without proper reflection...Before we stop, may we go back to Derek Parfit's famous teletransportation thought experiment, where a person is essentially destroyed and simultaneously recreated elsewhere, preserving all the person's memories and psychological states in a qualitatively identical body? In this case, is it not possible to say this?—'I can agree with Wiggins that the resulting person is not identical with the original. Nonetheless, when I think about what matters about my existence, I feel the teletransported being takes with him all that matters.' Does this perhaps show that one problem in the philosophical debate has been a failure to recognize that two very different questions of 'personal identity' can be asked, which have two very different answers, one logical and the other relating to our emotional attachment to selves past, present and future?

DW: I should resist that divorce on all sorts of grounds. But I am especially doubtful about this sort of plea for it. Logical reflection suggests, as you allow, that a process such as teletransportation simply cannot preserve x itself. I wonder though why you feel that it preserves 'all that matters'. The preservation of x matters to x and matters to all for whom x is dear or important. Doesn't x himself or herself matter? How can the teletransporter's producing a copy of x—even a unique copy of x—possibly preserve 'everything that matters about x'? The idea must be that in reality, identity with x is not a real property of x at all. But that is a mistake. Identity is irreducible, not a mere resultant of other properties and relations. (See *S&SR* pp. 183–8.) Despite your desire to separate distinct questions of personal identity, our concern for self-preservation—our 'emotional' attachment to self, our concern to survive and to persist—prompts reflections that are perfectly congruent with logic. If I am to walk into a machine at a certain place and be annihilated there, how on earth can I—or anyone else—be consoled for this annihilation by the promise that by the same process a replica or model will appear of me somewhere else—whether one model or two or three models? It is just imaginable, I suppose, that one who confused identity with similarity or particulars with universals could be talked into thinking that he himself would survive entry to the teletransporter. But I can't think anyone would *really* believe this, even if he or she had been fooled into believing in the identity of indiscernibles.

Here is one more question. When a teletransportee claims after the teletransportation process that he or she is (is identical with) NN him/herself, why should we take that seriously? Why believe them? They say they were in all sorts of places where they never were and say they did all sorts of things they were never in a position to do. Well, they quasi-remember them, I shall be told. But do we know what that means? And how can it help to constitute their survival?[5] (See Chapter 1, section 19.)

---

[5] It is a necessary condition of using the term 'quasi-remember' to mean anything that there should be a formally correct definition of the term, a definition stateable in the object language of the relevant branch of philosophy. In *S&SR*, pp. 213 ff. I point out that the now received definition

In its sober employment, the logic of identity, so far from taking us away from what matters, preserves for us the space within which *to conceive and then to follow through* the attachments that flow from the nature in which we share qua human beings who are persons.

An imaginary reader of TPM, entering the conversation in Spring 2014: I want to go back to the beginning of the discussion you two have been having—and to 'person'.

One might perhaps accept the indexicality that DW says is integral to the meaning of 'person', yet still hesitate to accept his exclusion of all non-human creatures from the status and full-blown companionship of fellow-persons. It is one thing (I would say) to insist that, if a creature is to count for a person, then it must be 'one of us'. It is another thing to narrow or confine the 'us' to human beings in the way in which DW seeks to do.

Suppose I claim in opposition to DW that *person* is a moral-cum-legal status concept celebrating a rational nature, the capacity to deliberate, and, consequentially upon these, the capacity to tell good from evil. If such are the marks of personhood, then I do not understand why there can't *in principle* be any non-human persons. In raising this question, I am not claiming that there are any. But I am not satisfied by DW's argument.

DW: Your thought is that rational nature, together with the capacity to deliberate, leads somehow into the distinction of good from evil and is sufficient for membership of the community of persons. But I have to ask: what does rational nature amount to here? What sorts of things does it give to us? Ordinary logic, the capacity to determine matters of fact and the capacity to find means to a given end? But is that enough to put the creatures that possess it within range of our efforts to make sense of them? If your suggestion is to support a case for the possible personhood of some non-humans, then the rational nature that you invoke must include some concern for the non-hypothetical or non-instrumental

---

(Parfit's definition) is a definition—*professedly* a definition—of 'accurately quasi-remember'. It is a non-trivial problem (an insoluble problem, I think) to turn it into a definition of plain 'quasi-remember'; and all the more so to do this in a manner consistent with the cognitive import that is part and parcel with the actual meaning of 'remember', even as that figures within the compound 'quasi-remember'.

I assume that this verb 'quasi-remember' is a compound rather than a mere fusion. I mean by a fusion a term to be understood without reference to the semantic import of its apparent components. If 'quasi-remember' is a fusion, then that only aggravates the problem with the way in which 'accurately' has got into the definiendum. If 'quasi-remember' is a compound then its sense depends upon our understanding of 'remember' unaltered and unreformed. See Chapter 1, section 17.

purposes that are discovered or revealed to us as we live our human life and ask ourselves and/or ask one another *what we should care about*. That same grasp of rational purposes is presupposed to the distinction of good from evil.

I think that your positive suggestion about personhood, when it is extended as I have just proposed it be extended so as to embrace understanding of rational ends or purposes, leads straight back to the question of the prerequisites for *any* being's catching on to the main drift of human conduct and the prerequisites for non-humans entering into mutual understanding with us. Human beings enter into that understanding by imitation and projection upon other human beings of their own cares, concerns and purposes. Human constitution takes care of most of this. (See Chapter 4.) But by hypothesis your non-human candidates to be persons will have a different nature or constitution from ours.[6]

In a remarkable passage near the beginning of his *Pro Milone* Cicero writes:

there exists this law which is not written but inborn. We have not learned it, received it, or read it, but we have snatched it from nature herself, snatched, imbibed and extorted it: a law to which we are not trained, but in which we are made, in which we are not instructed, but with which we are imbued...

On this view, our sense of the reasonable and the good must arise from our efforts to exercise the powers and capacities with which we are endowed by the constitution that we derive from 'nature herself'.[7] If we understand 'natural' as that which is specific to us as human beings, we need not traduce Cicero. Rather we find a contention closely comparable to that which we may discover and develop from Hume's account of the origin of the standard of morals.[8] But any such account depends on the constant back-and-forth of a specifically human converse—a converse that is refined and extended by our acting out our human nature and debating with one another as best we may what we are to

---

[6] I am told that we can read the dolphin as sharing with us in benevolence or read the elephant as sharing with us in the capacity for outrage or indignation against what is seen as an evil act. But would you say that that was all it takes for us to share with them or for them to share with us in any larger sense of good and evil or any more comprehensive sense of the reasonable. Suppose we allow that the dolphin and the elephant work to their own standard of the reasonable. We can rejoice that that standard coincides at some striking points with our own. We must not condescend to their standard. But we cannot seek fully to share in it. Can non-human animals really seek to share in ours when they cannot make sense of us by thinking of us as one of *their own*?

[7] Never mind the Stoic claim that Cicero's assertion belongs with—a conception of the natural world as divinely ordained, rationally intelligible and operating in accordance with providence to the benefit of humanity. There is a truth in the words quoted that is independent of commitment to that background.

[8] Cf. *ETL* where Hume's denials concerning the role of reason in moral matters are interpreted as relating to reason as his opponents conceive it—or (as I say) misconceive it.

care about and how much. *Ex hypothesi*, non-humans are not party to *that* nature.

Is this not enough to establish a difficulty *of principle* in the thought that a non-human might qualify as one of us who are persons? I stand by my claim that there are real difficulties of principle in the idea. Your point is that I have not said enough to prove that it is logically impossible for these difficulties to be transcended. I accept this.

Imaginary reader: Have you or have you not shifted your position about the thing I was reacting to?

DW: I have to accept that it is logically possible for a non-human to enter into full interpretive reciprocity with us. That is only to say that no logical or analytic truth excludes this possibility. What I doubt is that it is better than logically possible. But you have made me see that the most felicitous expression of my position is and always was that *the only satisfactory stereotype* we have of a person is a human being. (On 'stereotype' see again note 1.) You have also made me remember that, if I were to think of the noun 'person' as a substance-term in its own right—as self-sufficiently individuative in a manner independent of the status of human being—then that would create the danger of our cross-classifying a given subject, Peter or Paul or whomever, as both a human-substance *and* a person-substance and incurring in that way the risk of arriving in some case at logically discrepant judgements of identity: 'the same person but not the same human being'. (See Chapter 3, section 5 and see the first chapter of *ISTC*, *S&S*, and *S&SR*.) While seeking to amplify the idea of *person* by reference to our idea of human being, I avoid that difficulty by referring identity-questions about persons to identity-questions about human beings.[9] It is *human being* that is the plenary substance-concept. But not all questions about persons are identity-questions. It is by reference to the indispensable concept *person* that we bring out to ourselves the significance for us of human beinghood. A person, I say, is a substance of an animate kind that we human beings can accept as actually or potentially party to our own rational and moral nature and sensibility, and that we can accept as entitled by its origin and descent to count as our fellow and one of us. If we are to understand ourselves properly, we cannot do without either of the concepts *person* and *human being* or dissociate ourselves from either.[10]

---

[9] Sensing sometimes the temptation to antedate the demise of a person to a time before their biological death.

[10] Cf. 'Replies' in my *1996d*, p. 248.

Another imaginary reader: David Wiggins has explained the would-be metaphysical basis for his conservatism with respect to the human constitution of persons. In the light of this and his anti-artefactual conception of personhood, will he please summarize his objections to the idea that the transplantation of a person's brain to another body can sustain that very person's being and persistence?

DW: Let me begin by saying why I ever considered the matter. In *Identity and Spatio-Temporal Continuity* (1967), at a point where I was concerned to show what was wrong with the idea that there could be two distinct criteria of personal identity, namely the 'bodily criterion' and the 'memory criterion', I had recourse to the passage that everyone now knows in Sydney Shoemaker's book *Self-Knowledge and Self-Identity*. There would surely have been other and better ways, but this was the way I chose. My response to the Brown–Brownson example was this:

The brain does not figure in the *a priori* account of *person* or *same person* except perhaps under the description 'seat of memory and other fundamentally characteristic capacities'. But *de facto* it plays the role of individuating nucleus (*ISTC*, p.51).

Strange though the proposal appeared, continuity of the brain that supported and enabled the characteristic activity of a person (and of *this* person) seemed to hold the promise to supersede both bodily and memory criterion. It showed forth the incompleteness of each of these. But then, requiring as I did that any criterion of identity of *x* and *y* be a criterion for their indiscernibility, I had to be troubled by the fact that mammalian brains are roughly symmetrical. The two halves can be entirely separated to a great depth and separated *with only minimal disturbance of normal function*. Even if brain-continuity sufficed for the perpetuation (so to speak) of everything that was distinctive of Brown's way of being, brain-continuity could not as such be an adequate criterion for personal identity. Leibniz's Law forbad. It could only count as such a criterion if one were prepared to think of the person Brown not as a particular substance but as something plural or universal, as a very specific clone-type. (Compare the genotype Cox's Orange Pippin, a kind of apple.) But the trouble with this move to the level of the universal was that it had the effect of denaturing personal memory, experiential memory, intention, and other faculties which, at the outset, one had been philosophically so concerned for.[11]

---

[11] At almost interminable length, I tried in *S&SR* to demonstrate this point conclusively. See pp. 217–23. Another thing I regret is that when I wrote section 15 of *S&SR* I had not yet replaced the 'Only *a* and *b*' Rule (Dx) by the criterion of Adequacy now explained at Chapter 1, section 4.

In *ISTC*, staying with the individual substance conception but still under the spell of Brown–Brownson, the conclusion I came to was that the only way forward was to elucidate *person* in such a way that coincidence under the concept *person* required 'the continuance in one organized parcel of all that was causally sufficient and causally necessary for the continuance of essential and characteristic functioning, no autonomously sufficient part achieving autonomous and functionally separate existence' (p. 55).

If there and then I had settled down to think further what sort of thing such a 'parcel' would have to be like, then where would this have carried my thoughts? I needed to formulate a criterion of identity for persons which at one and the same time (a) exposed the judgements it generated to all the formal demands of the identity relation and (b) arose naturally from some plausible conception of what (sortally speaking) a person is. What then *was* a person? My eventual answer was a subject (potentially at least) of fine-grained interpretation by us, a subject for whom (potentially at least) we are such a subject—and a creature with whom we can have relations of solidarity and reciprocity. (I have said all this before, but it belongs here too.) And such a subject was a human being.

All this I would have claimed to extract from our shareable idea of *person*— even as I assumed that I could determine the extension of the indexical 'us' by reference to the pre-philosophical thoughts which had led long since to a use of the first person plural—one use among many others—that has now (in context) to embrace all human beings. The criterion of identity for persons draws upon the principle of activity and persistence for a human being.

A human being can lose arm or leg or lungs or stomach—even the face—and still persist somehow, as that very human being. But each loss or subtraction makes the next subtraction harder to reconcile with the idea that the human being can survive it. Suppose that all that remains is a brain or a cerebrum. That is not a human being. It is but the remains of one. Even if this remnant sustains some semblance of electrical activity, it is scarcely a *person*. If we hesitate (as I myself should) to plunge the remnant into formaldehyde or to cremate it, *that* hesitation will scarcely show that we think the remnant has 'everything that matters'. The person Brown, Brown himself, *he* is not there. But what if his remnant is housed in a vat that supports or sustains it? Or if it is housed in another body, what then? Even then the most that we can find—or so I claim—is not a person but a sad remnant (or remnants) of a human being.[12]

---

[12] Cf. my 'Reply to Shoemaker', *The Monist*, 87 (2004), p. 605. Such a remnant of a thing does not count as the thing itself. Matters have gone too far.

6

Heraclitus' Conceptions of Flux, Fire, and Material Persistence

> Even when they are most worthy of amazement, things of daily occurrence pass us by unnoticed.
>
> Seneca, *Quaestiones Naturales* 7.1.1

> It can hardly be supposed that a false theory would explain in so satisfactory a manner as does the theory of natural selection the several large classes of fact above specified. It has recently been argued that this is an unsafe method of arguing; but it is a method used in judging of the common events of life and has often been used by the greatest natural philosophers.
>
> Charles Darwin, *Origin of Species*

1 Heraclitus and the Milesians

1.1 In recent decades there has been a tendency among scholars to question whether Heraclitus was, in the same sense as the Milesians were, a *cosmologist*: '[Heraclitus'] real subject is not the physical world but the human condition, which for the Greeks means the condition of mortality... Like [his] substitution of Fire for [Anaximenes'] Air, any changes in detail must have been designed not to improve the physical scheme in a scientific sense but to render its symbolic function more drastic.'[1]

---

[1] Charles Kahn, 'A New Look at Heraclitus', *American Philosophical Quarterly*, 1 (1964), pp. 189-203. It would be wrong for me not to qualify the disagreement I shall note in the text by acknowledgment of how much I have found both to agree with and to admire on the subject of Heraclitus in Kahn's book *Anaximander and the Origin of Greek Cosmology* (New York: Columbia University Press, 1960), esp. pp. 187-97.

Kahn's later book *The Art and Thought of Heraclitus* (Cambridge: Cambridge University Press, 1979), came to hand as the essay now published as this chapter was reaching its penultimate draft. This enabled me to make a number of improvements in detail, and also to take over from Kahn the felicitous (and felicitously ambiguous) expression 'elemental form'. Since Kahn's later book was not a repudiation of the doctrine I have quoted from his 1964 article I ventured to let section 1.1 of the essay remain as it was.

It would be foolish to deny that problems about mortality, fallibility, and the human perspective were an important part of Heraclitus' main subject. But this is not inconsistent with his having seen himself as answerable in the first instance to the same questions as the Milesians, whatever his reservations about their would-be *polymathiē*:

One thing is wisdom: to understand the plan by which all things are steered through all things (B41).

One from all and all from one (B10).

It is wise to hearken not to me but to my *logos* and to confess that all things are one (B50).

Thales, Anaximander, and Anaximenes had been concerned not only with particular phenomena that aroused their curiosity but also with the description and explanation of the world as a whole: How did the world come to exist and to be what it is? And now that it does exist, what sort of thing is it, and how does it maintain itself? Heraclitus inherited these questions from the Milesians, and he asked others of his own, about the soul, and about human destiny, cognition, and language. I shall contend that the new problems were seen by Heraclitus as requiring an unconditional willingness on his part to attempt some better than merely symbolic response to those of the Milesians. Indeed, if the reading that I shall propose for certain passages is accepted, then it will appear that he saw himself as positively obliged to improve upon his predecessors' cosmological theories.

1.2 There is a second affinity I claim to find between Heraclitus and the Milesians. If we are to trace any pattern in the doctrines that have come down to us as his, we need to see him as exploiting just as recklessly as his Milesian predecessors did what is sometimes called the Argument to the Best Explanation:[2] If q is the best explanation why p holds, then, if p is true, q must be true too.[3]

Whatever G. E. L. Owen may make of the ascription of the method to Heraclitus, it is he who must bear some considerable part of any blame or credit that it provokes. For it is one of Owen's contributions to our understanding of Greek philosophy to have drawn attention to the central part (insufficiently remarked in modern times) that is played in Greek thought by the idea of

---

[2] See Gilbert Harman, 'The Inference to the Best Explanation', *Philosophical Review*, 74 (1965), pp. 88–95; Paul R. Thagard, 'The Best Explanation: Criteria for Theory Choice', *Journal of Philosophy*, 75 (1978), pp. 76–92. There is also an interesting affinity waiting to be drawn out with Collingwood's doctrine that '*questions* are the cutting edge of the mind'.

[3] The 'must' has 'if p then q' as its scope here; and of course it does not connote the metaphysical necessity of q.

Sufficient Reason.[4] Owen has traced the idea from Leucippus, Parmenides, and Melissus[5] back to Anaximander, where Anaximander's mastery of Sufficient Reason is brilliantly demonstrated by his replacement of Thales' supposition that water is what holds the world up by the insight (cf. Aristotle, *de Caelo* 295b11) that the earth is held up by nothing and simply stays where it is because it is in equipoise with other things, there being no reason for its shifting in any particular direction.

What is the connection between Sufficient Reason and the Argument to the Best Explanation? Suppose nothing holds true unless there is reason for its so holding. Then if p is true, something must be true which explains why p is true. But then it must be possible to argue backwards—albeit against the direction of implication—and infer from p's truth whatever best explains why p. The Principle of Sufficient Reason gives us the Argument to the Best Explanation[6] then, and in doing this it suggests a research strategy—the same strategy which Charles Darwin seeks to justify in the passage of *Origin of Species* prefixed to this chapter. Any phenomenon that is observed calls for explanation. But, wherever explanation is called for, one should postulate as true that which best explains the phenomenon, regardless of whether the putatively explanatory fact is in any way directly observable. Improving and amplifying the precept a little, it is natural to expand upon it as Plato did: when we have several explanations of distinct phenomena arrived at in this manner, we must test our explanations and the consequences of our explanations for consistency with one another and with everything else we believe. Then, in the light of our findings under that head, we must revise and modify or develop our explanations. Which being done, we must go on, find more phenomena to explain, use these explananda to gain favour for more hypotheses, and then collect all our hypotheses together in order to test the new accumulated total commitment for consistency, plausibility, etc...

No articulate statement of this method is to be found in Greek philosophy before Plato reaches for the Method of Dialectic in *Phaedo* and *Meno*, and tries in

---

[4] See, for instance, 'Plato and Parmenides on the Timeless Present', *The Monist*, 50 (1966), pp. 317-40. I understand that Owen developed the theme further in his Sather Classical Lectures (unpublished).

[5] For various statements of the principle or approximations to it, see Xenophanes A28; Parmenides B8, 9; Melissus B1-2; Leucippus A8, B2. Such references here and below are to H. Diels and W. Kranz, *Die Fragmente der Vorsokratiker* (6th edn, Berlin: Weidermann, 1952). See also Plato, *Phaedo* 98-9, 108E-109E; *Timaeus* 62E1 2ff.

[6] There are doubts about the opposite dependency—doubts that one may suppose can only be cleared up by an elucidation of 'reason' diverging from, e.g., Leibniz's interpretation of sufficiency. A full treatment of all this would divorce teleological conceptions of sufficient reason (Socrates, Plato, Leibniz) from anti-teleological conceptions. For Heraclitus' anti-teleological stance see B52, B124 ('The fairest order in the world is a heap of random sweepings').

the *Republic* to marry it up with the idea of ultimate explanation in terms of the Good, which Leibniz inherited from him and brought into a quite special relation with Sufficient Reason. Nor is there any fully explicit statement of anything resembling a Principle of Sufficient Reason before Parmenides. So sceptics will say that primitive natural philosophers such as the ones we are concerned with could not possibly have engaged in reasoning that wants so sophisticated a description. But to this I would reply first that Anaximander and Heraclitus and their successors were not primitive thinkers; and, second, that even if they were, we should still need to remember that very simple patterns of reasoning can satisfy very complicated theoretical descriptions. (Think even of the syllogism in Barbara.) The sophistication of the description we have to give in order to see the argument from the best explanation as a rational argument is no reason not to credit the Milesians with the corresponding procedure—or with the conviction that is made for the method, that we live in a universe (as Edward Hussey puts it) of 'order, lawlike regularity and intellectually satisfying construction',[7] hospitable to truly general, all-embracing explanatory hypotheses that stand in no need of qualification or adjustment *ad hoc*. (Cf. B41, etc., quoted in 1.1.)

1.3 From the nature of the hypothesis, the claim that Heraclitus and the Milesians have a common method can only be judged by the coherence and order that it will eventually discover to us if we see these men as building up their world-picture in response to the demand of Sufficient Reason. In the interim, some more immediate conviction of Heraclitus' continuity with the Milesians may be created by reconsideration of the familiar text where it seems that Heraclitus makes allusion to Anaximander. This is the correction that Heraclitus seems to offer of Anaximander's doctrine of mutual reparation. Anaximander had said:

Whence things originate, thither according to necessity they must return and perish [that is, back into the same components]; for they must pay penalty and be judged for their injustice in accordance with the assessment of time (B1).

It would appear that Heraclitus found much to agree with in this opinion, offering an excellent gloss on Anaximander's most probable meaning:

Cold things grow warm, warm cools, moist grows parched, dry dampens (B126).

But there was a fault that Heraclitus found with Anaximander:

One must understand that war is universal, strife is justice, and that absolutely everything happens by strife and by necessity (B80);

---

[7] Edward Hussey, *The Presocratics* (London: Duckworth 1972), p. 17.

and he denounced Homer (cf. Aristotle, *Eth. Eud.* 1235a26 [+ scholiast on *Iliad* XVIII 107] = A22) for saying 'Would that strife would perish from among gods and men', complaining that Homer did not see that he was praying for the destruction of the universe.

Now it is scarcely denied by anybody that B80 is a clear and (by Heraclitean standards) respectful allusion to Anaximander.[8] What has been insufficiently remarked is that such a disagreement between the two of them only makes sense against some background of agreement. What was this background? Only one answer readily suggests itself. They agree in wanting to explain the maintenance of the world order. Evidently they also agree that the maintenance of the world order (or the maintenance, had we better say in Anaximander's case, of this particular whorl off the *Apeiron*?) must be managed from within a definite store of something or other. Unless this were agreed, why otherwise should there be any need for what Anaximander calls *requital for injustice* and what Heraclitus prefers to see as *mere exchange*—one thing's superseding another, as one piece replaces another on a square in the game of *pessoi*? (Cf. B52.) If the two agree that this sort of process must be postulated, the disagreement between them relates only to the proper view to take of the justice or injustice of the process they otherwise agree about.

Here of course I am guessing—as I believe everyone interested in either Heraclitus or Anaximander ought to be obliged to guess. And obviously the guess must be pitted against any rival suggestion about what the background of agreement was. But this particular suggestion, together with the special idea that it imports of the autonomic steering or regulation of the world order, has the signal advantage of engaging well with information that we have from Aristotle about his predecessors. Aristotle says that one of their concerns was that coming to be and passing away should not give out.[9] On my reading, Anaximander and Heraclitus will be prominent examples of philosophers with this preoccupation.

1.4 Such familiar reflections will lead into others. In Anaximander certain questions appear to have been left open about the origin and continuous renewal of the world as we know it. Presumably B1 was his most striking contribution to the problem. But Heraclitus himself *closed* these questions. Not only was

---

[8] Cf. Gregory Vlastos, 'On Heraclitus', *American Journal of Philology*, 76 (1955), pp. 337–68.
[9] Cf. *Physics* 203b15–30, 208a8–9; *On Generation and Corruption* 336a14–18; John Burnet, *Early Greek Philosophy* (2nd edn, London: A. & C. Black, 1908), p. 60.

this cosmos made neither of god nor of man, but [it] always has been, is and always will be, an everlasting fire going out in measures and kindling in measures;[10]

the steering too (or the governance of the world as we know it) is said by Heraclitus to be from within, not, as Anaximander seems to have asserted, by the Boundless from without. (Cf. on Anaximander, Aristotle, *Physics* 203b7ff.) For whatever Heraclitus' thunderbolt is, whatever his Zeus may be, and whatever the relations may be between thunderbolt and Heraclitean fire (perhaps these things can be debated), thunderbolt is or stands for something inside the world; and

Thunderbolt steers all things (B64).

But then, if the steering of the *kosmos* was from within and if the maintenance of its order and vital activity was a question that required an answer, the idea of autonomic regulation that appears in the Anaximander fragment was exactly the idea that Heraclitus needed. One can scarcely imagine a more natural continuity between the doctrines of two independent thinkers, where the second knows the work of the first and improves or simplifies or develops it.

2 A Hypothetical Reconstruction of the Scaffolding of Heraclitus' Theory of Flux

2.1 I embark now on the hazardous and experimental work of the reconstruction of the philosophical motivation for Heraclitus' world view—a necessary task, but one that was speculative even in early antiquity. So far I have credited him with a Milesian method—the method of postulating whatever appears the best explanation of a phenomenon. I have quoted his conviction of the unity of things (which, as the reader will have guessed, I want to see as related to one consequence of that method). And I have implicated him in what I argue to have been a Milesian question about the maintenance of the world's motion, order and vital activity. To complete that stage of the reconstruction I have to ask what observations or phenomena can be expected to have given him the *question* of the

---

[10] B30 (in part). Aristotle is thought to have been the first to assert that the *kosmos* was not created. But B30 suggests that he was anticipated in this not altogether satisfactory move by Heraclitus.
Aristotle asserts (*De Caelo.* 279b12) that all his predecessors believed that the *kosmos* had a beginning, though many denied (280a11) that matter had a beginning. To reconcile B30 with Aristotle it seems best to locate the difference Aristotle sees between himself and Heraclitus in the *periodicity* of things. Aristotle contemplates little or no variability from *the kind of world order that is familiar to us*, whereas Heraclitus postulates an however orderly eternal periodicity. See 4.1, 4.2.

constant renewal of the world and made it as pressing as the fragments cited in 1.4 above suggest to me that it was. The most natural answer would appear to be:

(a) the everyday observation of the conspicuous but not manifestly ubiquitous disintegration of terrestrial *order*, and the observation of the constant transmutation and decay of terrestrial *substances*;
(b) the equally familiar observation of the habitual tendency of terrestrial *motions* to run down;
(c) the observation of the continuation, in spite of all this, of the world that we know, replenished by creation, growth, and new motion. When one substance ceases to exist, another takes its place. When one motion is spent, others appear and inherit its impetus.

Observations (a) (b) (c) suffice to justify the postulation of a theory of reparation. But what else beside these things did Heraclitus observe and seek to explain and bring into harmony with them? He is credited with all sorts of hypotheses about sun, moon, and stars as bowls of fire, and about the periodic and regular inclinations of these bowls. Such hypotheses, if Heraclitus really propounded them, were evidently designed to explain differences of night and day, or the warmth and coolness of the seasons. I am disposed to agree with the sceptical historian of science D. R. Dicks[11] that it is 'doubtful whether any of this [would-be astronomical detail] represents even approximately what Heraclitus thought'; but the detailed accuracy of the reports matters far less than the presumption which they help to sustain, that such celestial happenings were among the phenomena that Heraclitus treated as explananda. Dicks is surely right again when he declares, on the basis of fragments such as B94,

The sun will not transgress his due measure: otherwise the Erinyes, the ministers of justice, will find him out[12]

and B100,

the cycles the sun presides over, in order to determine and adjudicate the changes and seasons that produce everything,

that 'two things in particular struck [Heraclitus] when he contemplated [the cosmic] order, first the fact of its *continuity*, and second its *periodicity*'. But if this is what impresses one about the heavens, then how is the apparent anomaly, diversity, and small-scale disorder of terrestrial phenomena and the limited

---

[11] D. R. Dicks, *Early Greek Astronomy to Aristotle* (London: Thames & Hudson, 1970).
[12] Cf. B120, on which see Kahn, *Anaximander*, p. 197.

persistence of ordinary continuants to be subsumed under *one* order of nature with celestial imperishability, continuity, and periodicity? Surely what underlies celestial stability must be some regular lawlike process or processes. Nothing less will suffice to explain celestial phenomena. But if so, then, despite appearances, regularity of process must underlie terrestrial phenomena too—unless we are to breach the a priori requirement of unity (see B41, etc. quoted in 1.1). In the name of unity, which is only another aspect of Sufficient Reason, the orderly process that is manifest in the heavens must be something that the natural philosopher can recklessly hypothesize to hold absolutely everywhere, and so upon earth—in spite of the apparent contrast between the perishability of terrestrial bodies and the apparent imperishability of heavenly ones. The conviction of unity ('one from all and all from one') forces us to see the terrestrial order as continuously renewed in spite of disintegration and change; and the celestial order as subject to continuous processes of change in spite of its regularity, periodicity, and everlastingness. But if unseen elemental processes are uniformly regular and directed, then anomaly is an illusion that results from our imperfect understanding of their interaction; and, if all involve change, then permanence or apparent cessation of activity represents equilibrium (temporary equality, not proper peace or armistice) between unseen forces that are opposing one another actively.

2.2 When he reaches this point Heraclitus has advanced well past the observational-cum-hypothetical stage of scientific theorizing that I began by describing. He is offering redescriptions of phenomena themselves in terms more theory-contaminated than any that our senses could offer, and then reconceptualizing the classes of terrestrial and celestial phenomena in defiance of observed differences.

The hidden joining/harmony is stronger than the visible one (B52).

One hypothesis leads to the necessity for another. Inasmuch as every one of the elemental processes hypothesized must, unless resisted by others, take over the whole world, the belief in the continuance of the world obliges him to believe in the irresolubility (by treaty, by exhaustion, or by any other means) of the struggle in which they are locked. Strife is ubiquitous and universal. But being the instrument of renewal and restitution, it is also just.

2.3 So much for a first attempt at reconstruction of how we may find it intelligible that Heraclitus makes perpetual process or change the model by which to redescribe everything. We have motivated the idea of a flux that is ubiquitous, incessant, exceptionless, and all-embracing, and in virtue of which not only all living things flow but absolutely all perceptible things—stones, rocks, even the sun (cf. B8)—flow (cf. Aristotle, *Metaphysics* 987a33, 1078b14, Melissus DK B8). And, seeing Heraclitus in this light, we find nothing to astonish us in Plato's report that

> Heraclitus said that everything is in a stage of change and nothing stays stable, and likening things to the flow of a river he says that you could not step twice into the same river (*Cratylus* 402A).[13]

or in Aristotle's testimony:

> And some say that all existing things without exception are in constant movement, but this escapes our perception. Supporters of this theory do not state clearly what kind of motion they mean or whether they mean all kinds (*Physics* 253b9-12).
> It is plain that those physicists who assert that all sensible things are always in motion are wrong... They mostly conceive this as alteration (things are always in flux and decay, they say), and they go so far as to speak even of becoming and perishing as a process of alteration (*Physics* 265a2-7).

It is true that someone may still ask why we should believe that everything in heaven and earth is in flux and participates in a hidden harmony of opposites. But the ready answer to that question is that Heraclitus' argument or doctrine is simply a bold generalization from certain special cases or phenomena. It was the height of madness to extend his theory from these phenomena to absolutely everything. But before one derides the theory for that reason one should ask how else Sufficient Reason is to be reconciled with the convictions that our senses make it nearly impossible for us to abandon, about earth and sky and the seemingly continuous motion and renewal of the *kosmos*. (And how else, we can then reflect, is the ordinary behaviour of colliding bodies to be explained, unless *all* bodies contain opposing processes?)

2.4 What further ancient evidence can be adduced for Heraclitus' involvement in this way of thinking? Two points at least can be confirmed, one being general and the other an indispensable point of detail.

---

[13] In 'Natural Change in Heraclitus', *Mind*, 60 (1951), pp. 38-42, G. S. Kirk has sought to cast doubt on Plato's testimony here. He has done this in the name of doctrines of measure and reciprocity between opposites whose attribution to Heraclitus he has made very persuasive. My exposition of these doctrines is indebted both to this article and to Kirk's *Heraclitus: The Cosmic Fragments* (Cambridge: Cambridge University Press, 1954). I also believe Kirk reconstructs the river fragment correctly. (Cf. 2.5 below: if Heraclitus also said that you could not step into the same river twice, that is a hyperbolical restatement of what is said soberly and correctly in B12.) But against Kirk, I should claim that, on a more correct understanding of change than Plato achieved when he departed from the everyday conception to which Heraclitus was party, there is no conflict of any sort between the measure doctrine and the doctrine of universal flux.

First, the reconstruction makes goodish sense of a report of Plato's that is certainly intended to collect up Heraclitus' as well as other philosophers' opinions:

> Coming to be, and what passes for being, are produced by change, while not being and ceasing to be are produced by inactivity. For instance, the hot, or fire, which we are told actually generates and governs everything else, is itself generated by means of movement and friction; and these are changes. Moreover the class of living things is produced by means of those same processes... The condition of the body is destroyed, isn't it, by inactivity and illness but to a great extent preserved by exercise and change... *States of inactivity rot things and destroy them whereas states of activity preserve them*... So long as the heavenly cycle and the sun are in motion, everything is and is preserved, in the realms of both gods and men; whereas if that motion... were brought to a standstill, everything would be destroyed.[14]

In the second place, confirmation is to be found in Diogenes Laertius for the way in which I have claimed that Heraclitus combines an ontology of substances—the belief in what we should call substances—with his belief in universal flux:

> The totality of things is composed out of fire and is dissolved into it. Everything comes to be in accordance with fate, and the totality of things is harmoniously joined together through *enantiodromia* (running in opposition) (D.L. ix 7 [= DK Ai]).

The word *enantiodromia*—whatever it was that prompted it to Diogenes—is tailor-made for the account that our reconstruction has been forced to give of continuants, of permanency, and of the appearance of cessation of activity.

2.5 And here at last we arrive at the river fragment. For reasons that will become more fully transparent in 5.1 below and following, the version that I accept as likely to be closest to Heraclitus' official statement of his doctrine (no matter what other poetical or rhetorical effects he may have attempted) is Kirk's reconstruction:

> Upon those who step into the same rivers different and again different waters flow. The waters scatter and gather, come together and flow away, approach and depart.[15]

The river is at once an eminent and observable instance of flow and a metaphorical hostage for myriads of invisible cases of heavenly and celestial flux.[16] It is also

---

[14] Plato, *Theaetetus* 153A–D, trans. J. H. McDowell (Oxford: Clarendon Press, 1973).

[15] Fragments 12 and 91; text, contamination and translation after Kirk, *Heraclitus*, pp. 367–84.

[16] For the idea of a phenomenon going proxy for a whole class to which it may itself belong, I am greatly indebted to Edward Hussey (see 'Epistemology and Meaning in Hereclitus', in Malcolm Schofield and Martha Nussbaum (eds), *Language and Logic: Studies in Ancient Greek Philosophy* (Cambridge: Cambridge University Press, 1982), ch. 2). Cf. also here Philip Wheelwright, *Heraclitus* (Princeton, NJ: Princeton University Press, 1959), p. 44, from whom I borrow the Goethean phrase 'eminent instance'.

an eminent instance and metaphysical hostage for processes of renewal which Heraclitus sees as resulting from the equilibria or superpositions of opposing forces that underlie substance. In this reconstruction the fragment will remind one forcibly that Heraclitus' thinking is untouched by Parmenides. Heraclitus is not concerned with how it is conceptually possible for a substance to survive through change as that very same substance.[17] Why (unless one is sophisticated enough or muddled enough to be confused by identity and persistence) should that be a problem? What he asks is how a thing could survive unless it did change. A substance can persist through time, but only by virtue of constant process, and if *work* is done:

The barley drink disintegrates if it is not constantly stirred (B125).

The barley drink was a drink made of barley-meal, grated cheese and Pramnian wine (to which on one well known occasion when Odysseus was her guest, Circe added honey and magical drugs).[18] Being neither a mixture nor even a suspension, it separated and reverted rapidly to its constituents unless it was stirred vigorously. What the barley drink stands for is at once conditional persistence and the tendency towards disintegration which Heraclitus sees as so general that order, renewal and arrest of disintegration are what need explaining. He explains them without explaining them *away*, however; and if we accept that, with the barley drink as with everything else, what work explains is renewal and persistence, and if we also remember the correction to Anaximander, then we shall be led to one more reflection that belongs here: wherever one substance does persist by work and through process being set against process, there will always be other substances which, for just that reason, did not benefit by the application of work, or had it withdrawn from them.

2.6 I shall return in section 5 to the misunderstandings that Heraclitus' doctrine has provoked in the minds of those who have been schooled to put strange constructions upon ordinary descriptions of change and find philosophical difficulty in the idea of a changing substance. But in the interim, let us complete the first statement of the Heraclitean doctrine that persistence and numerical identity require change. It is important that this is not the doctrine that some continuant substance or stuff persists through *every* change—a Milesian idea which the Heraclitean doctrine of process is in flight from. Nor is it the doctrine that an individual substance can persist provided that just any change

---

[17] One of the editors of the volume in which this essay was originally published informed me that, in his courses of lectures on the Presocratics, Owen expressed a similar opinion.

[18] Cf. Homer, *Odyssey*, 10, 234, and 326.

befalls it. Admittedly, there is a great need for an account of what changes promote or allow the survival of a particular sort of continuant and what changes will entail destruction. This really is a good problem. (My own answer to the problem would depend on the natural distinction between answers to the question *what a thing is* and *what it is like*.[19] I claim that once we focus on the foundations of this distinction, which is almost the same as that between substantive and adjective (cf. Aristotle's *Categories* 1–5), it will appear plainly that particular concepts of continuants of this or that natural kind both *require* of their compliants certain sorts of change and also *delimit* the changes that such compliants can undergo except on pain of extinction: see 5.3 below.) But it is not clear that Heraclitus himself, enjoying the good fortune of writing before the waters had been muddied, saw any of this as an urgent or intractable problem, or even *as* a problem.[20] He takes the concept of change for granted. But he does not therefore misconceive it.

3 Fire

3.1 If 2.5 is correct, we must expect that, as one force or another force temporarily prevails in the struggle at any place, there will be a shift in the locus of equilibrium. And wherever this shift occurs we have seen that we must expect a gradual but continuous run-down of substances going past their acme in favour of others that are in progress towards their acme. We must expect this because Heraclitus supposes that there is a limited store of that in virtue of which there can be any processes at all. If, however, we now speculate with Heraclitus about the long-term general tendency of the struggle of elemental processes and of everything that depends on this struggle, then we have a chance to plait together at last the following ideas: the unity of things, perpetual flux, the just or equitable replacement of one thing by another thing, and *fire*.

The interpretation of Heraclitus' theory of fire that I want to propose rests on the following fragments:

This world or world-order, which is the same for all, no one of the gods or men has made; but it was ever, is now, and ever shall be, an ever-living Fire, kindling in measures and going out in measures (B30).

Fire lives the death of earth and air lives the death of fire, water lives the death of air, and earth of water (B76).

---

[19] See *S&S*, especially chs. 2, 3.
[20] Martha Nussbaum has put it to me that B36 and Heraclitus' other remarks about watery souls indicate an interest in this problem, and that the river fragment does too, though less clearly.

The turnings of fire are first sea; and of sea half is earth, half whirlwind (B31A).

Earth melts back into sea and is measured by the same tale as before it became earth (B31B).

All things are an exchange or requital for Fire, and Fire for all things, like goods for gold and gold for goods (B90).

B30 appears to assure us that the kosmos is a perpetual fire. Yet fire is extinguished. So fire itself is not the only elemental form. B31A and B31B tell us about fire's particular turnings or transformations into other things (e.g. into sea and earth). But B90 encourages us to suppose that, when sea changes into earth and back again, there is something that is not lost at all. And surely Heraclitus thinks the same applies in the cases where fire is condensed into sea or sea congeals into earth as when earth melts back into sea and sea evaporates back into fire (which Diogenes Laertius says Heraclitus says is the process by which fire is nourished). If so, then Heraclitus must think that, whatever happens, no fire is ever lost in the cycle of transformations ('Beginning and end are shared in the circumference of a circle', B103). If everything else is to fire as goods are to gold, then that cannot help but mean that the total fire-value of fire, sea, and earth (plus *prēstēr*, plus whatever else) taken together is constant. Suppose then that we were to try to think of Heraclitus' fire not as a particular form or stuff but as the agent of all process—or as the determinable of process itself. If we give in to this temptation, we are not the first to do so. See the discussion of the etymology of 'Zeus' and '*dikaion*' in Plato's *Cratylus* 412D:

Those who suppose all things to be in motion conceive the greater part of nature to be a mere receptacle, and they say there is a penetrating power which passes through all this and is the instrument of creation in all, and is the subtlest and swiftest element... this element which superintends all things and pierces all (*diaion*) is rightly called just (*dikaion*)... [When] I begin... to interrogate [these philosophers] gently... they try to satisfy me with one observation after another... One says that justice is the sun... [one says] it is fire itself... another says, No, not fire itself but the hot itself that is in the fire (quoted by Kirk, *Heraclitus*, p. 363).

Suppose now that we see some trace here of a Heraclitean conception of Fire, or of something that those who had the whole text of Heraclitus found that they had to say in order to sustain their stance as Heracliteans. Then what I believe we shall conclude is that, without having any notion of how the relevant measure of process would be constructed, Heraclitus committed himself to the idea that the total quantity of process is constant. I do not mean that he had the conceptual resources to make this last claim explicit. He has to prefer such expressions as the metaphor we encounter in B90. But if we try to transpose what he says there into something more literal, and then collate that with B31B, no smaller claim will do justice to the advance he has made from the Milesian standpoint. Fire is no more that out of which all things are made than gold is a constituent of all the things that buy and sell in the market place. Gold is one stuff among others. But it is that by reference to which, or that in terms of which, all other stuffs can be measured there. Fire is for the world order, then, what gold is for the *agora*—the measure. Extending Heraclitus' metaphor, one may go on to say that, notwithstanding the local extinguishing of fire, and notwithstanding temporal variation in the proportions of the elemental forms (see section 4), the great cosmic enterprise as a whole trades neither at a loss nor at a profit; but, in virtue of a reciprocity between processes that are getting their way and processes that are falling back, the books always balance exactly. However much the assets are redeployed or transformed, the capital is constant as measured in measures of fire.

A comparison between fire, conceived as Heraclitus conceived it, and energy, as that was conceived in eighteenth–nineteenth century physics, would be anachronistic, yet only relatively mildly so. Many plain men have scarcely any better idea of what energy is than Heraclitus had of what fire was. But most of us have *some* conception of energy. The common idea, and the idea that holds our conception of energy in place and holds Heraclitus' conception of fire in place, is the idea of whatever it is that is conserved and makes possible the continuance of the world-order. 'Fire' is Heraclitus' counter for that, 'energy' (or energy plus matter, matter being conceived independently of energy in nineteenth-century fashion) is ours. A physicist would be needed to take the point further. But that does not mean that Heraclitus cannot have taken it this far.

3.2 This sort of reading of B90 and B31A, B is not new. I find that Vlastos and others[21] have long since anticipated it:

[B90] identifies fire as the thing that remains constant in all transformations and implies that *its* measure is the same or the common measure in all things... The invariance of [fire's] measure is what accounts for the observance of the *metron* in all things, and fire is therefore that which 'governs' or 'steers' all things.[22]

But the very mention of energy in the modern sense will prompt others to remind me that it took European science two hundred years from the death of Galileo and at least one long and vexatious metaphysico-scientific controversy concerning *vis viva* to assemble the ideas of work and of potential energy (as distinguished from kinetic energy), to gather the other fruits of the conceptual labours

---

[21] e.g. Kahn, in his *Anaximander*, and J. L. Mackie, in an unpublished paper of 1941.
[22] Vlastos, 'On Heraclitus', pp. 360–1.

of Leibniz, Bernoulli, Helmholtz, and others, formulate the principle of the conservation of energy, and then at last see the principle of the conservation of the *sum* of kinetic and potential energy tested by the efforts of Joule and others. I also expect to be informed that by the importation of the idea of energy one lays oneself open to the charge of systematic falsification of Heraclitus, a thinker much more primitive (it may be said) than any who can be recognized in this portrait.

Such a charge would rest on a misapprehension both of what I am saying, and of the conceptual provenance of the conservation principle. To make out my interpretation I do not have to credit Heraclitus with any conception at all of that which is the sum of kinetic and potential energy, where kinetic energy is $\frac{1}{2}mv^2$, or even to credit him with our conception of energy as the power of doing work, where work is conceived as force times distance moved (or whatever). I have only to credit him with having asked a question and then conceived of there being something or other whose conservation would help to answer that question. I cannot forbear however to add that, whatever the complexities of arriving at an idea of energy sufficiently precise for the conservation principle to be tested and proved, one part of what eventually and painfully discovered it to human beings was a stubbornly ineradicable prejudice that is even older than philosophy:

An effect is always in proportion to the action which is necessary to produce it. (René Descartes, *Oeuvres* I [A.T.]. See pp. 435–48.)

There is always a perfect equivalence between the full cause and the whole effect (Leibniz, Reply to Abbé Catelan in *Nouvelles de la Republique de Lettres*, Feb. 1687).[23]

No working cause can be destroyed totally or in part without producing an action equal to a decrease in the cause (Johannes Bernoulli, *Opera Omnia* Vol. 3, p. 56, Essay no. 135, ch. 10, §1).

The author [Clarke] objects that two soft or non-elastic Bodies meeting together lose some of their *Force*. I answer, No ... The *Forces* are not destroyed but scattered among the small parts; but the case here is the same as when men change great Money into small (Leibniz: Fifth letter to Samuel Clarke).

Why are Leibniz and Bernoulli so sure? Though they proved to be right, they had no rigorous empirical evidence that it was so. Maybe the answer to this question has to do with the ultimate unintelligibility of the idea that anything could come from nothing. But the most striking demonstration of the naturalness and simplicity of this underlying thought can be found in the words that Joule

---

[23] Quoted in Hidé Ishiguro, 'Pre-established Harmony *versus* Constant Conjunction: A Reconsideration of the Distinction between Rationalism and Empiricism', *Proceedings of the British Academy*, 63 (1979), p. 241.

spoke in St Anne's Church Reading Room, Manchester, in the 1847 address in which he first described for the world at large his experimental demonstration of the conservation principle:

> You will be surprised to hear that until very recently the universal opinion has been that living force could be absolutely and irrevocably destroyed at any one's option. Thus, when a weight falls to the ground, it has been generally supposed that its living force is absolutely annihilated, and that the labour which may have been expended in raising it to the elevation from which it fell has been entirely thrown away and wasted, without the production of any permanent effect whatever. We might reason, *a priori*, that such absolute destruction of living force cannot possibly take place, because it is manifestly absurd to suppose that the powers with which God has endowed matter can be destroyed any more than that they can be created by man's agency; but we are not left with this argument alone, decisive as it must be to every unprejudiced mind. The common experience of every one teaches him that living force is not *destroyed* by the friction or collision of bodies. We have reason to believe that the manifestations of living force on our globe are, at the present time, as extensive as those which have existed at any time since its creation, or, at any rate, since the deluge—that the winds blow as strongly, and the torrents flow with equal impetuosity now, as at the remote period of 4,000 or even 6,000 years ago; and yet we are certain that, through that vast interval of time, the motions of the air and of the water have been incessantly obstructed and hindered by friction. We may conclude then, with certainty, that these motions of air and water, constituting living force, are not *annihilated* by friction. We lose sight of them, indeed, for a time; but we find them again reproduced. Were it not so, it is perfectly obvious that long ere this all nature would have come to a dead standstill.[24]

Since we are struck by a phenomenon and have the wit to find it remarkable, sufficient reason carries us inexorably onwards into hypothesis.

4 Periodicity and Variation

4.1 Among the many loose ends I have left hanging here (many of which would still hang loose even if we had the whole book instead of fragments), let me attend to just one. What in this picture will explain periodicity, and night and day and the seasons? It seems clear that Heraclitus thought of these as corresponding to variations in the quantity or distribution of the elemental forms air, sea, *prēstēr*, earth, etc. Diogenes Laertius reports Heraclitus as maintaining that the earth gave off bright exhalations which nourished fire and produced day by igniting in the circle of the sun; whereas the sea gave off dark exhalations which nourished

---

[24] See *The Scientific Papers of James Prescott Joule* (London: Physical Society of London, 1884), vol. I, pp. 265–76.

moisture and by their periodic increase produced night. But however it is interpreted, the report (like the *verbatim* fragments themselves) leaves unanswered what is the most pressing and interesting question: what causes or steers or controls these variations themselves?

Perhaps we can supply the deficit in our evidence here (or in Heraclitus' own book) by adducing the words of the zealously Heraclitean author of the Hippocratic treatise *de Victu*, which Bywater had the happy idea of printing with his collection of fragments of Heraclitus:[25]

Fire can move all things always, while water can nourish all things always; but in turn each masters or is mastered to the greatest maximum or the least minimum possible. Neither of them can gain the complete mastery for the following reason. The fire as it advances to the limit of the water lacks nourishment, and so turns to where it is likely to be nourished. The water as it advances to the limit of the fire finds its motion to fail and at this point falls back.[26]

The explanation is thoroughly Ionian in spirit and it fills a gap in the Heraclitean theory. If we wished, and if we trusted Diogenes Laertius enough, it could be complicated and diversified by deployment of the two sorts of exhalation he mentions. The thing that matters though is the leading idea. Every elemental process or force wants to take over the whole world, but, the closer it comes to that objective, the harder it finds it to follow up its victories, and the better conditions then become for the forces that are ranged against it to rally themselves. If we see this as a sort of feedback arrangement, then we have only to suppose that the requisite and inevitable adjustment is always slightly delayed, or that there is always overcompensation in the adjustments, in order to explain periodicity. We can see periodicity as resulting from a kind of 'hunting' between opposite and equally unstable or unmaintainable states of an unceasing struggle.[27]

---

[25] I. Bywater, *Heracliti Ephesii Reliquiae* (Oxford: Clarendon Press, 1877), p. 61.
[26] *de Victu* 1.3, in *Hippocrates*, vol. IV, trans. W. H. S. Jones (London: Heinemann, 1931), p. 233.
[27] We can take this idea over from the author of the *de Victu* as a complementation of Heraclitus' doctrine. But of course we should note that he has resolved in an overdefinite way certain difficulties—most notably Heraclitus' apparent need for some matter-principle independent of fire. Anticipating Aristotle's criticism of monistic condensation and rarefaction theories (*On Generation and Corruption* 330b10), this author allows water to enjoy an autonomy for which we have no Heraclitean authority. Insofar as Heraclitus himself offered any account of the differentiation of kinds of process or kinds of thing, he seems to have explained differentiation of things by reference to the difference of the processes underlying them, and differentiation of processes simply by an analogy: 'God is day and night, winter and summer, war and peace, surfeit and hunger, but he takes various shapes, *just as fire, when it is mingled with spices, is named according to the savour of each*' (B63, trans. Burnet).

4.2 The *De Victu* fills out the Heraclitean world-view. But more still needs to be said about periodicity. It has often been supposed that there is a conflict here between the testimonies of Plato and Aristotle. Aristotle says in the *De Caelo* 279b12:

That the world was generated they are all agreed, but generation over, some say that it is eternal, others say that it is destructible like any other natural formation. Others, again, with Empedocles and Heraclitus believe that there is alternation in the destructive process, which takes now this direction now that and continues without end.

There is other evidence of a complementary kind that is hard to dismiss. Simplicius says (*De Caelo* 94, 4):

And Heraclitus says that at one time the kosmos is burned out and at another it rises again from fire according to certain definite cycles of time in which he says it is kindling in measures and going out in measures. Later the Stoics came to be of the same opinion.

And again in *In Physica* 23, 38 Simplicius quotes Heraclitus as saying that:

There is a certain order and determined time in the changing of the kosmos in accordance with some preordained necessity.

There is also DK A13, which consists of passages of Aëtius and Censorinus and amounts to the claim that Heraclitus thought that there was a great year whose winter was a great flood and whose summer was an *ekpurōsis* (conflagration). It appears that Heraclitus and Linus supposed that the cycle consisted of 10,800 years. This is a not inconsiderable body of evidence. But many have felt that there was some conflict between all this and what Plato says in *Sophistes*:

The stricter Muses [e.g. Heraclitus] say 'in drawing apart it is always being drawn together.' The milder [e.g. Empedocles] relax the rule that this should always be so and speak of alternate states, in which the universe is now one and at peace through the power of love, and now many and at war with itself owing to some sort of Strife (*Sophistes* 242E).

What scholars have concluded from these testimonia is that we have to choose between an oscillatory or Aristotelian interpretation of Heraclitus and a Platonic interpretation in terms of instant reciprocal tension between opposites. Heraclitean scholarship itself has long oscillated between the two interpretations. Tension theorists have ignored or sought to discredit A13 and Aristotle *De Caelo* 279b12, while oscillationists have even supposed that they had to tinker with the interpretation of what seems to me to be one of the clearest of Heraclitus' fragments. This is B51, a fragment whose proper paraphrase is surely:

They do not grasp how the discord of things is in fact a perfect accord. [What we have here], as with a bow or lyre, is the harmonious reciprocation of opposites, or opposing tendencies.[28]

Now anyone who sees a conflict here should start by noting that there is in fact no consistent opposition between Plato and Aristotle in this matter. In another place Aristotle confirms a steady state reading of B51:

Heraclitus says that 'it is what opposes that helps' and that 'from opposing tones comes the fairest harmonia' and 'that everything happens in accordance with strife' (*Nicomachean Ethics* 1155b4).

And, so soon as we understand the doctrine of fire properly, I suggest that there need be no real conflict at all between oscillation and reciprocal tension. The world is in a steady state of rapid flux;[29] but this steadiness simply consists in the conservation of process or fire. (Compare Leibniz on 'Force'.) Heraclitus' theory of the world requires reciprocal tension if it is to accommodate substance; and it requires oscillation if it is to accommodate periodicity. But there is simply no problem in combining both features, or in allowing continuous variation in the overall proportions of the elemental forms, if we will only see the conservation of fire in terms that are abstract enough. What then about *ekpurōsis*, which oscillationists such as Charles Kahn now admit into Heraclitus (in reaction against Burnet and Kirk)? The idea of periodic annihilation of everything by fire is rationally objectionable (how can fire differentiate itself again?), and it spoils the accord with the *de Victu* passage. But nor is it forced upon us by textual evidence. For there is nothing in the conservation of fire, seen now as the conservation of quantity of process, to exclude the possibility that Heraclitus thought that every 10,800 years (or whatever) the sea rises to its maximum possible extent and takes over all it can, provoking an equal and opposite reaction in which fire conceived as an elemental form reaches out to *its* maximum extent, scorching almost everything.

---

[28] Whether we read *palintonos* or *palintropos*—whether we consider the lyre or bow in repose, strung in tension against itself (*palintonos*), or consider the bow or lyre's tendency to return into that state after the withdrawal of the interfering force of the archer or lyre player (*palintropos*)—it makes little difference, I believe. Either way, this is a steady state theory, presented in a manner consistent with a potentially very abstract account of what the steadiness consists in (it is a steadiness such as to require a total balance of universal agitation), and consistent also with periodicity or seasonal variation.

[29] A phrase I steal from Rudolf Schoenheimer: see *The Dynamic State of Body Constituents* (Cambridge, MA: Harvard University Press, 1942).

5 Identity through Time

5.1 Finally I turn to flux and identity through time. In point of general Heraclitean doctrine I have accounted Plato a reasonable witness.[30] But as a critic I think he was less excellent; either that, I would claim, or his influence has been pernicious.

An entirely typical statement of the mental condition into which we have lapsed in certain matters ever since Plato is to be found in Frege's introduction to *Foundations of Arithmetic*:

> If everything were in continual flux, and nothing maintained itself fixed for all time, there would no longer be any possibility of getting to know anything about the world and everything would be plunged in confusion.[31]

The general context is of course arithmetic but the assertion itself carries no such restriction, and the confusion it evinces between flux and chaos echoes a well known argument in Plato's *Theaetetus* 182. This argument distinguishes between two kinds of change—moving in space and undergoing alteration—and it then claims that nothing can be involved in both simultaneously:

> SOCRATES Let us ask them 'Are all things, according to your doctrine, in motion and flux?'
> THEODORUS Yes.
> SOCRATES Have they then both kinds of motion which we distinguished? Are they moving in space and also undergoing alteration?
> THEODORUS Of course; that is if they are to be in perfect motion.
> SOCRATES Then if they moved only in space, but did not undergo alteration, we could perhaps say what qualities belong to those moving things which are in flux, could we not?
> THEODORUS That is right.
> SOCRATES But since not even this remains fixed—that the thing in flux flows white, but changes, so that there is a flux of the very whiteness and a change of colour, so that it may not in that way be convicted of remaining fixed, it is possible to give any name to a colour, and yet to speak accurately?

---

[30] Even though he offers us a misstatement of the river paradigm. But here there is interaction between the virtues of the witness and the vices of the critic.

[31] Gottlob Frege, *The Foundations of Arithmetic: A Logico-Mathematical Enquiry into the Concept of Number*, trans. J. L. Austin (Oxford: Blackwell, 1980), p. vii.

THEODORUS How can it be possible, or possible to give a name to anything else of this sort, if while we are speaking it always evades us, being, as it is, in flux?[32]

The standard interpretation of this passage reads the argument as pointing to a precondition of identifying or individuating anything through time. Thus Owen wrote in his article on Plato's *Timaeus*:

Plato points out that if anything... were perpetually changing in all respects, so that at no time could it be described as being so-and-so, then nothing could be said of it at all—and, *inter alia*, it could not be said to be changing. If an object moves, we can say what sort of thing is moving only if it has some qualitative stability (182C9–10); conversely, to have complete qualitative flux ascribed to it, a thing must have location...[33] So no description of any process is possible if we can say only that its constituents are changing from or to something and never that they are something (cf. *Tim.* 37E5–38A2, where it is allowed to say only what a *gignomenon* was and will be; the White Queen offered Alice jam on the same terms).[34]

On the basis of *Theaetetus* 182 it has seemed that Plato either concludes that knowledge of material particulars is impossible (a familiar nineteenth–twentieth century interpretation) or concludes that, if there is to be intelligible description of perception and the objects of perception themselves (which are never this or that in themselves,[35] but only becoming), then the contention that 'everything flows' or 'everything constantly changes' must be mitigated somehow.[36] And here the enemies of Heraclitus have rejoiced in Plato's supposed refutation of him, and the friends have either (Kirk, Reinhardt) sought to deny that Heraclitus ever said that 'everything flows' or (in the case of Guthrie) acknowledged their embarrassment but sought other Heraclitean concessions to stability and permanence (e.g. the doctrine of fire).

Both these reactions are equally mystifying. How could Plato's demonstration, however it should be interpreted, possibly prove the incoherence of the claim that

---

[32] Plato, *Theaetetus*, trans. H. N. Fowler, Loeb Classical Library (London: Heinemann, 1921).

[33] The omitted passage reads: 'Nor can any quality of the object, such as its whiteness, be claimed as a subject of this unqualified change: any change would be "change to another colour", and to apply "whiteness" to a colour-progression is to deprive it of determinate sense (182D 2–5).' This anticipates a variant interpretation offered by John McDowell at pp. 180–4 of his annotated translation (Oxford 1973).

[34] G. E. L. Owen, 'The Place of the *Timaeus* in Plato's Dialogues', *Classical Quarterly*, n.s. 3 (1953), pp. 85–6; cf. I. M. Crombie, *An Examination of Plato's Doctrines*, vol. 2: *Plato on Knowledge and Reality* (London: Routledge & Kegan Paul, 1963), pp. 11, 27.

[35] Cf. Plato, *Timaeus* 49D7–E6.

[36] At least for instance to the extent of according sufficient stability to a class of *qualia* in terms of which the perception and description is possible of *gignomena* (cf. McDowell's 1973 translation).

'everything flows' or 'everything constantly changes', which is all that Plato says that Heraclitus said? The accepted answer seems to be that for a world to be rationally intelligible there must be some landmarks, and for there to be landmarks there must be some continuants. But continuants have to be individuated (the argument continues) and under conditions of Heraclitean flux it is impossible that there should be any rational basis in the properties or behaviour of things for a difference between good and bad hypotheses about which changeable continuant x, included in an inventory of items existing at one time, should be counted as coinciding with which changeable continuant y, included in an inventory of items existing at a later time. Heraclitean flux, it is then said, removes the whole point of the questions that these hypotheses set out to answer. But if that is the argument, it is unconvincing. Only if one confused flux with chaos could one possibly suppose that this basis was lacking in the world that Heraclitus describes. Why should not the principle that 'steers all through all' and the unending and irresoluble struggle of opposites furnish us with a natural order in which there is a sound, non-arbitrary basis on which to distinguish between good and bad hypotheses about which perishable continuant coincides with which? Heraclitus' *kosmos* is lawlike, and lawlike at several levels of description. There is constant change, and most substances eventually perish. But the perishable changeable substances are *continuants*, which can be traced through time so long as they persist—right up to the moment when they are replaced by other things. There is nothing in Heraclitus' worldview that excludes the application to it of conceptions of natural kinds that impose on their members specific notions of coming to be, activity, and passing away that delimit the changes which they can indulge.

5.2 A logical difficulty may perhaps seem to lurk in elucidating how exactly we understand as readily as I think we do understand the phrase 'all the time everything is changing in all respects'. There are puzzles of what Russell and Whitehead called impredicativity to be uncovered here. But these are not the difficulties that Plato and his latter-day followers are urging; and 'all the time everything is changing in all respects' is not quite what Plato reports Heraclitus as having said. Plato says that Heraclitus said that everything was on the move, was in a state of change, or flowed. But even if Heraclitus had said that all the time everything was changing in all respects, we could still dispel impredicativity in the natural way (whatever that is) that controls our manifest intuitive understanding of the claim (e.g. reading Heraclitus as saying that all the time everything there is at that time is changing in respect of all its completely determinate *qualia* in every empirically definable property range): and it would then be hard to see why, even in a world satisfying this stringent specification, a persisting thing should not remain for the while within the set limits of transformations that preserve its integrity, and be reidentified there through simultaneous continuous change of position, continuous motion, continuous replacement of its constituent particles *and* continuous change of qualities. What is the difficulty supposed to be?

'If anything...were perpetually changing in all respects, so that at no time could it be described as being so and so, then nothing could be said of it', someone might say. But I protest that 'man' or 'river' or 'barley drink' or whatever does not stand for a respect of change in which a thing 'perpetually changing in all respects' changes. That is not what we let ourselves in for when we say that a thing is changing in all respects. And that is not what we ought to mean by such a respect—or what Heraclitus would have meant if he had said this (see section 5.3 below). Indeed, if we say of an individual thing that *it* is changing all the time, then we must already have excluded counting 'man' or 'river' as a respect in which that thing changes. It is true that the objection might give trouble if Heraclitus wanted to assert of rivers and men and such things that they only *come to be* (become) and never *are* anything. But there is no evidence that he did want to confine the being of rivers and men to 'becoming'; and it is evidence against his having had this desire that there is no trace of the Cratylean denial of substance in Heraclitus' writings. Heraclitus writes happily of 'rivers', 'souls', 'the barley drink'—of continuants, that is. To insist that he really thinks of these things as processes, not as continuants, is to try to make a contrast that is quite anachronistic—and, on top of that, a category mistake. Processes are regular or gradual or fitful, take time, have temporal parts. None of this holds of rivers, even if rivers correspond to a certain class of processes, or supervene (as Heraclitus could be paraphrased as saying) upon certain classes of processes. In fact the nonsense that philosophers have sometimes talked about rivers or men not being but only becoming seems to be entirely of Plato's and other post-Heraclitean philosophers' confection. If (as I suppose) there is no clear trace of such linguistic revisionism in Heraclitus, then we should not carry this philosophical hang-up to the fair-minded assessment of the claim which is the strongest claim that anyone can prove Heraclitus to have made about flux, viz. that everything is on the move or flows.

5.3 Aristotle derides Heraclitus; but there is an Aristotelian insight from which any even-handed critic might see Heraclitus' doctrine as properly entitled to benefit.[37] 'River' or 'man' answers in the category of substance the question 'What is it?', and this is a question that Aristotle found good reasons of theory to

---

[37] Which makes it all the worse that Aristotle was simply helping himself in his *Meteorologica* (357b28–358a3), without acknowledgement of any sort, to the thoughts and perceptions of the philosopher he belittled so frequently.

contrast with the question 'What is it like?' The two questions correspond to a categorial distinction among predications of *substance* and predications of *quality*, and our very identification of continuants depends on our distinguishing the first sort of predication from the second. Surely this is the distinction that we have just seen to be presupposed to the proper understanding of the claim that individual substances are changing all the time in all respects. No doubt there are many changes which do not consist of any substance's changing. But every time some substance does change, what we typically have is a qualitative change. (When a thing ceases to exist, that results from a change in it. But existing and then ceasing to exist, though a change, is surely not itself a respect in which the thing itself changes.) To change is to come to deserve a different description in respect of *what one is like*, not to become different in respect of fundamental predication in the category of substance or in respect of *what one is*. Thinking that substances supervened upon universal process, Heraclitus is not charitably interpreted by anyone who accepts or understands Aristotle's distinction as maintaining that at every moment every substance changes in respect of its being this or that very supervenient substance.

Appendix

6.1 It is sometimes claimed nowadays (by Michael Dummett,[38] for instance) that the proper foundation of philosophy is not the theory of knowledge but the theory of meaning. The theory of meaning, as we have got it, was born out of the theory of logic, which is a subject that pre-Socratic speculations such as Parmenides' played their indispensable part in bringing into existence. Except perhaps by serving as a butt for Aristotle, who needed to find a philosopher open to the charge of denying the Law of Non-Contradiction, Heraclitus contributed nothing to these speculations. Nor did logical or semantical puzzles impinge upon Heraclitus. They were not the sort of thing to engage with the intellectual passions of such a man. A fortiori, Heraclitus did not have the logical equipment to distinguish opposition from contradiction (say), or identity from exact similarity. But so far from concluding from this that he must then have been tempted to confuse them, I have drawn the conclusion that, not having the equipment to distinguish them, he did not have the logical equipment to confuse them either. (Just as he lacked the equipment to formulate the absurd hypothesis that a thing's principle of individuation is a respect in which that thing can change.)

---

[38] Michael Dummett, *Frege: Philosophy of Language* (London: Duckworth, 1973).

A finished philosophy of logic will be an instrument of special philosophical power. Our hope is that, removing all distortions and obstructions that now impede us from getting a clear view of this aspect of ourselves, it will purify our understanding of our own beliefs; and, working in this way, it may one day reveal to us, as through a medium of utter transparency, a world of wonderful plainness. Such a philosophical instrument (however easy it is to describe) is neither easily invented nor easily manufactured. Compare the long history of the lens. Even now, after the logical labours of many men of genius and good sense, our philosophy of logic and language is scarcely in sight of partial completion; and even now the colours of the rainbow vexatiously and constantly obtrude themselves upon the philosophical magnifications that have been achieved. One need not deny that, if philosophy needs any foundation, then its ultimate foundation is the theory of logic and meaning. But so long as such instruments only approximate to perfection, it is no bad thing if at least some philosophers proceed as if philosophy needed no foundation. And one such philosopher is Heraclitus, a thinker best seen as relying on the language itself (not on a philosophy of logic or language or some theory of names or reference or predication) to fix the meaning of what he says.

6.2 It would be an error to suppose that a reliance like Heraclitus' on natural language as non-philosophically construed will automatically entail naivety, or will carry with it any insensitivity to the question how, if the *kosmos* is as unlike the vulgar conception as Heraclitus says, a human being can think or find expression for the thought that matters are really thus or so. Nor need this reliance entail some blindness to the problem of how the initiated theorist can express his new thoughts in the very same language that the ignorant employ (and he himself employed when he was ignorant of the unity of things). Heraclitus knew that there were those problems. Since the theory of meaning or philosophical logic (as many still call it) has just got us to the point where we can appreciate his contribution to their solution, I shall conclude with some account of this.

Nature loves to be hidden (B123), Heraclitus says, but there are places where the workings of the cosmos will peep out. What can be seen in these places may be interpreted by anyone who has the sense to heed and reflect upon such clues as the river, the barley drink, or the motion of the heavens. If he will attend then, just as the Delphian Apollo 'neither speaks nor conceals but makes a sign', these phenomena can exemplify for him the whole nature of things. He must lay himself open to such eminent instances.

Now it is only by a transaction between things and minds, or a transaction between designata and their designations as held together by a practice, that language itself, not excluding vulgar pre-philosophical language, has come into being and been invested with sense, reference, and denotation. It is no accident even that *bios* means 'life' and 'bow', and again no accident that *ergon* can mean 'work' or 'thing' or 'reality' and that these ambiguities all combine in such a way that the same set of words can mean either

> The name of the bow is life but its work is death (B48)

or

> Life is the name assigned but the reality [to which we give the name] is the process of dying (cf. B21).

These are bizarre instances, but what they show is a byproduct of the general process by which language comes into being.

When we ask how the *logos* of the world can be grasped by the soul, we must remember that the soul itself is not for Heraclitus something that is alien to reality; it is all of a piece with what it seeks to interpret,[39] being fire or air (and, like all fire or air, at hazard from the peril of too much wetness).[40]

Heraclitus lived before the moment when concepts became ideas and took up residence in the head. But, even if concepts had by then taken up residence in the head, Heraclitus' view of the *psuchē* might have saved him from the absurdities of psychologistic accounts of concepts that seek to identify a concept by reference to some mental state somehow annexed to it, and specify the mental state itself not *de re* but in isolation from any outward feature of the reality that impinges on the mind or serves as the intentional object of the state. Unlike most philosophers in our tradition, Heraclitus cannot even be tempted by the theory that Austin parodies in 'Pretending':

> It is only the hair on a gooseberry that stops it from being a grape: by a 'gooseberry' then, we may mean simply a hirsute grape—*and* by a 'grape' likewise simply a glabrous gooseberry.[41]

---

[39] J. L. Austin, *Philosophical Papers*, ed. J. O. Urmson and G. J. Warnock (2nd edn, Oxford: Oxford University Press, 1970), p. 254 n. 1. Cf. Hussey, 'Epistemology and Meaning in Hereclitus'; Martha Nussbaum, '*Psuchē* in Heraclitus, 1', *Phronesis*, 17 (1972), pp. 1–16.

[40] Kahn argues that air, not fire, is the stuff of the soul. See Kahn, *The Art and Thought of Heraclitus*, pp. 238–40, 248–54, 259.

[41] These theories stem from Locke, but Locke's own opinions are too complex, too highly elaborated, and too much of a compromise between empiricist and rationalist elements to be fairly parodied. For a perfect statement of a sub-Lockean model, richly deserving such parody, see e.g. James Mill, *Analysis of the Phenomena of the Human Mind* (London: Baldwin and Cradock, 1829), ch. IV, section 1.

If one element in that which identifies the concept of what it is to be a gooseberry (identifies the concept the predicate 'gooseberry' stands for) is what the predicate is true of (viz. gooseberries, as they are out there in the world, ready and waiting for us to find out what they are and what they are like);[42] and if the predicate's denominating what it in fact denominates is determined not by the match between a mental content and certain objects but by some causally conditioned, practically reliable lien that ordinary men can depend upon *without* knowing what they are depending upon or knowing the nature of the terms of this relation; then what the thinker who follows Heraclitus' way to truth must refine is not language *per se* or predicates such as 'gooseberry' but conceptions. He needs conceptions that are inaccessible to ordinary men who use predicates like 'gooseberry' without true understanding.

Reading Heraclitus' several fragments about sleeping and waking and grasping how things are, one is struck by the similarity between the state of ordinary men as Heraclitus conceives them and men sleepwalking. If one sleepwalks one finds one's way without knowing what one is doing. Similarly, ordinary men conduct the business of everyday life without getting lost or suffering the sad fate of Elpenor. But they do not grasp properly what they encounter, nor understand what things are, even after they learn to recognize and reidentify them (B17, 26). Here, once more, Heraclitus would appear to be in a fortunate position. He does not have the theory and technical vocabulary that it requires to confuse the concept of gooseberry—what it is in nature to be a gooseberry—with thinkers' *conceptions* of gooseberry. (What I mean by the conception of gooseberry is a rudimentary recognitional capacity of ours that may or may not mature into distinct theoretical knowledge of gooseberries.[43]) But, had he possessed the technical vocabulary required to enter into these matters, and had he wished to pronounce on the issue, it would have been open to him (at least in cases like these) to agree with Frege's declaration that 'what is known as the history of concepts is really a history either of our *knowledge* of concepts or of the meanings of words'.[44] The man who has awoken and learned to expect the unexpected (B18) and to exploit whatever signs nature does afford to him, gains new understanding of what, without thinking, he did already in the world at large.

---

[42] Cf. *S&S*, ch. 3, section 1, cited at note 19 above.

[43] Cf. Leibniz, *Meditationes de Cognitione, Veritate et Ideis*, Gerhardt, iv, on clear but non-distinct ideas.

[44] Frege, *Foundations of Arithmetic*, preface—adjacent to the sentence criticized in section 5.1 above. For the Fregean theory of predicates' sense and reference here espoused see especially Frege's letter to Husserl, 24 May 1891, and *S&S*, ch. 3 *ad init.* (with note 2). See also the Introduction to the present volume, section 4.

It is in gaining this that he transcends the valueless subjective opinions he once entertained about the world and its contents:

So one must follow what is public, that is what is common and universal to all. For what is public *is* what is common and universal to all. But, although the logos is something common and universal to all, the many live as if they had their very own private wisdom (B2).

It is the universality and publicity of the *logos* and of the reality that the *logos* ordains that makes the philosopher's or scientist's task possible:

Of the *logos* that is given in my book, men are always uncomprehending. They do not understand it before they hear it from me, or when they first hear it. For, although everything happens in accordance with this *logos*, men have no cognizance of this, even though they have encountered the words and things I put before them, as I dissect each thing according to its real nature and show forth how it really is. Other men are not aware what they do when awake, just as they are forgetful of what they do in their sleep (B1).

As for those men who can see no unity and no connections between different phenomena even when they are afforded clues in perception, Heraclitus likens them to the deaf. Because they understand as little of the working of their own language as a Greekless foreigner understands of Greek among Greeks,[45] the senses of ordinary men deceive them instead of informing them.[46] For so long as they use their language only by habit, bad testimony is all they will ever be able to get. Yet even this does not mean that the human condition is simply hopeless, closed in upon its own hopelessness. What determines the identity of concepts and attaches common nouns to their denominata is what men *always did*—even before some men awake from their deafness to their own language. Practice is the anchor (and practice, I would add, can only be adequately described if we describe the objects[47] themselves which men uncomprehendingly responded to in perception and action, and spoke of without knowing what they were saying).

All this, in his own special way, Heraclitus understood. But we have only just begun in philosophy to understand the significance of the thing that he understood. We have found it so hard to understand that thing ourselves that we have never seen how close Heraclitus came to understanding it.

6.3 Parmenidean puzzles of being and non-being were no doubt as indispensable to the infancy and maturation of the philosophy of logic and language as the

---

[45] Cf. Nussbaum, '*Psuchē* in Heraclitus, 1'.

[46] Cf. Leibniz: '[Les hommes] sont empiriques et ne se gouvernent que par les sens et exemples, sans examiner si la même raison a encor lieu.', *Nouveaux Essais*, Gerhardt, v, p. 252.

[47] For this reading of the doctrine that meaning is use see my *S&S*, pp. 1-4.

alchemical speculations of some of Aristotle's scientific successors were to the development of chemistry. But the power of Heraclitus—his claim to be the most adult thinker of his age and a grown man among infants and adolescents—precisely consisted in the capacity to speculate, in the theory of meaning just as in physics, not where speculation lacked all useful observations or where it needed more going theory to bite on, but where the facts were as big and familiar as the sky and so obvious that it took nothing less than genius to pay heed to them.

7

The Concept of the Subject Contains the Concept of the Predicate

1

In the *Discourse of Metaphysics*, in the correspondence with Arnauld, and in numerous other works dating from the same period, Leibniz says that a proposition is true if and only if the concept of the subject contains the concept of the predicate. For instance:

> In every true proposition, necessary or contingent, universal or particular, the concept of the predicate is in a sense included in that of the subject, *praedicatum inest subjecto*, or I know not what truth is. (Letter to Arnauld, 14 July 1686)[1]

In Leibniz's later philosophy he sees the need further to qualify the containment principle. But, as in the quotation just given, wherever Leibniz propounds the doctrine, he applies it to necessary and contingent propositions equally.

Philosophers have found difficulty in understanding how Leibniz can have supposed that this was a good principle of truth for the case of contingent propositions. Less excusably, they have even questioned Leibniz's sincerity when he insisted that his recognition of contingency was one of the points that distinguished his whole philosophy from Spinoza's.

The first aim of this chapter is to explain what commended the principle to Leibniz and how it leaves room for contingency. I claim that the problem that some modern scholars have found with the principle can be solved quietly and simply by reference to suggestions that Leibniz himself makes in the *Discourse of Metaphysics*. This will come with a suggestion about why, in the decade after the *Discourse of Metaphysics*, Leibniz becomes uneasy with the *praedicatum inest*

---

[1] Gottfried Wilhelm Leibniz, *Philosophical Papers and Letters*, trans. and ed. Leroy R. Loemker (2nd edn, Dordrecht: Reidel, 1969), p. 377.

subjecto principle. I hold that this need have nothing to do with any problem about contingency. It has to do with logic.

The second aim is to say something about a distinct problem that Leibniz himself thought he saw in the accommodation of contingency. This problem has at best an indirect connection with anything that might motivate the claim that, by virtue of containment's being a necessary relation, the containment principle must render contingent true propositions 'analytic' (in Kant's sense). What I think is happening is that a doctrine of possible worlds devised for the understanding of God's choice and creation of the actual world proves to be seriously mismatched with questions about what this or that individual might or might not have done. At this point, where the question at issue relates to the identification *de re* of particulars, I think Leibniz is less sure-footed than I give him credit for being in his treatment of containment and necessity. In fact, I think he ignores at least one point that he has himself quite clearly perceived in another connection. The oversight that I attribute to him is underdetermined, however, by Leibniz's rationalist starting point in the theory of truth. It is also instructive metaphysically.

2

What commended the containment principle to Leibniz? Suppose one thinks, as Leibniz does—this is his principle of sufficient reason—that nothing holds true, obtains, happens, or exists without a reason and that there must always be a reason why this rather than that holds true, obtains, happens, or exists.[2] And suppose that, to avoid an infinite regress of causal explanatory reasons,[3] one gives a teleological construal to 'reason', insisting with Leibniz—this is the effect of his Principle of the best—that any finally adequate explanation of anything must locate the thing to be explained within a total state of affairs that would commend itself as the transparently, self-evidently best to a rational omniscient mind that singled out from all others as the most perfect the world that is 'simplest in hypotheses, and richest in phenomena'.[4] Then a proposition will hold true if and

---

[2] Compare, for example, *Die philosophischen Schriften von Gottfried Wilhelm Leibniz*, ed. C. I. Gerhardt (Berlin: Weidmannsche Buchhandlung, 1875–90), vol. VII, p. 289, translated in *Philosophical Writings*, ed. H. Parkinson (London: Dent, 1973), p. 145.

[3] Gerhardt, VII, p. 302, trans. Parkinson, p. 136.

[4] *Discourse of Metaphysics*, §VI. In connection with Leibniz's confusion in this sentence between laws in rerum natura and hypotheses, which are *judgements* about the world, compare the general tenor of the criticisms I urge in section 9. For the *Discourse* I have used the translation of P. G. Lucas and L. Grint (Manchester: Manchester University Press, 1953).

only if it holds in the world that has the simplest laws but is richest in essence, or richest in the variety of real substances that it furnishes.

What then is a world? And more to the point, what sort of thing is a world that is even a candidate to be chosen by the rational omniscient mind as fit to be made real? Well, at least this much is clear from the numerous Leibnizian texts that bear on this matter: no world that is a serious candidate to be chosen by God could contain more substances than it does.[5] Each of the worlds that God chooses between is as rich in quantity/variety of essence as it can be given the set of laws that regulates it.[6] In the second place, once the substances are specified for some world, there is no simplifying the laws of that world. For the specification of the substances (even the specification of their kinds) fixes the laws.[7] So looking at the matter as if from the point of view of God and as if from a moment 'before' there are any created substances—hence from a moment at which there *are* no actual substances to 'pick' (or 'select' or 'recruit') for the best world, and at which all choice has to be purely on the basis of description—one can say that the choice God makes is between rival specifications. And since it is the substances in a world that furnish both its variety/quantity of essence and realize or embody its laws, these specifications must be rival specifications of *substances* or, in more Leibnizian language, rival sets of individual concepts. God's choice qua specificatory is the choice of a set of substances: the set will be maximal (that is, a set that cannot consistently contain more substances); and the members of the set will jointly embody the simplest set of laws there can be for any world that furnishes so much richness or variety as this one does.[8]

A point we must notice here, though its importance will not be clear until later, is that where the issue is one of the relative merits or titles to be realized of the

---

[5] No doubt other worlds are possible worlds, but what I am concerned with here is that they are not, as I shall say, *Leibnizian* possible worlds.

[6] Compare Bertrand Russell, *A Critical Exposition of the Philosophy of Leibniz* (Cambridge: Cambridge University Press, 1900), p. 67. Disagreeing so much as I do with some of Russell's interpretations, I seize the opportunity to salute the sharp insight and strong sympathetic grasp that inform his exposition here of Leibniz's theory of the compossibility and incompossibility of individual substances.

[7] Compare Louis Couturat (ed.), *Opuscules et fragments inedits de Leibniz* (Paris: Alcan, 1903), pp. 16-24:

> I think that in this series of things there are certain propositions that are most universally true, and which not even a miracle could violate. This is not to say they have any necessity for God but rather that when [God] chose the particular series of things he did choose, he decided by that very act to observe these principles as giving the specific properties of *just this* particular series of things.

[8] Here and elsewhere one struggles with the fact that Leibniz's criterion of excellence is a two-factor criterion.

worlds projected in different world specifications, the question of whether this individual concept and that individual concept belonging to different maximal sets are or are not concepts of the same substance simply does not arise. God has no need either to ask or to answer this question. And if it were asked, well, no basis has been provided on which to answer it. (Contrast 'If I had made a table yesterday, would that have been the very same table as I shall actually make tomorrow?' which is an inherently silly question, at least in most contexts, with the question 'Could the table I made yesterday have been made two days later?' which might reasonably collect the answer yes.)

Suppose now, naturally enough, that everything that is real in a world is either a substance or some sort of a dependency of substances. Then everything that is actually true will either be a truth about the substances of the actual world or stand in some relation of dependency to such truths. But what then are substances? Leibniz's idea of substance is neither that of a qualityless substrate nor that of a shifting crowd of concepts or universals struggling to be seated on one another's laps. Indeed his concept of a substance is more or less the same as Aristotle's, even if, as his system develops, his idea of the extension of the concept diverges more and more strikingly from Aristotle's. Pace what is suggested or assumed in many comments and criticisms that distinguish insufficiently between the individual concept and what the concept is of, a Leibnizian substance is a real thing, not a congeries of characters, or a concept. What is true, however, and may have given rise to such misconceptions is that, in the Leibnizian framework within which we have to speak of God's choice, each and every substance will indeed *answer* to a complete concept or divine specification. This complete concept fixes everything bearing on the question of the eligibility of the whole world that contains the substance. A fortiori it fixes thereby everything that there is to know or understand about the substance itself.

All true predication has some foundation in the nature of things, and when a proposition is not identical, that is to say when the predicate is not expressly comprised in the subject, it must be comprised in it virtually and that is what the philosophers call *in-esse* when they say that the predicate is in the subject. Thus the term of the subject must always include that of the predicate, so that whoever understood perfectly the notion of the subject would also judge that the predicate belongs to it.

This being so, we can say that the nature of an individual substance or of a complete being is to have a notion so complete that it is sufficient to comprise and to allow the deduction from it of all the predicates of the subject to which this notion is attributed. Whereas an accident is a being the notion of which does not include all that can be attributed to the subject to which this notion is attributed. Thus, the quality of King which belongs to Alexander the Great, in abstraction from the subject, is not sufficiently determined for an individual, and does not include all that the notion of this Prince comprises; whereas God seeing the individual notion of *haecceity* of Alexander sees in it at the same time the foundation and reason of all the predicates that can be truly said of him, as for example that he would conquer Darius and Porus, even to the point of knowing it *a priori*.[9]

3

Given Leibniz's starting point, the containment principle is an entirely natural principle for him to have adopted.[10] It is not the love of necessity nor any essentialist passion that suggests the principle. Nor is it Leibniz's 'enslavement to the Aristotelian logic of subject and predicate' that underlies Leibniz's metaphysics. It is the principle of sufficient reason, working in concert with philosophical ideas that are really quite ordinary and are neither silly nor readily replaceable. These are ideas about what a world is and what there is to talk about in one (namely, substances and their dependencies). Nevertheless, this conjunction of the ordinary with the peculiarly rationalist or Leibnizian comes with implications that we might not have expected.

Finite beings such as we are can learn that a substance has property F only in isolation, through our senses or a posteriori, and without seeing this truth's connection with other truths. But for God 'Fa' is one part of the specification of the world whose title to be realized is rationally and morally self-evident and quite independent of the sense perception of anything. The a priori determination of the truth that the substance a has the property F cannot, however, be a determination of this truth taken by itself. The determination must arise from the identification of the most perfect world, and this identification will have depended on the comparison of all the members of an infinite or indefinite series of complete specifications of infinitely or indefinitely many worlds, specifications that fix simultaneously both the laws and the set of substances in each of them.

The world that defeats all rivals defeats each one overall with respect to simplicity and diversity taken together. So the rationale of any *actual* substance's being as it is will depend on everything in virtue of which the world that contains it, namely the actual world, defeated all rivals. But then it follows that under the a priori aspect of things—or under their *praedicatum inest subjecto* aspect—every contingent truth about the actual world presupposes every other contingent truth about it.

---

[9] *Discourse of Metaphysics*, §VIII.
[10] Nevertheless the astute and the logically minded will wonder whether, in addition to making the containment principle seem natural, we have *derived* the containment principle from sufficient reason. In section 8 we shall find such doubts confirmed.

[E]very substance is like a whole world, and like a mirror of God or of all the universe which each expresses after its own fashion, much as the same town is variously represented according to the different situations of the man who is looking at it. Thus the universe is multiplied as many times as there are substances, and the glory of God is also redoubled by the same number of wholly different representations of his work. One can even say that every substance bears in some sort the character of God's infinite wisdom and omnipotence, and imitates him as far as it is capable. For it expresses, albeit confusedly, all that happens in the universe past, present, or future, and this has some resemblance to an infinite perception or knowledge; and as all other substances express this one in their turn and accommodate themselves to it, one can say that it extends its power over all the others in imitation of the omnipotence of the creator.[11]

The a priori proof that the substance a is F is something we can describe, but it is not something we can imagine (or even imagine ourselves imagining) ourselves giving. But for Leibniz it is enough that there must be such a proof or determination. And so long as there must be, the next step is natural enough. Since the divine notion of each substance involves the notion of each and every other substance that belongs in the same world, Leibniz draws the conclusion not only that all the truths about the other substances in a world can be read off the complete concept of any one of them but also that each substance is self-sufficient and autonomous, that each substance is *itself* a world apart, as if nothing else existed besides God and it; that substances are windowless, do not causally interact, and are adjusted to one another by a divinely conceived pre-established harmony.[12] And then yet other things are supposed to follow.

---

[11] *Discourse of Metaphysics*, §IX.
[12] See, for example, 'A Specimen of Discoveries about Marvellous Secrets', Parkinson, p. 79. If Leibniz had distinguished carefully, as I have tried (wherever something depends on it) to distinguish, the specification of a set of substances from the set of substances themselves that *answer* to that specification (instead of employing the language of concepts or notions, which permits interpretation in *either way* and then both at once), then maybe this conclusion would not have appeared quite so obvious. There is no absurdity in the idea that there should be causal relations between entities e_1, e_2, e_3, even though there is no possibility, within the not necessarily yet actualized specification itself, of saying which entities each of e_1, e_2, and e_3 are without mentioning all the others.

On the other hand, maybe Leibniz's argument was not an argument from the supposed need for it to be possible to specify the individuals in a world independently of their causal relations. Perhaps the point was that, when the world is put together so that it will run as God wills but without God's intervention and adjustment, each substance must be 'wound up' exactly, in the light of how all other substances will act, so that substances will *combine* to produce the outcome that is good. So each substance must be wound up to have precisely its own positive active force. Compare again, 'A Specimen', Parkinson, pp. 84–5.

4

Some links are stronger than others in this marvellous and questionable sequence of deductions, all resting or purporting to rest on the idea of sufficient reason as teleologically interpreted.[13] I shall not pause to assess any of these further deductions here, because that system of metaphysical ideas is simply the backdrop for the claim I do wish to defend. Not only, my claim goes, is *praedicatum inest subjecto* a natural principle for Leibniz to have chosen to try to spell out his 'goodlike' conception of truth,[14] but also the principle itself is modally innocent. To try to show this, I need to make three preliminary points, however.

First, an a priori proof is a proof that does not rest on materials provided by sense perception. Formally, Leibniz's use conforms to the definitions of 'a priori' and 'a posteriori', which Kant was destined to propose in the preface of the *Critique of Pure Reason*. This is to say that, since God's criterion of perfection is not dependent on experience or a posteriori, God's determination of '*Fa*' is a priori in Kant's sense. But this sort of determination, being in part axiological, is unlike anything that the expression 'a priori' would lead anyone to expect nowadays, unless his thinking were insulated from all Kantian, post-Kantian, and positivist influences. What we, who are subject to these influences, should expect an a priori proof or determination of $F(a)$ to need to rest upon is considerations that are purely logical or mathematical, not axiological considerations. But Leibniz was not to know what a strange note his use of the term 'a priori' was destined to sound in our ears.[15] And as things are, the only way to understand fully what Leibniz meant by an a priori proof of a proposition that is a posteriori for us is to understand the elements of the rest of his theory of truth. The reader has my own interpretation of this in section 2.

In the second place, Leibniz never calls a proposition in which the concept of the predicate is contained in the concept of the subject *analytic*. So nor should we—if Leibniz is the philosopher we want to discuss—even if many Leibniz scholars do talk like this. It is simply not Leibniz's fault that Kant defined an analytic judgement as one in which the predicate was contained in the subject or that, in doing so, he created the expectation that all analytic judgements would be necessary. Had Leibniz been available to comment on Kant's proposals then, at a

---

[13] Elsewhere, I have traced the continuity (and the differences) between Leibniz's teleological conception of explanation and the teleological conception that Plato puts into Socrates' mouth in the passage of Plato's *Phaedo* that Leibniz quotes so often (96c following). See *Wiggins 1986b*.

[14] For the expression 'goodlike', see Plato, *Republic*, 509b 14.

[15] Nor was he to know that the time would come, after Kant, when it would be expected, however lazily or naively, that all a priori proof would be 'analytic'.

cost I shall compute in due course (section 9), he could have made two points: (1) Unless it is given a special nonexistential interpretation, 'the F and G thing is F', which Russell would have rendered 'there is just one F and G thing and it is F', is not a necessary judgement at all. Surely the unique F and G thing, that thing itself, even though it is F and G, might not have been F or G. I shall return in due course to this point, and to the complex question of Leibniz's right to insist upon it.[16] (2) Given his intention that all analytic judgements should be necessary, Kant could have had an in every way better definition of 'analytic': a judgement is analytic if and only if it can be reduced to a truth of logic (whatever logic may turn out to be) using only logic and noncreative, a priori for us definitions.[17]

The third preliminary must be to furnish some semantical explanation of the *praedicatum inest subjecto* rule that will show how Leibniz could have supposed it would apply equally and indifferently both to quantified, as we should say, and to singular sentences, or apply equally, as Leibniz would say, to the case in which A stands for an individual concept and the case in which A stands for a general concept.

The background to the rule is of course Aristotelian syllogistic in the various modifications and extensions that Leibniz proposed to it. A typical Aristotelian syllogism is expressed in the form

If A belongs ($ὑπάρχει$) to all B, and B belongs to all C, then A belongs to all C.[18]

Here 'A', 'B', 'C' typically hold places for substantives or adjectives, rather than for singular terms like 'Caesar'. So far from fitting smoothly into the theory, those always gave trouble to its traditional exponents, because the way in which 'Caesar' is a subject of 'Caesar crossed the Rubicon' is really quite different from the way in which 'broad-leaved plants' is the subject of 'All broad-leaved plants are deciduous'. We shall come in due course to Leibniz's method of aligning these two kinds of subject. But concentrating first on the case where the theory of the syllogism is at its best, one surmises that the modern preference will probably be to follow the view that Frege would have taken of 'A', 'B', 'C' as they occur in sentences that are typical of syllogistic and to say that these letters hold places for expressions that stand for concepts. Understood so, 'All broad-leaved plants are deciduous' asserts that a certain subsumptive relation holds between the concepts *deciduous* and *broad-leaved plant*, or that whatever falls

---

[16] See sections 6 to 8.
[17] See Gottlob Frege, *The Foundations of Arithmetic: A Logico-Mathematical Enquiry into the Concept of Number*, trans. J. L. Austin (Oxford: Blackwell, 1980), §3.
[18] Compare *Generales Inquisitiones*, §16 (Couturat, p. 366) and §132 (Couturat, p. 388).

under the concept *broad-leaved plant* falls under the concept *deciduous*. Most modern views descend from this idea. It is very different from the idea that has prevailed in traditional expositions of syllogistic. But oddly enough, this is really the view that Leibniz wants to take too.[19]

There are all sorts of important differences of terminology and of detail between Leibniz and Frege or Russell. Following Aristotle, who paraphrases 'All broad-leaved plants are deciduous' as '*deciduous* belongs to (ὑπάρχει) every broad-leaved plant' Leibniz would prefer to say that *deciduous* is contained in (*inest* or *continetur*) all of the subject, viz. broad-leaved plants. But there is at least one similarity to which we must pay special attention—namely, that Leibniz is in a position to be party to the thought that the terms of Aristotle's proposition are the concepts *deciduous* and *broad-leaved plants* and not these terms taken together with their sign of quantity. If so, the 'all' has really to be syncategorematic in function. Insofar as it is expressed, it must be seen as going with the 'belongs' or 'contains'.[20] In the 'universal calculus' it is *absorbed* into the sense of 'contains'.

Two questions remain. The first, which I can postpone to the end of section 8, is how to preserve the containment rule for other kinds of quantified sentence. The other is the Leibnizian treatment of expressions such as 'Caesar'. We can say, if we like, that the concept *broad-leaved plant* contains or comprises the concept *deciduous* if and only if broad-leaved plants are a subset of deciduous

---

[19] Had Russell studied Leibniz a few years later, at the point when his own view of generality had advanced to the same stage as Frege's, he would not have failed to notice Leibniz's anticipation:

> When in a universal affirmative proposition I say 'every man is an animal' I wish to say that the concept of animal is involved with the concept of man. (For the concept *man* is the concept *rational animal*.) And when I say 'every pious person is happy'. I mean that anyone who understands what it is to be pious will understand that in this concept true happiness is included. (Couturat, p. 85)

> When I say that every man is an animal I mean that men are to be sought among the animals, or that whatsoever be not animal is not man either. (Couturat, p. 235)

Furthermore, what Leibniz meant by a notion or concept coincides quite well enough for the purposes of the analysis of generality with what Russell and Frege meant. Note for instance the following formulation of Frege's:

> The word 'some' states a relation that holds in our example [viz. 'some numbers are primes'] between the concepts of number and of prime. Similarly 'all' [in 'all bodies are heavy'] states a relation between the concepts *body* and *heavy*. (Review of Schroeder, in Gottlob Frege, *Philosophical Writings*, ed. P. T. Geach and M. Black (Oxford: Basil Blackwell, 1952), p. 93n.)

In case we doubt that this is essentially the same account as Leibniz's, we should note that Leibniz gives no signs of wanting to suggest a different account of the logical form that is involved in necessary truths and the logical form present in contingent generalizations such as 'all gold coins are circular'.

[20] See especially Couturat, pp. 49, 85, 243.

plants, or the concept *deciduous* applies to everything that falls under the concept *broad-leaved plants*. But Julius Caesar is not a set or subset of anything. Nor is he a concept that can contain another concept. This, however, is not necessary for the solution to Leibniz's semantical problem, if we will transpose that to the Leibnizian metaphysical context of God's choice and 'the objective foundation' of the contingent truths about substances that determine the whole actual world.

It is unnecessary because, for purposes of the divine calculations that fix these truths, a truth such as 'Julius Caesar crossed the Rubicon' is arrived at not through the identification of Julius Caesar himself or any actual stream but through concepts that are divine *specifications* of things that are to answer to certain descriptions. These specifications or concepts will comprise one small part of the larger specification of the complete world whose complete specification will commend that world to God over all others as the most perfect world. And, unlike the name 'Caesar' or the demonstrative 'this man', these substance-specifications themselves, being purely general, *can* be conveyed by complex concept expressions that will fit smoothly into Aristotelian syllogistic.[21]

5

With these preliminaries completed, I quote the *Discourse of Metaphysics* statement of the difference between necessity and contingency:

All contingent propositions have reasons for being so rather than otherwise, or (which is the same thing)... they have proofs a priori of their truth which make them certain, and which show that the connection of the subject and the predicate of these propositions has its foundation in the nature of the one and the other; but they do not have demonstrations of necessity, since... these reasons are only founded on the principle of contingency or of the existence of things, that is to say on what is or appears the best among several equally possible things; whereas necessary truths are founded on the principle of contradiction and on the possibility or impossibility of essence themselves, without regard in this to the free Will of God or of creatures.[22]

The task will now be to put this together with the containment doctrine and to show how the principle of the best really does distinguish the necessary from the contingent.

Let us write

$(Ax)[\ldots x, \underline{} x]$

---

[21] For evidence of Leibniz's actual awareness of the detailed intricacies of characterizing all this in terms of containment, see Couturat, p. 51. Also see section 8.

[22] *Discourse of Metaphysics*, §XIII.

to state that the concept designated by '...x' contains the concept that is designated by '_____ x' or that whatever satisfies the condition '...x' satisfies the condition '_____ x'.[23] Then Aristotle's sentence 'all broad-leaved plants are deciduous' will be rendered as

(Ax)[Broad-leaved plant x, Deciduous x].

And 'Caesar crossed the Rubicon' will be rephrased to make it formally suitable for the neosyllogistic framework as (in the first instance)

(The x)[Caesar = x, Crossed Rubicon x].

This last sentence will be true (Leibniz could stipulate) just if all things that uniquely fall under the individual concept *identical with Caesar* fall under the concept *crossed the Rubicon*[24] or (as Russell could stipulate) just if one and only thing falls under the concept *identical with Caesar* and the concept *crossed the Rubicon* belongs to this concept. At this point I refer back to the account we have just given of how it is to be told whether or not this thing (person) is so included. Ordinary human beings look in history books. But someone who came to understand God's purpose could proceed as follows: 'Caesar' being the name of an actual substance to be encountered in the world and the actual world being the world that combines the greatest variety of forms ordered by the simplest and most beautiful laws, what s/he has to do is to ascertain which concept the concept *identical with Caesar* is, that is, identify the concept through some other specification(s) also true of Caesar but more illuminating of the grounds for God's choice of the world he has chosen containing Caesar. 'Embracing the infinite in one intuition,' s/he has to recapitulate God's grounds for his choice of the actual world, discover the identity of the concept *identical with Caesar* with the concept designated by the choice-relevant specification of Caesar, and show that this concept comprises the concept of crossing the Rubicon.[25] Starting out with

---

[23] For these 'binary quantifiers,' see *Wiggins 1980a*.

[24] So long as we see ourselves as making extensions of Aristotelian syllogistic, then we must attend here to the question, much worried over by Leibniz, of existential import. If we were to take 'all' as having existential import, as Aristotle does, then the upshot would be that the 'all' conditions for a 'The' quantifier would coincide exactly with Russell's truth condition for the upside-down iota quantifier, a sign normally of course explained with the use of an existential quantifier.

[25] For 'embracing the infinite is one intuition', see Gerhardt, VII, p. 309 ('A specimen', Parkinson's translation, p. 80). For the account that Leibniz would have needed of the sense and reference of predicates and of concept-identity, see Frege's letter to Husserl dated 24 May 1891 and my commentary on this in *Wiggins 1984*. But note that, in order to complete/correct Frege's account of concept-identity, it would be necessary to extend Frege's object-language by the addition of a modal operator.

the substance Caesar himself, picking him out as that very individual,[26] someone with this insight is already assured by the principle of sufficient reason and the best that there is *some* choice-relevant specification Caesar answered to. So, understanding the interconnection of all these things with all things, s/he must find a way to replace the courtesy concept-expression 'identical with Caesar' by some more complex expression comprised in the overall world specification by reference to which it can be shown that the corresponding world combines the greatest variety of forms with the simplest laws. This new complex expression would stand for the same concept. So the new sentence would be bound to have the same truth value as 'Caesar crossed the Rubicon'. The truth-value would be truth if and only if *crossed the Rubicon* were one constituent (or Fregean mark) of the concept that the new specification stood for.

6

It may be suggested that this is already enough to make 'Julius Caesar crossed the Rubicon' necessary. For it is surely necessary, indeed analytic, someone may say, that anything that uniquely satisfies the condition '(_____ and crossed the Rubicon),' where '_____' holds a place for the rest of the specification of Caesar's individual concept, crossed the Rubicon.

To this there are two replies, however. First, a necessity of this sort, attaching as it does to the new sentence, is highly sensitive to sense as well as to reference. Even if the new sentence is necessary, it does not follow that the sentence that it replaces was necessary. What binds together the truth values of the old and the new sentence is not logical necessity but only 'the principle of contingency or of the existence of things' (that is, the principles of sufficient reason and the best). Surely the sense of the name 'Julius Caesar', which we all understand passably well, cannot be the same as that of a vast conjunction, still less that of a conjunction accessible only to God. So the intersubstitution is not *salvo sensu* but at best *salva veritate*. It may be said that for God the sense of the name 'Caesar' would correspond to that omniscient or omnipotent way of thinking of Caesar. But if that is said, then the objector has lost sight of the question of the modality of *our* sentence, which employs the name 'Caesar' in *our* sense, a sense

---

[26] For Leibniz's recognition of his right to such direct or demonstrative reference, see, for example, *Generales Inquisitiones*, Couturat, p. 360, especially

At certum individuum est Hic, quem designo vel monstrando vel addendo notas distinguentes.

that we explain in a way that has at some point to be entity-invoking.[27] It is Leibniz's right to insist on this.

In the second place, even the analyticity of the new sentence, if it were analytic, could show nothing about Caesar himself, no more than the analyticity of the sentence 'All who sit and smoke in the corner smoke in the corner' shows that anyone who sits in the corner and smokes *must* smoke there.

At this point, those who are determined to find necessity in the containment relation may try another tack. Surely the concept that the predicate '____ and crossed the Rubicon' stands for is the same as the concept that 'identical with Caesar' stands for, but the concept that '____ and crossed the Rubicon' stands for necessarily contains the concept *crossed the Rubicon*; so, the concept *identical with Caesar*, since this is the same concept, necessarily contains *crossed the Rubicon*.

If this were not only a good route but also the only route to the objector's desired conclusion, it would be fair to point out that, by virtue of its reification of concepts, it disregards Leibniz's professed nominalism.[28] But that is a last-ditch defence (and no more secure than Leibniz's claim that it is always possible to see general terms as *compendia loquendi*, or as a handy way of speaking of substances). And in any case, I do not think we should make the concession that the objector has even a good route here to his conclusion.

Is everything that a concept contains (every mark of the concept) essential to it? It may be said that there can be nothing more to the identity of a concept in Leibniz's scheme than the set of its Fregean marks (and that the identity of the object itself that falls under the concept is not a distinguishable or individuating element in Leibniz's scheme). But that is questionable. Maybe Leibniz inadvertently discourages us from questioning it in the *Discourse of Metaphysics*, where he seems to be prepared to equate the individual concept of x with the nature or essence of x. (Perhaps everything in an essence is essential to that essence itself? Perhaps that is something special about essences—though even this claim might merit a little argument.) But later this point about concept and essence was sorted out clearly and definitively:

---

[27] Compare again the account of direct and demonstrative identification cited from *Generales Inquisitiones* in note 25. Note that this is the counterpart for singular terms of the extension-involving account of general terms that I attribute to Leibniz in *S&S*, pp. 10–11, 76–86.

[28] See, for example, 'Preface to Nizolius', Gerhardt, IV, pp. 138–76.

of the essence of a thing is what belongs to it necessarily and perpetually; of the concept of a singular thing, however, is also what belongs to it contingently or by accident, or what God sees in it when he has perfectly understood it.[29]

And once we respect Leibniz's distinction between concept and essence, the whole objection begins to wilt. Suppose that concept A = concept B if and only if everything that belongs to concept A belongs to concept B, and vice versa; and suppose that identity itself is a necessary relation. It *still* does not follow that whatever A contains it necessarily contains.[30]

7

At least two distinctions are relevant here. First, there is the distinction Leibniz might have wanted between the essential and the non-essential. Thinking about that in terms of worlds, one may reflect that what is essential to *worlds* in Leibniz's scheme is the range and variety of substances that they contain and the laws that these substances exemplify. No world is better than any other, for instance, simply by containing a certain particular individual as such (as opposed to another one like it). If so, and if a set of substances constitutes the form and matter of a world, then it may seem—this is speculation—that what is essential to a Leibnizian substance is *at most* something non-individuating, either something that is essential to substance as such or something that is essential to a substance's exemplifying a certain general form or conforming to some general law.[31] But, as I say, this is speculation. There is very little in Leibniz about this question, and it seems to me that no one who examined the texts with an innocent eye could attribute to Leibniz any strong interest at all in the issues that we debate nowadays under the label of 'essentialism'.

The second distinction to be borne constantly in mind is the distinction between concepts and the objects that fall under them. So far, the objector has failed signally to offer even the appearance of getting beyond divine specifications, or individual concepts, and engaging individual substances themselves in his necessitarian argument.

---

[29] G. W. Leibniz, *Textes Inedits d'après les manuscrits de la Bibliothèque provinciale de Hanovre*, ed. G. Grua, 2 vols (Paris: Presses Universitaires de France, 1948), 383. This important passage was first brought to my attention by a discussion of it on page 263 of Robert Merrihew Adams's 'Leibniz's Theories of Contingency', in Michael Hooker (ed.), *Leibniz: Critical and Interpretive Essays* (Manchester: Manchester University Press, 1982).
[30] One might as convincingly argue that, because substance A = substance B if and only if A and B occupy all and only the same places and because identity between substances is a necessary relation, any place that A or B occupies it necessarily occupies!
[31] Compare the conclusion I reach in another way in *S&S*, p. 120.

8

In a last effort to engage individuals themselves, someone may ask us to consider the sentence

The man sitting in the corner smoking is smoking.

Obviously, the objector may say, the man sitting in the corner does not have to smoke. This (it is now evident) is not a necessary truth but a contingent one. But the trouble for Leibniz, the objector will now say, is that the sentence already has an a priori proof. We do not need to appeal to the principles of sufficient reason and the best or to embark on any reduction of the proposition to prove it. For it is already in the form

The *F G* is *F*,

which is the terminus of reduction; so ex hypothesi nothing more than we already have is required to prove it. All we need is what Leibniz calls the Principle of Contradiction. Therefore, by Leibniz's doctrine, the sentence must be necessary.

But this objection is mistaken. We cannot get a proof for a proposition by hiding one part of it away in a presupposition. (Compare standard criticisms of certain traditional arguments for the existence of God.) Putting that presupposition back into the judgement itself, we should get

(The x)(x is a man sitting smoking in the corner, x is smoking),

which, for Aristotle, Russell, and Leibniz alike (although for different reasons) will both have existential import and be contingent. What is more, the a priori proof of the existential part of the judgement would have to proceed, as the *Discourse of Metaphysics* has it, through 'the principle of contingency or the principle of the existence of things, that is to say [through] what appears best among several equally possible things'. It would need to be shown, but it *could not* be shown using only the principles of identity and contradiction, that the man in question enters into 'the most perfect series' or the series that pleases God or that he was 'compossible with more things than anything incompossible with him'.[32]

This account of the matter suggested by what Leibniz wrote in 1686 is so straightforward that it may seem it must be inadequate. For if it is right, then why did Leibniz eventually give up the containment doctrine of truth? And why did he take such pains to develop an analogy (seen by many commentators as a new answer, not as a further elaboration of a *Discourse of Metaphysics* answer)

---

[32] Compare Couturat, pp. 9, 360 (sub 'existens'), 405.

between the specification of substances or the identification of their concepts on the one hand, a task that Leibniz comes to see as entailing infinitary analysis (because the specification of every substance involves the specification of all the others), and the computation of surds, irrationals, asymptotes, etc. on the other? (See *Generales Inquisitiones*, dated later in the same year as the *Discourse*, namely 1686, §130–§137.)

My brief answer to these questions would be to suggest first that Leibniz's giving up the containment principle of truth had nothing at all to do with necessity and contingency but arose from his perception of the complexity of achieving in terms of relations of containment any general statement of the truth conditions of *all* true sentences and from the enhancement of his awareness of the complex role played by negation in what we should call quantified sentences. 'All A's are B's' and 'All A's are non-B's' conform well enough to Leibniz's rule, but what about their contradictories? Already in 1679, we see him hard at work on this problem. 'The concept of the subject either in itself or with some addition involves the concept of the predicate.' (See Couturat, p. 51.) He distinguishes 'direct' from 'indirect' connections of subject and predicate. In due course, Leibniz enters a qualification—'the concept of the predicate is *contained in some way* in the concept of the subject'. (This occurs in 'On Freedom', cited later (section 9).) The final blow to the containment formula, I surmise, was Leibniz's long-delayed but finally clear perception, in the decade after the *Discourse*, of the general character of the interaction that we describe as the interaction between quantification and negation.[33] In a pure calculus of containment, it is only where A is an individual concept that 'A non continet B' will be equivalent to 'A continet non-B'. ('A does not contain B' may be true because some A's are non-B's. 'A contains non-B' will be true, where it is, only if every A is a non-B.) Even after seeing this clearly, Leibniz could have gone on saying that a proposition in whose truth conditions the concepts A and B occur essentially will be true only if the A stands in *some* relation one could specify in terms of containment between concepts to B. But this is so vague as to be almost vacuous. It is not what Leibniz first had in mind when he wanted to state a simple rule of truth.[34] I surmise also that Leibniz noticed that the abandonment of the general containment doctrine did not undermine his doctrine of the

---

[33] Compare Wolfgang Lenzen, '"Non est" non est "est non"', *Studia Leibnitiana*, 18(1) (1986).

[34] Compare the way in which some modern philosophers have started out wanting to characterize truth in terms of the predicate of a sentence applying to its subject—and then found in due course that that special case will not generalize. Either they have then fallen silent, or they have been forced into an account of 'application' or 'truth of', which is (1) at least as language relative, and (2) at least as complex, as Tarski's definition of satisfaction.

individual concept of an individual substance and its determination of what is true of that substance.

So much for the first of the two questions that I announced in the paragraph before last. About the other, I should say that the analogy with infinitary analysis seems not to have been introduced as a *substitute* for the containment rule. In the paper *Generales Inquisitiones* it stands side by side with it in a complementary relation. Surely the analogy starts out as a striking dramatization of the mind-boggling complexity of the interconnection of things and of all the considerations that would be involved in showing that any particular series of things would be the most perfect.[35]

9

When Leibniz eventually saw the inadequacy in detail of the containment principle to his doctrine of truth, this did not need to disturb the metaphysical principles that had suggested the principle to him in the first place. As always, these principles were in a state of development, but there were other reasons for that. Nor did his doctrine of contingency in the *Discourse* become superfluous in the absence of the doctrine of truth. For the doctrine of the individual concept remained and the idea remained that all truths ultimately repose upon the title of some set of these to be realized. That doctrine and the Leibnizian account of the simple subject-predicate (unquantified) case still stood in need of the *Discourse* defence. (Indeed the same defence is surely both presupposed and required by the doctrine of infinitary analysis.) It is true that Leibniz continued to speculate actively about problems of necessity and contingency. But it is hard to believe that this was because Leibniz did not recognize what had been achieved in §XIII of the *Discourse*. Surely, it was because there were *other* modal worries in the offing, most of them perfectly visible in some shape or form to Leibniz himself, worries that had little to do with the individual concept's containment of all the truths about the object that fell under it. These were worries about the modal status of statements of God's nature and existence, of the principle of sufficient reason, of the principle of the best, of the claim that God chooses the best, and of the fact that this or that is the best or most perfect.[36] Because my concern here is with the principle of containment, I do not need to address any of these other

---

[35] Note also the calm with which Leibniz registers the manifest imperfection of the analogy at *Generales Inquisitiones*, §136. Such calm would be harder to understand if the infinitary analysis analogy were intended to be a self-sufficient solution to some problem seen as otherwise insoluble.

[36] See again Adams, 'Leibniz's Theories of Contingency'.

difficulties or try to relate any of them to Leibniz's conception of the problem of freedom. There is, however, one problem that persists beyond the *Discourse* and that may still appear, contrary to everything I have been claiming, to rest on the idea that the relation between a concept and its marks ought for Leibniz to have been a necessary one.

In an essay entitled 'On Freedom' (1689), Leibniz begins by saying that at one time he used to consider that

fortune, as distinct from fate is an empty word, and that nothing exists unless certain conditions are fulfilled, from all of which together its existence at once follows. I found myself very close to the opinions of those who hold everything to be absolutely necessary.[37]

But Leibniz had been pulled back from this precipice, he says, by considering possibles that are not actual. Then, he continues:

Having recognized the contingency of things, I raised the further question of a clear concept of truth, for I had a reasonable hope of throwing some light from this upon the problem of distinguishing necessary from contingent truths. For I saw that in every true affirmative proposition, whether universal or singular, necessary or contingent, the predicate inheres in the subject or that the concept of the predicate is in some way involved in the concept of the subject. I saw too that this is the principle of infallibility for him who knows everything *a priori*. But this very fact seemed to increase the difficulty, for, if at any particular time the concept of the predicate inheres in the concept of the subject, *how can the predicate ever be denied of the subject without contradiction and impossibility or without destroying the subject concept?*

It ought not to be assumed that the problem being mentioned in the words I have italicized is that Leibniz thinks that every sentence in which the concept of the subject has as a constituent the concept of the predicate somehow *ought* to have expressed a necessary truth. For we know that he did not think that. Perhaps the problem is that, not having the sense/reference distinction, he cannot see quite how the sentence reduced can fail to have the same modal status as the sentence it is reduced to. But, even though the sense/reference distinction would have clarified and assisted here, Leibniz surely solves that problem well enough in the *Discourse* by making it clear that, wherever a proposition is contingent, the process of reduction will itself rest on something non-logical and non-necessary. It seems then that the problem that worries him is rather that we still need to know how the predicate can be denied of the subject, as Leibniz indeed puts it, *without destroying the subject concept.*

---

[37] Parkinson, p. 106; Loemker, p. 263. I have followed Parkinson's dating.

This supposed problem, which I declare to be different from the supposed problem of the necessity of containment, surfaces in one of the initial misunderstandings on the part of Arnauld that got the Leibniz–Arnauld correspondence off to such a bad start.[38] Over and over again, among the many good points Leibniz makes, he rashly concedes to Arnauld that, if he himself, that is, the actual Leibniz, who went of his own free will upon a certain journey, had not gone upon that journey, then

> there would be a falsity which would *destroy my individual or complete notion*, or that which God *conceives of me*, or did conceive even before he decided to create me. For this notion involves *sub ratione possibilitatis*[39] existences or truths of fact, or decisions of God, on which facts depend. (Letter of 14 July 1686)

Suppose that it is contingent that Leibniz went on a certain journey. Then it might seem that nothing prevents us from making sense of his not doing so. But then either we *can* make sense of Leibniz's 'destroying' Leibniz's individual notion—which sounds totally unintelligible—or better, Leibniz thinks, the man who refrained from the journey would not have been Leibniz (the Leibniz of whose refraining from the journey we supposed that sense could be made). Surely Leibniz ought to have looked again at the first horn of this dilemma. Instead, he builds the difficulty into his presentation of his system by his seeming to rule positively, in *Theodicy* and other writings, that no particular individual—no actual Adam or Tarquinius Superbus or Leibniz or whoever—can figure in each of two possible worlds that differ in any respect at all; so that, if a necessary truth is one that holds in all possible worlds, then it will be necessary that Adam—if one means literally Adam—should have had the posterity he did have and necessary that Leibniz—if one means *literally* Leibniz—should have gone on the journey he went on. 'Leibniz could have refrained from making the journey he made' has then to be saved by a system of reinterpretation.

What is it that prevents Leibniz from re-examining the first horn of the dilemma? Putting the question that it raises more literally, what incoherence is there in the idea that the very person who went on a certain journey, the person whom it so happens we can identify in that particular way, might not have gone on that journey—in which case he would have had to be identified in some other way? Well, given his doctrine of the individual concept as determinant of the whole being of a thing, Leibniz attaches no sense to the idea of the very same

---

[38] These misunderstandings were not really Arnauld's fault—or even the fault of the text of the *Discourse*. Arnauld was working from an abstract. (This was conveyed to him, at Leibniz's request, through the Duke of Hessen-Rheinfells.)

[39] 'In general terms' (Parkinson).

individual's figuring in a different Leibnizian world from the one it actually figures in. Yes. But why is this? Why insist, in the face of the question of the contingency of the journey (a contingency Leibniz does not doubt), on that particular form of the doctrine of the individual concept?

The answer to these questions is speculative; but the question itself is nothing short of compulsory. And my own provisional suggestion would be this: Leibniz's system of possible worlds starts out as a device for the comparison of possible worlds in respect of ontological richness and nomological simplicity; and within that framework (or so I have claimed) questions of identity and difference across possible worlds are simply not provided for. At the 'moment' of God's choice that the system is intended to illuminate, *there is* nothing except God and the ideas in the mind of God. There can be no question therefore of the criterion of identity for individual concepts being given in the form that concept C_1 = concept C_2 if and only if C_1 is of the same individual substance as C_2 is of. Rather, the model must supply in advance all the marks of every individual concept for every Leibnizian possible world, and then $C_1 = C_2$ if and only if every mark of C_1 is a mark of C_2 and vice versa.

Where the question of creation is under consideration, this is fair enough; and the framework that delivers this result really does not enable us to pick out one and the same individual in two different possible worlds (two Leibnizian ones, I mean). But this finding should not distract attention from the fact that the question of the different titles to realization of different possible worlds is an utterly different question from the question of whether or not an identified individual, a given particular encountered in the world or thought of *de re*, might have refrained from a journey that he actually made. With Saul Kripke's semantics for modal logic laid out in front of us, it is not hard for us to conclude that the question of the alternatives for such an individual needs to be explored in a different framework. This framework will require possible world specifications to include *explicit* information, quite inappropriate for Leibnizian specifications, about the identities of the individuals that figure within some world. And then, once we have actual individuals to talk about, there will be no difficulty in imagining circumstances under which individuals fail to conform to their actually given individual concepts. What is more, nothing will prevent us from adopting the Leibnizian framework for one sort of question and the Kripkean for the other.

If we decide to look at things in this way, there is scarcely any temptation to slide from the claim that no sense attaches within the Leibnizian framework to cross-world identity to the claim that different Leibnizian worlds must contain *different* individuals. Indeed Leibniz too would have seen this as a lapse, as so described. ('It is one thing not to understand a thing, and another for us to understand its contradictory,' he says.) Nevertheless I yield to the temptation to think that it is something like this slide that, without benefit of the Kripke semantics, Leibniz was himself involved in.

As always with Leibniz, however, there is more than one thing at stake here, philosophically speaking. Had he warmed to the proposal just made and come to regard both conceptions of possible worlds as available to him, then he would have been faced with the need to allow that, strictly speaking, God's deliberative thoughts of substance are not properly referential at all. He would have been forced into allowing a bifurcation between properly referential thinking ('hic homo quem designo etc') and completely determinate specification effected by complete individual concepts which, being still general in character, fix every last detail of Adam's or Julius Caesar's life without ever reaching down to these substances themselves in the manner that referential thinking does. Such a bifurcation, once admitted, would have had the effect of reopening the question of the principle on which Leibniz had so often depended (for instance in his theory of God's choice, where it enabled him to equate the variety of forms with the quantity of created substances), namely, the identity of indiscernibles. And it would have signalled a real gap between something's being a member of 'the most perfect series' or being 'compossible with more substances than any substance incompossible with it'[40] and its being something actual or real. These definitions suggest that creation is a metaphor for something outside time. Once such a gap looms, however, it is hard to avoid interpreting the idea of God's act of creation much more literally than is suggested by the Leibnizian definition of existence. And then we have to wonder how God's creating some substance can come within a time series *after* his conceiving of the maximal set of concepts that contains it as a member but *before* the beginning of a time series that stretches, according to Leibniz, infinitely[41] back into the past.

10

There is no question, on the general interpretation I offer, of Leibniz's having confused an object with its complete concept. What is at issue is not a mistaken identification of these. Nor is there any doubt that Leibniz recognized that there was thought such as demonstrative thought that essentially concerned individuals. After all, his whole account of human a posteriori knowledge of the world

---

[40] Compare Couturat, p. 360 (sub *existens*).
[41] See Gerhardt, VII, p. 302 (Parkinson, p. 136).

and its substances depended on this. What he failed to appreciate was rather the sharpness of the divide between the thinking that goes into such a choice as God makes and properly referential thinking. Once we recognize what is so special in the latter, however, then we must recognize the possibility of singling out Caesar or Leibniz, the man himself, a sort of singling out that Leibniz does recognize, and saying of that person within whose specification it is written that he will choose to go on a journey but *choose freely* to do so, that he (literally, he, that very man) *might* have refrained from making the journey.[42] And we must recognize the possibility of imagining the possible world in which that very individual does not make the journey, albeit a possible world that does not belong in the set of possible worlds between which God has to choose. Leibniz too could have recognized all this, consistently with the principles of sufficient reason and of the Best—if not consistently with absolutely everything else that he albeit wanted to say.

Acknowledgements

I have been greatly influenced in my thoughts about the topic of this paper by Hidé Ishiguro, both by conversation with her and by her writings on Leibniz. It is to her reading of Leibniz that I owe the very thought that it is possible for contingency to be saved in Leibniz's system. In this connection, see especially her 'Contingent Truths and Possible Worlds', in *Leibniz: Metaphysics and Philosophy of Science*, ed. R. Woolhouse (Oxford: Oxford University Press, 1981); *Leibniz's Philosophy of Logic and Language* (London: Duckworth, 1972).

This paper was written while I was a Fellow at the Center for Advanced Study in the Behavioral Sciences, Stanford University, in the 1985–86 academic year. I acknowledge gratefully the financial support provided there by the Andrew W. Mellon Foundation and the additional support of a grant in the humanities from the British Academy.

---

[42] The other thing that must be noted, at least where Leibniz's difficulty with Leibniz destroying his own individual concept is concerned, is that a concept is not in itself such as to determine anything at all, whether fatalistically or causally. It is not the concept but the actual nature of each individual and the individuals that are coexistent with it in the same world that fixes or determines the history of the world. And note how badly Leibniz *himself* will need to say this when he engages with the problem of human freedom.

8

Putnam's Doctrine of Natural Kind Words and Frege's Doctrines of Sense, Reference, and Extension: Can They Cohere?

1. Hilary Putnam has been apt to emphasize all the differences between the deictic doctrine that he advocates for the understanding of our understanding of natural kind substantives and the various accounts of the meanings of these expressions that his predecessors in the philosophy of meaning offered or would have had to offer. Delighting in iconoclasm, he has sought at various times to include within the ambit of his entertaining criticisms of his predecessors such figures as Aristotle, the Scholastics, Locke, Mill, Frege, linguistic philosophers, analytical philosophers, philosophers of linguistics, indeed practically everyone.[1]

In this chapter, I set out Putnam's proposal and show how, in the later nineteen-sixties, it helped to break the mould for one kind of philosophical analysis. But I also try to show that we may deploy Putnam's proposal most convincingly if, flying in the face of Putnam's own wish, we try to place it within the framework of Fregean sense and reference. Then I try to show that, having done that, we can improve our understanding further if we seek to integrate the deictic proposal—significantly but desirably adjusted at one key point—with an extant, neglected but even more time-honoured tradition of semantic speculation, a tradition, not empiricist, in which there is already a clear place for Putnam's insight concerning the functioning of natural kind words.

---

[1] See for instance the exposition that he gives in *Representations and Reality* (Cambridge, MA: MIT Press, 1988).

2. I begin by reminding you of the contents of 'Is Semantics Possible?'. This is a paper that Putnam read to a conference in Brockport, New York, in 1967.[2] It was in this paper that he first introduced the idea that to impart the meaning of a natural kind term is to impart certain core facts: (1) the *stereotype*—consisting of the facts an ordinary speaker needs to know in order to use a natural kind term—and (2) the *extension*, the identification of the latter being the province of experts. Or, as I would rather say,[3] it was in this paper that Putnam introduced the idea that the sense of thing-kind words standing for natural kinds is reality-invoking or extension-involving.

Putnam led up to his conclusion by criticizing incisively and amusingly the easy (or fall-back) supposition that the right way to give the meaning of 'lemon', 'tiger', 'water', or whatever, would have to be by analysis into simpler terms or by giving necessary and sufficient conditions. I worried, when I read de Sousa's notes, that Putnam filed no report of an analytical philosopher (contrast one philosopher of linguistics) with his trousers down actually attempting such a thing. But then, by 1967, linguistic philosophers were a canny bunch; and it quickly appeared that Putnam's failure to identify such an attempt was not a cause to criticize him. The thing that mattered was that the problem of natural kind words was not to be solved by the tact or good taste in which analytical philosophers then excelled, or by the refusal to recognize that these expressions constituted a special question for the philosophy of meaning.

On this matter, as on others, ideas were at that time in short supply. But it must be recorded that, for the slightly similar case of proper names, there had existed from well before 1960 an important minority opinion which (perhaps under the influence of Geach and Anscombe) Michael Dummett took very seriously and which (under Dummett's influence) I myself took maximally seriously (indeed believed and preached to my students from 1959 onwards). This was that a proper name has its meaning, and thus affects the truth-conditions of the sentences in which it occurs, by standing for its bearer—and that there is no other way to give the sense of a proper name than to say which object it is that the name stands for.[4] It was not out of the question then, even in that distant epoch,

---

[2] For a long time this paper was known only by report. I came to know it myself from the notes taken at the conference by Ronald de Sousa, to whom I owe my first appreciation of its significance. Eventually it was published in H. E. Kiefer and M. K. Munitz (eds), *Language, Belief and Metaphysics* (Albany, NY: State University of New York Press, 1970), pp. 50–63, and in *Metaphilosophy*, 1 (1970), pp. 187–201.

[3] See below and *S&S*, Preamble.

[4] See G. E. M. Anscombe, *An Introduction to Wittgenstein's Tractatus* (London: Hutchinson, 1959), pp. 41, 42, 44; Michael Dummett, 'Truth', *Proceedings of the Aristotelian Society*, 59 (1958–9), pp. 141–62.

to say that the senses of proper names were reality-invoking or object-involving or that a proper name had its sense by being assigned to something, not by the laying down of some specification such that a bearer of the name bears it by virtue of meeting that specification. Nor, among those who held the minority opinion I have just described, was it an unfamiliar question what it would involve to find room for this in Fregean semantics. (Frege's notion of *Art des Gegebenseins* seemed to be ready-made for such an attempt. See Section 8 below.) Rather, that which was still missing in linguistic philosophy and in the philosophy of science of those times was any strong perception of the need to say something similar for potentially predicative expressions such as 'lemon', 'tiger', 'water', or to try to *generalize* from the direction of semantical fit that is so strikingly exemplified by the assignment of an ordinary name to something.[5]

Back now to 'Is Semantics Possible?'. Not only, Putnam insisted, were philosophical analyses of substantives such as 'lemon', 'tiger', 'water' laughably inadequate. The only explanation of anyone's even supposing that it might be possible for there to be such an analysis was sheer negligence of the whole *mise-en-scène*, the whole social-cum-technological context, on which we all depend in order to come to understand one another. Even to understand what we find in the dictionary we depend upon that context. Philosophers who were ready to suppose that there could be a philosophical analysis of the meaning of 'lemon' or 'tiger' were ignoring the division of mental labour and the role of the authorities or experts who sustain our shared understanding of natural kind words. Philosophers should cease to complain, Putnam said, about the fact that dictionaries are 'cluttered up with colour samples and stray pieces of empirical information (e.g. the atomic weight of aluminium) not sharply distinguished from purely linguistic information'. They should take that fact seriously as a clue to the real situation, the situation that Putnam himself wanted (however schematically) to describe.

3. Confining oneself to the ideas of 'Is Semantics Possible?', but departing a little from Putnam's mode of exposition there, one can put the positive proposal he wanted to advance as follows: where the instructor's grasp of extension is authoritative (or is downstream from an authoritative identification of that extension), an instructor could initiate a learner into the meaning of the word 'lemon' as follows:

---

[5] If you doubt that, read the reply to Putnam in the Brockport volume or trust my recollections of the experience of trying to expound Putnam's theory to an incredulous audience at a meeting of the British Association for the Philosophy of Science in the early 1970s. For 'direction of fit', see J. L. Austin, 'How to Talk: Some Simple Ways', reprinted in his *Philosophical Papers* (Oxford: Clarendon Press, 1961), and M. J. Woods, as cited in S&S.

This is a lemon. [Here the instructor displays a specimen.] A thing is a lemon if it resembles this [the specimen] or this [another displayed specimen] or this [a third specimen] in the relevant way. I say *the relevant way*. But to understand better what that way is you must inquire, just to the extent necessary for your purposes, into the *nature* of these three things that I am showing you.

The philosophical claim is that (however artificially) such a demonstration or ostension reconstructs the ordinary teaching and learning of thing-kind words. It reconstructs that which is essential to the transactions that take place between those who know and those who do not know what a given substantive means.

4. I suspect that it is hard for those who have been introduced to philosophy by anyone who understood the point of such a proposal to appreciate the novelty it once enjoyed, at the time when Putnam introduced it. But before I say any more of this novelty or touch upon the tractability of Putnam's doctrine to the theory of sense and reference or trace its affinity to certain rationalist ideas, four points need to be registered.

First, the doctrine, which is sometimes loosely called 'the indexical theory', does not, on a true understanding, imply any close similarity between natural-kind substantives and indexicals or demonstratives. If 'lemon' or 'tiger' or 'water' had any real resemblance to 'this' or 'that' or 'now' or 'today', these substantives might in other contexts, and without change of lexical meaning, pick out other kinds of things than the kinds that we denominate lemons, tigers, or water. But the point of the theory is to attach the meaning of these words to the real natures, more or less well known, of the actual lemons, tigers, and water that we have encountered. Therefore we must not compare 'water' to a demonstrative. The theory is a deictic theory in just one sense: it is the theory of the *deixis* by which we can, under special and favourable conditions, attach a word to a kind of thing.

Secondly, the doctrine does not extend to all thing-kind words. Occasionally, in later papers, Putnam was tempted to apply it to functional or instrumental substantives like 'pencil'.[6] But that was a pity, indeed threatened—however momentarily—the shipwreck of a good idea. We can perhaps learn the word 'pencil' by ostension—but only imperfectly in so far as this disprepares us for the

---

[6] In discussion at the meeting at St Andrews for which this paper was written, Hilary Putnam reminded me that at this point he had been reporting a discussion with Rogers Albritton, in which they had been envisaging circumstances under which it was found that all extant pencils had a certain microstructure. But *all* pencils, however manufactured and for whatever specialized purpose? This would be magic. Or (more likely) there would have to have been a practical joke somewhere in this story.

possibility that almost anything at all—any old thing—can be a pencil if one can write or draw with it (or achieve analogous goals). It is unsatisfactory too if the learner is left with the impression that pencil is a natural kind. Indeed functional or instrumental kinds are among the best candidates for old-fashioned definition. Moreover, with 'pencil', there is little or no resemblance to the case where the ostension of a natural kind invites us to extrapolate freely across the observed properties of its exemplars in the search for interesting generalizations about its nature.

Thirdly, it is wise to leave room for a certain kind of exception to Putnam's account of these matters. Consider the element gallium, a natural kind if ever there was one. Gallium was not discovered by finding specimens and seeking to determine what they were. It was predicted that such an element would be found at an apparently vacant place in the periodic table. In the terms of that table, gallium is even definable. Here, however, reference and sense are *cantilevered* upon a structure set up in another way. Maybe almost anything (well *almost* anything) can be cantilevered. But not everything can be cantilevered. The disruption that this creates for Putnam's picture is minimal. It presupposes that picture.

This point leads to a fourth, which might itself have been the occasion for a whole chapter, but is not the occasion for the whole of mine. In this area there are problems of the underdetermination of meaning by *deixis* and problems of the proper representativeness of specimens (problems analogous to those that Goodman calls 'constant companionship' and 'imperfect community'). Room must be made within the theory of this demonstrative practice for an instructor to make his pupil understand whether it is a species that is being indicated or a subspecies/variety (is it rose or Rosa rugosa?); and room must be made for the instructor to make the pupil understand whether something specific or something generic is to be identified (tiger, say, or Felis).[7] Ostension had better not be the magical solution to the problem of natural kind predicates. We shall return to this point in section 13.

5. So much in outline for the new theory of natural kind words. Why though was it so difficult for so long for our sort of philosophy to arrive at this deictic or extension-involving conception of their meaning? And how indeed was the barrier (whatever it was) ever surmounted?

---

[7] These problems are more tractable than the problems they superficially resemble and that were thrown up by the resemblance (or no-universals) theory of universals defended by Bertrand Russell and H. H. Price. They are more tractable because here, in this context, we may expect that *deixis* can be supported by context and by verbal explanations that are unconstrained by special requirements of ontological parsimony. See the explanations envisaged below, especially section 13.

Well, I shall leave it to Hilary Putnam to answer the second question—unless modesty forbids. But about the first, one thing is very obvious, but, since it occurred to me altogether afresh, when I was reading a review in *Mind and Language* (Autumn issue, 1989) of the book *Representations and Reality*—which was Putnam's critique of many positions in present-day philosophy, not least of functionalism—I yield to the temptation to begin there.

After expounding Putnam's deictic theory in his own way, the reviewer writes:

But why should water beliefs, so understood, pose a problem for the functionalist? He will not be able to capture the content of such beliefs by alluding to their characteristic causal connections with experience alone. Rather, the important connections will be those between the current water thought, a past demonstrative thought about certain samples then in front of the subject, and the theoretical belief that such substances fall under some fundamental classification which may be revealed by investigating the causal properties of those substances. It is these connections which will ensure that the thought is indeed about water and they are part of that thought's causal role.[8]

Even as I read the words 'water beliefs' and 'current water thoughts', something stirred in memory: 'There will not be books in the running brooks until the dawn of hydrosemantics.'[9] But now that philosophy is well into hydrosemantics—now that the running brooks are into the books[10]—it is time to ask why in the 1950s and well into the 1960s it seemed so irresistibly comical to contemplate the very idea of hydrosemantics—even for 'hydor' ('water'). This was unthinkable to most philosophers of Austin's era because, even though everyone knew that Quine had exposed a grave circularity in all extant attempts to explain the analytic/synthetic distinction from a standing start, that did not seem to matter very much. It did not matter because analytic philosophers thought that, in practice, they could still reach principled consensus on what was analytic. So what good reason was there to question the separation of language from the world, to contemplate letting water itself into the semantics of 'water'? What reason was there to modify the idea that philosophy consisted in analysis? Analysis and the search for non-circular necessary and sufficient conditions could continue.[11]

---

[8] David Owens, 'Review of Hilary Putnam, *Representation and Reality*', *Mind and Language*, 4 (1989), pp. 246–9.

[9] J. L. Austin, 'Truth', *Proceedings of the Aristotelian Society*, suppl. 24 (1950), 121.

[10] For a closer approximation to the hydrosemantics or natural meanings that the exiled Duke must really have had in mind at *As You Like It*, II. i. 16: see Paul Valéry's celebration (however ill-calculated to evoke Austin's approval) of the Source Perrier.

[11] Indeed at the time of writing (1993) it still continued, to judge by the aims and ambitions that were prescribed by most of the participants in the group-effort to solve for x—if necessary by brute force—in the equation: (knowledge) = (belief + x). In easel painting, pointillisme was a short-lived experiment. In philosophy, it seemed destined to continue for ever.

By attacking the very idea of analyticity (a supposedly salutary exaggeration), the Quinean onslaught had overextended itself and miscarried. The point about Putnam's 'Is Semantics Possible?' is that it was part of a more modest but far more effective second onslaught on the idea of analyticity. This second attack is not targeted on definable single criterion concepts, *vixen* (= *female fox*), *oculist* (=*eye-doctor*). Nor is it an attack on the analyticity of 'a vixen is a female fox', 'an oculist is an eye-doctor', etc. That is scarcely worth attacking. It is targeted upon the attempt to *generalize* from those however undeniable small successes. 'A theory which correctly describes the behaviour of perhaps three hundred words has been asserted to correctly describe the behaviour of the tens of thousands of general names.'[12] In other words, what obstructed the discovery (or rediscovery, as I shall claim) of the necessity to frame a deictic view of natural kind names was the failure to think through exactly and all the way to the end the problems and the limitations of the analytic/synthetic distinction. It is no accident that Putnam, who had spent as long as anyone in re-examining the distinction, should have been the rediscoverer (or co-rediscoverer with Kripke) of the deictic view of natural kind words. What I think *is* strange, if anything is, is that these matters have still [1990] not been thought right through[13] and have still not impinged as they should on the practice of philosophy. It is stranger still, I think, that in the philosophy of science those who now concern themselves with the meaning of theoretical terms still [in 1990] show so little inclination to explore the possibility of sense-giving relations between predicates and kinds that might mimic the direction of fit we now take for granted in our understanding of the setting up of the relation of designation. (See again the third paragraph of section 2 above.)

It is time now to show how the extension-involvingness of nature kind words will cohere with the theory of sense and reference.

6. On 24 May 1891 Frege wrote Husserl a letter about the sense and reference of predicates, and he included in it an instructive and remarkable diagram (Figure 8.1).

---

[12] Putnam in Kiefer and Munitz (eds), *Language, Belief and Metaphysics*, p. 52.

[13] Not anticipating that Kripke would be charged with violating some supposed distinction between metaphysics and the philosophy of language (another distinction Quine and Putnam subverted) and, falsely supposing that, after Kripke's excellent observations on the differences between the statuses of necessity, analyticity, and a priority, all these things would inevitably be thought through to the end, I rashly elected in *S&S* to call certain truths and necessities that were neither analytically nor formally nor combinatorially guaranteed *conceptual truths*. (Such truths arose from the individuative sorts that things fall into.) I little thought that this 'conceptual' would be read as an evasive synonym of 'analytic', or that I would be seen as seeking to save some of the most implausible theses of linguistic philosophy. Why should a concept such as *man, horse, tree* be something that arises on the language side of a barrier that keeps the world from flowing into the word? It was expressly denied in *S&S* that language can be protected by such an exclusion zone.

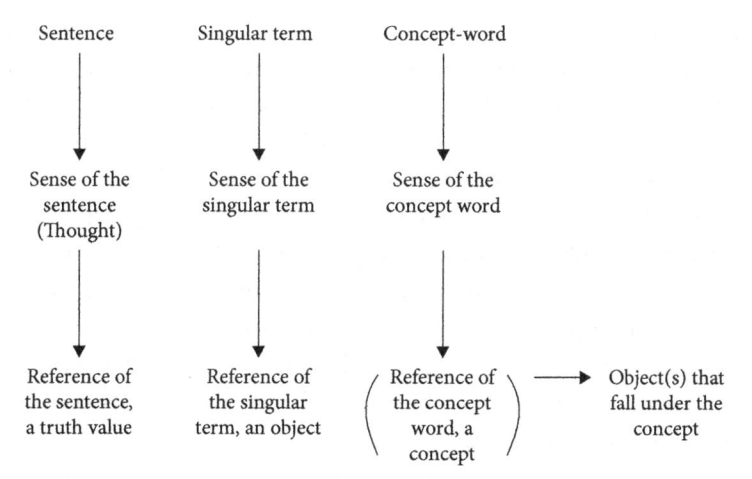

```
Sentence          Singular term      Concept-word
   │                   │                 │
   ▼                   ▼                 ▼
Sense of the      Sense of the      Sense of the
 sentence         singular term     concept word
 (Thought)
   │                   │                 │
   ▼                   ▼                 ▼
Reference of      Reference of      ⎛ Reference of ⎞  ──▶  Object(s) that
the sentence,     the singular      ⎜ the concept  ⎟       fall under the
a truth value     term, an object   ⎝ word, a      ⎠       concept
                                      concept
```

Figure 8.1

Let me first gloss this diagram in familiar ways. Then, after proposing a small repair to Fregean doctrine under the third column, let me try to show how well the deictic proposal can be assimilated within the scheme.

7. About column 1, let us simply remark that grasping the sense of a sentence is a matter of grasping under what conditions it attains to the True. In preference over saying that, in the strict sense of 'designate' or 'refer', the True is the reference or designation of a sentence, let us say that the True is the semantic value—Dummett's term—of the sentence. (Let us think of reference itself as a special case of semantic value.)

8. Now column 2. Here let us bear it in mind that, strictly and literally interpreted, the claim that 'sense determines reference' is compatible with the denial of the *priority* of either.

Because it is rarely quoted, let me start by pointing to Frege's remark, in *Ausführungen uber Sinn und Bedeutung*, about the fictional names 'Nausicaa' and 'moly'.[14] In so far as 'Nausicaa' is allowed any sense, Frege says its literary signification depends upon its behaving *as if* it designates some particular young woman.[15] But implicit in the claim about fiction is a simpler claim about the case of fact. The simpler claim is that in the non-fictional case a name has a sense by

---

[14] Gottlob Frege, *Posthumous Writings*, ed. Hans Hermes, Friedrich Kambartel, and Friedrich Kaulbach, trans. Peter Long and Roger White (Oxford: Blackwell), p. 122.

[15] Similarly, the kind name 'moly' gets what sense it has by behaving as if it designates a particular herb, namely the herb which in *Odyssey*, Book X, Hermes gives to Odysseus in preparation for his encounter with Circe. The name is still there, ready and waiting for any pharmaceutical product with similar or comparable apotropaic powers.

behaving as if it has—indeed simply by having—a reference. A name has its sense then by somehow presenting its object. To grasp the sense of a name is to know (in the manner correlative with the mode of presentation that corresponds to this particular designation) which object the name is assigned to. To impart the sense is to show (in that manner) which object the name stands for.

To speak as Frege does of sense as 'mode of presentation' suggests nothing less than this: there is an object that the name presents and there is a way in which the name presents it. So the name carries with it a conception of that object—an account of how things are with it, a body of information (not necessarily correct in every particular) in which the object itself plays some distinct and distinguishable role.[16] Such a conception or body of information will normally be open-ended, imperfect, and corrigible.

Properly possessed then, the conception of an object x that sustains the sense of a name which is keyed to that conception is a way of thinking about x that fixes (with the help of the world, the world being what helps create the conception) which object it is. Which object it is is precisely what is mastered by one who comes to understand the name with the sense corresponding to that conception.

9. Now the transition to Frege's third column. Even as grasping the sense of a name or singular term and its contribution to truth conditions is grasping the particular conception of that object that corresponds to the name's mode of presentation of what it stands for, and even as we give the term's sense by saying in a manner congruent with that conception what the term stands for, so grasping the sense of the predicate (understanding what it contributes to the truth-conditions of sentences that contain it) consists in grasping the predicate's mode of presentation of the concept that it stands for. Thus we give the predicate's sense by saying what concept it stands for. And just as, in the case of a singular term, we show or exhibit one sense in preference over another sense by drawing upon one body of information in preference to another in filling out our identification of the object—so similarly, in the case of a predicate, we show or exhibit this sense in preference to that, e.g. the sense of 'horse' rather than the sense of say '*Equus caballus*', by exploiting one mode of presentation rather than another to say which concept this is. We prefer the body of information one might expound by saying 'A horse is a certain animal with a flowing mane and tail; its voice is a neigh; and in the domestic state it is used as a beast of burden and draught, and for riding upon' over the body of information that identifies such creatures by classifying them as perissodactyl

---

[16] See John McDowell, 'On the Sense and Reference of a Proper Name', *Mind*, 86 (1977), pp. 59–85.

quadrupeds, locates their species among the genus *Equus* and the family *Equidae* and then dwells on other zoological features.

10. With this suggestion—entailing that there can be different accounts of one and the same kind of thing, namely *horse* or *Equus caballus* and (more generally) one and the same property—I can look forward to a possible conclusion about stereotypes (see section 2), namely this: that Putnam's stereotypes approximate to those special conceptions that serve to explain the senses of expressions that stand for natural kinds; that stereotypes are particular or special ways of thinking in identificatory fashion about such kinds and their specimens. That will indeed be my proposal. But there are confusions to be avoided here, and there is a departure from Putnam. We must hasten more slowly.

11. To avoid confusion, we must take care to present Frege's theory in column 3 as perfectly general with respect to all predicates and *then* say what is so special about natural kind words among predicates. It will also be necessary to indicate at some point what sort of thing Fregean concepts are. Finally, conceptions of a horse being in this picture conceptions *of* the concept horse (i.e. conceptions of what it is for something to be a horse), we must be as clear as possible about the difference between a conception, something belonging on the level of sense, and a concept, which is something on the level of reference.

Let us return to the analogy between names in general and predicates in general, that is the analogy between columns 2 and 3. If we take the analogy in the manner proposed, then it makes good sense of Frege's insistence, in the letter to Husserl and elsewhere, that the reference of a predicate cannot be any object or objects that it is true of. Just as singular terms without reference are unfitted to figure in the expression of a judgement possessed of a cognitive significance that enables us to move forward, as we must, to a truth value, and just as a name capable of figuring in the expression of a judgement that can constitute knowledge *must* have a reference, so must any predicate that aspires to this status have reference. But many predicates essential to the expression of good information do not have anything they are true of. Therefore their Fregean reference is not any object they are true of. Thus, as Frege says in the letter cited:

> With a concept word, it takes one more step to reach the object than it does with a proper name, and this last step may be missing—i.e. the concept may be empty—without the concept word's ceasing to be scientifically useful. I have drawn the last step, from concept to object, horizontally in order to indicate that it takes place on the same level, that objects and concepts have the same objectivity. In literary use it is sufficient if everything has sense; in scientific use there must also be *Bedeutungen*.

So on this account of things, the claim that a predicate has a concept as its reference does not bring out what is distinctive of natural kind terms or of Putnam's proposal concerning them. 'Round square' has a reference, 'blue' has a reference, 'pencil' has a reference. You come to know this reference, which is nothing other than the concept, by coming to know what it would take (whether that be possible or impossible) for a thing to be a round square, blue, or a pencil. And now, *as one special case of this*, there are terms, such as 'lemon' or 'tiger', where to grasp what it would take for something to be a lemon or a tiger or whatever it is, you need exposure to the extension of the term. In this case—if the argument of 'Is Semantics Possible?' is correct—there is no grasping the reference or concept otherwise than through the extension. (See the fourth column of Frege's diagram and its sole member: objects that fall under the concept.) Here (at least) we cannot have reached the understanding that we do in fact enjoy by coming to grasp a strictly lexical definition. So whereas the reality-involvingness of proper names amounts to their being reference-involving, the reality-involvingness of natural kind terms amounts to their being *extension*-involving. The schema itself of sense and reference neither demands that idea about extension nor excludes it, but it accommodates it.

12. On this account, we could say that one who understands 'horse' and knows what Victor and Arkle both are, viz. horses, grasps a general rule for accepting or rejecting the sentence '*x* is a horse' according as it collects or fails to collect for arbitrary item *x* the verdict True. And, equally we could say that one who knows what Victor or Arkle are has got a grasp of the concept *horse*. These two accounts of the concept come to the same thing.[17]

At this point, it is necessary to digress for a moment to say a word about one well known and entirely general difficulty in Frege's scheme, a difficulty which has nothing to do with extension-involvingness, namely Frege's supposed need to deny that concept horse is a concept. If the view I take of these things is right, then the reference of 'horse' is indeed something predicative but only in the following restricted sense. The term 'horse' can be combined with the copula and article to give the predicative phrase 'is a horse'. The phrase 'is a horse' is indeed, in Frege's terminology, an unsaturated expression. You can, if you wish, assign the phrase a semantic value. But to say that is not yet to say that the predicative

---

[17] What then does it turn on whether concept C_1, is or is not the same as concept C_2? The question is difficult (indeed impossible if we are confined within Frege's object-language), but the difficulty is not one that we bring down on ourselves by exercising an escapable option to speak or not speak of concepts. Concepts are not philosophical artefacts. They are general things we are already committed to thinking about when we quantify (as we frequently do) over what predicates stand for. For some important contributions to the proper (that is the piecemeal) treatment of the problem, see Hilary Putnam, 'On Properties', in *Philosophical Papers*, vol. 1: *Mathematics, Matter and Method* (Cambridge: Cambridge University Press, 1975).

phrase has a reference. Without permission from Frege, I declare that the predicative phrase 'is a horse' isn't what has the reference. 'Horse' is what has the reference. In other words, the way back to the truth that the concept *horse is* a concept is to take the presence of the copula seriously and distinguish 'horse' from 'is a horse'. If I say that there is something that Victor and Arkle both are, then the thing they both are is *horse*, not *is-a-horse*. What we quantify over are simply concepts. But a concept is the sort of thing which we can connect to a subject of discourse by linking a subject term and a predicate term by the copula. The concept has a predicative role because it plays such a role in predication but, pace Frege, it is complete in itself, not unsaturated.[18]

There is much more to say on this subject, as there is on the analogy that Frege wanted to see between predicates and functors, but the time has come to sum up and move on to the next stage, which is to show how easily the deictic theory can be placed at column 3 within the framework of Fregean semantics.

13. In the case where we can only explain what the reference of a predicate is by something like the method that Putnam describes, because no strict analytical definition exists or could exist, the thing that we who do know the sense of a given substantive have to recapitulate for someone who does not know it is something that we have ourselves learned by commerce in the world at large with the objects that satisfy, fall under, or exemplify the concept. In practice, and so in the theory of this practice, any specification of such a concept will have to depend directly or indirectly on exemplars. That is Putnam's point. But surely that point does not commit Putnam to think that the exemplars themselves can be given by bare unfocused presentation, unsupported by collateral explanation. (Cf. section 4 above.) No presentation, one might say, without focus, and no focus without elucidation. When we fix the sense of an expression with a predicative role by giving its reference and give its reference by demonstrating or alluding to exemplars, what we need to impart to one who would learn the sense is both factual information *and* a practical capacity to recognize things of a certain kind, the information sustaining and regulating the recognition, and the recognition making possible the correction and amplification of the very information that first sustained the recognition. What we need to impart, we might say, is an identificatory or recognitional conception. So to grasp the sense of a natural kind term is to be party to a recognitional conception that is unspecifiable *except* as the conception of things like this, that, and the other specimens exemplifying the concept that this conception is a conception of.

---

[18] For the semantics of the copula and other aspects of the difficulties that Frege encountered with the concept *horse*, see my *1984*, pp. 126–43.

14. At this point it may be objected that what I have just claimed isn't the same as what Putnam claimed. I shall attend to that in a moment. And there may be a more basic disquiet—disquiet at the fact that, if you follow my suggestion about accommodating the doctrine of extension-involvingness, then you will find yourself saying: 'that which supports the sense of the substantive "horse" is a certain identificatory conception of the concept *horse*'. Is this not an intolerable convergence in terminology? I shall attend to the first of these two worries only in the course of allaying the second.

15. The convergence of 'conception' and 'concept' is ugly perhaps but it doesn't signify any confusion. It is clear what the terms 'conception' and 'concept' mean here, and it is clear what they have to do, namely, quite different work. But not only that. It is perfectly possible to replace the term 'conception'. There are at least three ways of doing this, each of them illuminating in its own way.

16. In the first place, we can replace the term 'conception of the concept horse' by saying with Evans that there are two 'ways of thinking about' the concept of horse—or (in effect) about horses.[19]

17. The second possibility applies chiefly to natural kind words and the like. It is to replace the word conception by Putnam's word 'stereotype'. Or should this be doubted?

At the beginning of his article 'Is Semantics Possible?', Putnam introduced the deictic theory by saying that in order to impart the meaning of a thing-kind word one has to impart certain central facts, the stereotype and the extension. But what did Putnam mean by stereotype? And what did he think was the relation of stereotype and extension? When Putnam spoke of the stereotypes that support our normal understanding of the meaning of thing-kind words, he may sometimes have been thinking of something like the little engravings one finds in dictionaries such as the old *Larousse*. (Indeed such engravings are full of theoretical interest in these connections. They are reminders of what deixis has to do in bringing language up to the world and the world up to language.) Normally, however, what Putnam means by a stereotype is a fund of ordinary information or a collection of idealized beliefs that one needs to grasp in order to get hold of the meaning of a thing-kind word. So a stereotype is rather like what you find—or one proper part of what you find—in the text of a good dictionary or encyclopedia (which is not of course to say that it resembles an analytical definition).

What then must be the relation between the stereotype and the extension? Putnam himself was insistent that the core facts that determine the meaning of a

---

[19] See Gareth Evans, *The Varieties of Reference*, ed. John McDowell (Oxford: Clarendon Press, 1982), ch. 1.

thing-kind word were two separate kinds of fact, as if the stereotype could be explained or specified in a manner entirely independent of the question of its extension. The extension was the special province of experts and what belonged to it could be dark to possessors of the stereotype. But there is something strange in this separation. Of course the stereotype is different from the extension, but this is not to say that the first can be explained without any allusion to the second. To defend his own way of separating stereotype and extension Putnam himself claimed that he possessed the stereotype of elm and the stereotype of beech but didn't know the difference between an elm and a beech.[20] Reports have it that (mischievously, no doubt) he has studiously defended this ignorance over decades in order to defend his opinion that one can understand a word by grasping the stereotype without having any grasp of what the extension is. Nevertheless, if Putnam is as vague as he says he is about the difference between an elm and beech, then I think one has a good right to doubt the *degree* of his comprehension of these words. If he entirely lacked the capacity to tell elms and beeches and to distinguish them, then there would be something that he was missing. To insist that this thing he is missing is nothing *semantic* might become an upholder of the separation of language from the world or of the old understanding of the analytic–synthetic distinction. But these are separations that Putnam's own work has done so much to discredit. Would it not be better to say that the stereotype is the stereotype of this or that concept and that grasping the stereotype represents the beginning of an identificatory capacity, a capacity that the expert manifests more completely than the non-expert? In the case of the non-expert the capacity can be rudimentary, but surely it is identificatory. It is a capacity which could *advance* to the point where it became the capacity of an expert.

18. There is a third way to avoid saying that the conception which supports the sense of the word 'horse' is a conception of the concept horse. This is to redraft one's description of the whole situation in terms inspired by Leibniz's theory of clear and distinct ideas. The thing we most badly need here is what Leibniz called a clear but confused (i.e. non-distinct) idea.

In Leibniz's account of ordinary human knowledge, a clear idea of horse is not an image or a likeness of horse. It is that by the possession of which I recognize a horse when I encounter one. (What clarity in an idea contrasts with is not confusedness or non-distinctness, but obscurity.) A clear idea of horse is confused (or non-distinct) if, even though I can recognize a horse when

---

[20] Hilary Putnam, 'The Meaning of "Meaning"', in *Philosophical Papers*, vol. 2: *Mind, Language and Reality* (Cambridge: Cambridge University Press, 1975).

I encounter one, I cannot enumerate one by one the marks which are sufficient to distinguish that kind of thing from another kind of thing. My understanding is simply practical and deictic. What I possess here I possess simply by having been brought in the right way into the presence of the thing. ('Being brought into the presence of a thing' translates Leibniz's own words.)[21] Our idea of horse will begin to become *distinct* as we learn to enumerate the marks that flow from the nature of a horse and that distinguish a horse from other creatures.

What Leibniz shows us how to describe here is nothing less than the process by which clear but indistinct knowledge of one and the same concept begins life anchored by a stereotype to examples that are grouped together by virtue of resemblances that are nomologically grounded. But then, as it grows, this knowledge gradually unfolds the concept in a succession of different and improving ideas (or conceptions—as we might have said). Rather than tell again the old Lockean story of nominal and real essence and face again the question what, if anything, makes them essences of some one and the same thing, we can now describe the process by which a clear indistinct idea is replaced by a clear more distinct idea, and then by a clear more adequate idea.[22]

This brings me to my last remark. When we reconstruct the first stages of the process, from the moment where there is ground to credit language-users with possession of a stereotype for horse, and ground to credit them with possession of a stereotype of the very same thing as we have a better and more informative stereotype for, and when we reflect that at that stage there could scarcely have *been* any experts—well, we may think that strictly speaking, what Putnam wanted to stress was not the necessity of experts but the necessity of the possibility of experts.[23]

---

[21] See 'Meditationes de Cognitione, Veritate et Ideis', Gerhardt, IV, p. 422; *Discourse on Metaphysics*, Gerhardt, IV, sections 24–5; *New Essays on Human Understanding*, trans. and ed. Peter Remnant and Jonathan Bennett (Cambridge: Cambridge University Press, 1981), pp. 254–6.

[22] But only in a sense of 'adequate' that must (I hold) be purged of certain Leibnizian preoccupations, e.g. the idea that, at the limit, as human knowledge approximates to God's knowledge, a posteriori knowledge will be able to be replaced by a priori demonstration.

More generally, and against the idea that extension-involvingness itself only reflects a stage in the development of scientific understanding, see *S&S*, pp. 210–13.

[23] At page 283 of his 'Comments & Replies' in Peter Clark and Bob Hale (eds), *Reading Putnam* (Oxford: Blackwell, 1994) Putnam points out that what I say he should have said, he had *always* said.

9

The *De Re* 'Must', Individuative Essentialism, and the Necessity of Identity

I

Preamble

Between 1974 and 1979, I published a series of multiply overlapping studies (1974, 1975, 1976b, 1976d, 1976e, 1980d) concerned with identity, necessity, essence, and a position that I defended in *Sameness and Substance* (and still defend) under the name of *individuative essentialism*. This doctrine derived from the general idea that the essential properties of a thing are part and parcel with what it takes for that very thing to be singled out from the rest of reality, and all of a piece with the necessary conditions for one who conceives the thing under a variety of counterfactual circumstances not to lose hold of that very thing while seeking to conceive it under this or that variation from its actual circumstances.[1] The present chapter consists of a sequence of extracts selected and arranged to present two or three trains of thought in which these pieces participated. In advance of the extracts themselves, I begin by setting out some of the arguments that connect them.[2]

---

[1] See *S&SR*, pp. 108, 121, 127. Could these criteria diverge? The thought was that it is our understanding of the first that sustains our grasp of the second. On these matters see now Nicholas K. Jones, '*Object* as a Determinable', in Mark Jago (ed.), *Reality-Making* (Oxford: Oxford University Press, 2016), pp. 121–51.

[2] Among the extracts, the footnotes are numbered consecutively and no longer have their original footnote numbers. In Extract Five the propositions originally numbered (4) and (5) have been renumbered as (14) and (15) to separate them from Kripke's propositions (4) and (5) discussed in Extract Three.

In order to make the extracts self-sufficient and make plain their connections, a variety of omissions and additions (marked where significant by square brackets) have been made, some of them substantial.

It is sometimes represented that there is a 'choice' to be made between an ontology-cum-ideology of substance and an ontology-cum-ideology of events and processes along a world-line in space-time. See Extract One. Here I think one will be wise to hold back from the automatic assumption that such different ways of thinking and inquiring are simply bound to find out and confront in reality the very same things or kinds of thing. (See Chapter 1, sections 15–16.) Suppose, for instance, that we are persuaded by Bertrand Russell as he is reported in Extract One and, on that basis, we take against the ontology of substances. What, if anything, should we think then, in our role as Russell's new disciples, about (say) the human being Socrates? In so far as any such subject is there to be discerned within Russell's preferred ontology, Socrates can only be a logical construction from events or processes. (Cf. Chapter 1, sections 14–15.) But can one say that such a construct is essentially and necessarily a man? Human beinghood is inherent in the individuation of Socrates the substance. But can the very same apply in the case of the logical construction? How do I think of myself as a logical construction?

This is not the place to try to advance that particular question beyond the doubts rehearsed at Chapter 1, section 15, and the pluralistic reflections of section 22 of the same chapter. For something else comes first. We need a more complete understanding of the *de re* 'necessarily'—the 'necessarily' that essentialists apply so apparently freely and so frequently. Moreover, where not all essentialists explain themselves in the same way, the defender of individuative essentialism will have in the end to explain how he can start from the business of singling out a thing or tracking it and then advance so quickly from there to a modal claim about how the thing *must be in itself.*

Here we arrive at Extract Two. Suppose you try to conceive of Socrates while withholding from him the fundamental sort *human being.* Suppose you put aside the answer to the Aristotelian question *what is it?* and look instead to the mathematics of spatio-temporal continuity to identify and track this subject. Then in a whole variety of cases the result is a very poor fit with the judgements that we actually make about the objects we recognize and are familiar with. Pace Eli Hirsch, I think we need something much more specific to the kind of thing we are singling out. Or so I argue in the second extract. Continuing from there, I remark that Hirsch and I are agreed that what it takes to track a given object is central to the question of individuation; but then, where he looks for something rather general to guide or regulate the business of tracking a thing through space and time, I myself think one should work outward from a much more specific thought, the thought that the given object is—for some f that answers the question *what is it?*—this very *f*. What then remains of the idea of tracking that object? Well this. To complete that specific thought about the *f* in question will involve nothing less than an account of the kinds of *alterations, shifts and actions or reactions* that one who sought to track that kind of object would have to be ready to pursue it through. Where Socrates is the object in question, the principle of activity and the mode of being of the thing is that of a human being. Nothing could count as Socrates' escaping into some other mode of being. Transposing that into the material mode one may say Socrates cannot help but be a human being.

So far so good. But how are we to understand modalities such as these? If any modalities are *de re*, surely these are. How then do they work? What others are there? Another variant on the same theme is surely the 'necessarily' that we encounter in Ruth Barcan's formal argument for the conclusion that, if x is y, then x is necessarily y. (If x is y, one might ask, then how can x help but be y?) If, as it appears, this is the very simplest case of a *de re* 'necessarily', let us try to understand this case too.

Extract Three begins with Kripke's careful presentation of the Barcan theorem to the effect that $x=y \rightarrow \Box\, x=y$. In its own terms, the proof is faultless. Yet it confronted the doubt or scepticism of a considerable body of considerable philosophers—to name but a few, E. J. Lemmon, W. V. Quine, A. J. Ayer, and Ian Hacking (see Extract Four). Salient among the various reservations that Barcan's and Kripke's defence of Barcan's theorem provoked, there were two questions: first a question about apparent counterexamples to Barcan's result, and second, a question whether the open sentence 'necessarily identical with x' can determine the genuine property that is invoked at step (2) of the Barcan derivation. As we shall see, there is a link between these problems.

We learn from the conclusion of the Barcan derivation as Kripke presents it in Extract Three that, if Hesperus is Phosphorus, then Hesperus is Phosphorus in every possible world (or in every possible world in which Hesperus or Phosphorus exists). It does not matter—it does not count against this conclusion—that the identity itself is an empirical discovery. Seeking to soften the strangeness of such a claim, Barcan Marcus urges us to liken planet-names such as 'Hesperus' to logically proper names—that is to simple 'tags' which are devoid of further content beyond standing for the object that the name gets its sense by designating. As a claim about names of planets, however, there is something implausible in the comparison with a bare tag. It is true that neither 'Hesperus' nor 'Phosphorus' is a definite description. But each name is associated with one or another particular conception of the planet Venus, a morning conception in the case of Phosphorus and an evening conception in the case of Hesperus. Oughtn't these conceptions to suffice for the construction of a possible world that counts against Kripke derivation of the necessity of identity?

The Babylonians, reportedly the first people to consider the question of Hesperus and Phosphorus, decided eventually that Hesperus *was* Phosphorus. But in debating the question before it was decided, mightn't one Babylonian have spoken like this to another?

'One possibility is that that heavenly body that goes down with the sun in the evening [Hesperus] should still accompany it when it returns the next morning from the East. But that of course is only one possibility. There is another. Maybe, after the sun goes down and we can no longer see it, another heavenly body joins up with the sun and leads it back to us at dawn. In that case, what we see in the morning, the body we call the light bearer [Phosphorus], is a quite different celestial body from that which we see escort the sun over the western horizon at the end of the day. We are quite ignorant of what the celestial bodies do when they are out of our sight.'

On the basis of his (4)—see Extract Three—Kripke can, of course, protest that one of these supposed possibilities, even before it is released from the primitive ideas and the improbabilities we are imagining a Babylonian deploying, is simply impossible. Kripke can insist that there are not two possibilities here, only one. Yes, that can be said—once (4) is secure. Indeed, once (4) is secure, we can sharpen our understanding of what to count as a possible world and define rigid designation just as Kripke defines it.[3] Moreover, once (4) is secure, the very idea of a possible world can be purified. But at *this* point in the argument, is (4) yet *available*? Well, not everybody thinks so. As matters stand, counterexamples seem to stand in its way, counterexamples which can create (and did once create) the suspicion that semantical difficulty must lurk in the very idea of a modal property such as that which yields Miss Barcan's theorem.

Here we arrive at the second reservation concerning that theorem. Twenty years before Kripke took his stand, W. V. Quine had doubted what could make it unconditionally necessary that, if there were life on the Evening Star, then there would be life on the Morning Star. Quine was not alone in this doubt. For it was

---

[3] A designator such as 'Hesperus' (or 'Phosphorus') is rigid according to Kripke in the sense that it designates the very same thing in every possible world in which it designates anything. This rules out from the start the alternative that the Babylonian speaker claims to envisage. But is it all right to rule it out as soon as this? Doesn't Kripke need (4) *before* he can rule it out?

standard opinion that identities such as that of the Evening Star and the Morning Star were contingent. Extract Four cites the opinions of E. J. Lemmon and A. J. Ayer.[4]

In order to assess claims such as these on behalf of the contingency of identity, it may be useful to return to Quine's original text[5] and to consider the would-be Leibnizian but evidently problematical inference:

Necessarily (7 < 9)
9 is the number of the planets
Necessarily (7 < the number of the planets).

The inference depends upon the open sentence 'is necessarily less than x' determining a genuine predicate. But how *can* it determine a genuine predicate, Quine asks, if substitution for x of different designations of the same thing yields sometimes a truth but sometimes a falsehood such as we find in the third line of the foregoing derivation? (There was never any necessity that there should be more than seven planets.) So Quine says that the presence of the word 'necessarily' induces a kind of intensionality which he calls referential opacity. It follows, he claims, that

> Being necessarily or possibly thus and so is in general not a trait of the object concerned, but depends on the manner of referring to the object. (p. 148)

In other words, the truth or falsity of a sentence of the form 'necessarily S is P' depends, given the particular predicate P, upon how the subject S is specified. In so far as there is any such necessity as *de re* 'necessity', there can be nothing more to it than a *de dicto* 'necessarily' that is governed by the principle I have just quoted from Quine's p. 148.

There is one last hope for the *de re* 'must', Quine then says, and a last hope for 'Aristotelian essentialism'. It involves finding some principled way of favouring some one particular description over other descriptions of the object that is in question. In the case of the inference just rehearsed the essentialist would

---

[4] Contemplating a different kind of example, Ian Hacking asked how it could be necessary rather than contingent that Hacking, a philosopher at that time harmlessly occupied in analytical philosophy, should twenty years from thence be one and the same person as 'a vicious cardsharper called Doncaster' who we know, from 'a crystal ball employing physics not magic', would be around twenty years from thence. 'I assert [Hacking wrote] that in this story "Doncaster" and "Hacking" are being used as proper names, that H=D, but H *could have...been* other than D.' See Ian Hacking, 'Comment on David Wiggins's "Identity, Necessity and Physicalism"', in Stephan Körner (ed.), *Philosophy of Logic* (Oxford: Blackwell, 1976), pp. 147–8.

[5] Willard Van Orman Quine, *From a Logical Point of View* (Cambridge, MA: Harvard University Press, 1953), pp. 139–57.

naturally prefer the canonical designations '9' or 'nine' over the designation 'the number of the planets'. On some such basis an essentialist can try to find some way to discredit the unwanted inference just rehearsed while preserving those that he favours.[6] But there is no question, Quine suggests, once we depart from the world of numbers or similar abstracta and we engage with concrete things, of justifying any parallel system of preference there.

Rather than watch the essentialists try to challenge the last claim, let us revert to a much more fundamental consideration concerning the would-be Leibnizian inference that Quine puts in front of us. Let us distinguish names or simple designators ('nine', '9') from definite descriptions ('the number of the planets'), insist that the definite descriptions of ordinary language have *scope*, and distinguish two different possible placings of 'necessarily' with respect to the scope of 'the number of the planets'. (Compare the third extract, third paragraph.) On these terms the Quinean inference appears manifestly fallacious, as Smullyan pointed out.[7] The most we can obtain from Quine's premises is the harmless conclusion 'for some x, x numbers the planets and anything that numbers the planets is x, and necessarily $7 > x$'.

Advancing from this point, let us look at a parallel inference that Quine invites us to consider. It begins from the truism

Necessarily, if there is life on the Evening Star, there is life on the Evening Star.

But, mindful of Smullyan, let us replace descriptions by names and reformulate the sentence using only the name 'Hesperus'. Let us start from the truism

Necessarily, if there is life on Hesperus, there is life on Hesperus.

Now consider the open sentence 'Necessarily if there is life on Hesperus then there is life on x'. If that open sentence stands for a genuine property or attribute, then Hesperus has it. But then Leibniz's Law and the mere fact that Hesperus is Phosphorus suffice to give:

Necessarily, if there is life on Hesperus, then there is life on Phosphorus.

---

[6] According to the individuative essentialist, it is indeed a test of someone's veritably conceiving the number nine that they should locate it within the number series *two steps after* seven, and something similar can surely be contrived—he will say—with empirical examples. But, as we shall see in one moment, Smullyan (see note 7) offers the essentialist a more immediate and better response to Quine's argument.

[7] See Arthur F. Smullyan, 'Modality and Description', *Journal of Symbolic Logic*, 13 (1948), pp. 31–7. Cf. also Dagfinn Follesdal, 'Essentialism and Reference', in Lewis E. Hahn and Paul Arthur Schilp (eds), *The Philosophy of W. V. Quine* (La Salle; IL: Open Court, 1986), pp. 97–113.

On the conditions stated the inference is valid. Nevertheless, according to Quine, the conclusion is simply false. It is false because Hesperus (he says) is only contingently Phosphorus. What to blame? Quine blames the supposed modal property on which the inference depends. The 'necessarily' in the open sentence that purports to define that property induces an opaque context. Whether or not a sentence of the form 'necessarily...' is true must depend upon how the objects in question are specified, etc. There is no question here of *de re* necessity.

At this point, followers of Barcan and Kripke will declare that, given the evident validity and plain meaning of the inference that employs proper names, not descriptions, and given that no considerations of scope can complicate things, everything accords entirely with Kripke's defence of the Barcan theorem. They will insist that there is nothing wrong with the inference.

Contingency theorists will say that they *can* conceive of a world where Hesperus and Phosphorus are distinct, one planet inhabited and the other not inhabited. Kripke will respond by ridiculing the contingency theorists' claim to describe the possibility of Hesperus' and Phosphorus' being distinct. But in the absence (as yet) of (4), that is not so easy as previously it seemed. Kripke may appeal here to his doctrine of rigid designation. The idea of designation seems unproblematic but, in so far as 'rigid' adds anything (see note 3 above), what it adds is not independent of (4) either.

In the papers of mine represented by the extracts reprinted here, I wanted to re-examine Quine's intentionality objection, to try to answer it in its own terms, and *then* to restore (4). Noticing how natural it sometimes is to prefer 'it is impossible *for Socrates* not to be a human being' over saying 'Necessarily Socrates is a man', 'Socrates is necessarily a man', or 'it is impossible that Socrates be not a human being',[8] I thought I saw the way forward. Could one not take the 'necessarily' in 'Socrates is necessarily a man' not as a sentence-adverb governing a whole sentence (it was this that suggested that the subject-term would lie within the scope of an operator that could induce opacity), but as qualifying *only* the application of the property of manhood to the subject Socrates? Representing the property of being a man as (λx)(man x) and seeing 'necessarily' not as governing a sentence but as signalling that property's manner or mode of inherence, I replaced '□' by 'NEC' and rewrote '□(Man(Socrates))'

---

[8] Compare Ian Hacking, 'All Kinds of Possibility', *Philosophical Review*, 84 (1975), pp. 321–37; see also Extract Four.

thus: NEC[λx (Man x)] <Socrates>. In other words, it is necessary for Socrates to have the property of being a man. He cannot help but be a man. And, similarly for the context of identity, I said that in 'Hesperus is necessarily Phosphorus' the 'necessarily' governed not a whole sentence but only the application of the identity relation to the subjects of the sentence. What the sentence says of Hesperus and Phosphorus is that they must be the same/cannot help but be the same.[9]

In Extract Four these thoughts are applied to the Barcan proof by the provision of a proof of the necessity of identity in which the subject-positions are not open even to a suspicion of opacity. Formulation and proof are given there in second-level terms. Here is a more perspicuous first-level version.

(1λ) Hesperus and Phosphorus are such as to be identical. [Fact]
(2λ) Hesperus and Hesperus are necessarily such as to be identical. [Truism]

Putting x here for (say) the second occurrence of 'Hesperus', we have the open sentence

(3λ) Hesperus and x are necessarily such as to be identical.

Given the simple truth of (1λ) and the non-opacity of the frame (3λ) and given Leibniz's Law, we can take Phosphorus as a value of x and obtain

(4λ) Hesperus and Phosphorus are necessarily such as to be identical.

Since the necessity of identity can be settled entirely intuitively, as it now appears, without there being any question of opacity and without any reference at all to the theory of possible worlds, this finding can *then*, in its turn, shape the theory of possible worlds. In the light of the new version of Kripke's (4), we have now to *expect* that empirical facts concerning particular identities can constrain the construction of possible worlds. We must not be surprised if some however harmless-looking world-specifications are excluded from entering into the determination of any genuine possibility at all.

---

[9] Quine himself had had a similar idea in 'Quantifiers and Propositional Attitudes', *Journal of Philosophy*, 53 (1956). In that essay Quine introduced the suggestion that, in addition to the ordinary use of 'say' governing a whole sentence and creating there an opaque context, we need another use of 'say' by which someone can *say of* something x identified in whatever way (this may remain unspecified) that it, x, is F. *Saying of* is then a three-place relation between the sayer, the object, and the attribute $\hat{x}$ (Fx)—or, as I might prefer to write, λx(Fx)—which is said of the object. (It will be a tetradic relation where the speaker attributes λxy(Rxy) to two subjects, as the speaker would in the utterance λxy(loves x,y), <Peter, Paul>...) Thus construed, *saying of* was innocent even of the possibility of creating opacity.

II

This last finding, independently established, coheres very well with a number of other Kripkean insights. See Extract Six. Some philosophers, Leibniz and David Lewis for instance, have supposed that, if in a certain possible world someone called Caesar did not cross the Rubicon, then *that* Caesar cannot be the same Caesar as the historical Caesar, only a sort of counterpart. Others such as Hintikka explored the view that identities must be determined from whatever information is provided concerning the world in question. But Kripke takes a third and more plausible view. According to Kripke, we construct in thought a possible world in which we place the real Caesar—at the same time altering Ceasar's decision in 49 BC to cross the Rubicon. In the process of constructing the alternatives to the actual course of events, we speculate about what else would or might in that case have happened. But all the time we know who we are speculating about. It is *our* construction and it is up to us to say who or what it relates to.

In Chapter 4 of *Sameness and Substance Renewed*, I point out that, even though we do not have to speculate about which Caesar it is who figures in the possible world that we are constructing, we cannot place the real Caesar we are concerned with in just any possible world or conceive of Caesar's doing just anything! We have to respect something I call the anchor constraint. (See *S&SR*, pp. 121, 131.) It is not certain that there are no other constraints. There is a temptation to look for a perfectly general theory of possible worlds sufficient to endorse as possible or else to exclude as impossible, on grounds wholly integral to it, any putative possible world that presents itself for consideration. But on reflection one sees that this must be a mistake. We have seen that we must not construct a possible world in which there is life on Hesperus without there being life on Phosphorus. But such exclusions, like others not here entered into, depend crucially upon empirical discoveries. And empirical discoveries are endless and endlessly diverse. Bare logic underdetermines the possibility of worlds.

III

In the decade or so represented by the extracts that are given here, it seemed important that a proper answer be mustered to Quine's contention that modality can induce a referential opacity which would obstruct both the Barcan theorem and philosophical essentialism. I believed that I had arrived at such an answer. But the satisfaction I felt with that answer is qualified by justifiable complaints some make about the uncertain prospects for constructing a proper logic for NEC, read as a predicate modifier.[10] I have not even attempted to create such a logic. I can, however, conclude by noting certain constraints and suggestions (α) (β) (γ) (δ) to which I have committed myself.

(α) See the last sentence of Extract Four (to follow). Within a context governed by NEC, can we not expect NEC-identicals to be intersubstitutable?

(β) See the last paragraph of Extract Six and consider the would-be scientific claim

(i) $(\forall x)(x$ is necessarily such that if x is a human being then x is such as to be G)

where G is some phylogenetic or genomic determinable. Then consider the the historical claim

(ii) Julius Caesar was such as to be a human being

and the characteristically essentialist claim

(iii) Julius Caesar was *necessarily* such as to be a human being.

Now let us muster the natural or intuitive thought that, where one property implies another property, the necessity of the first will imply the necessity of the second. Compare the axiom of modal propositional logic $(\Box(p \to q) \& \Box p) \to \Box q$. If there is room for some formal proposition (iv) corresponding to that thought within the construction of a logic of NEC, then we can conclude

(v) Julius Caesar is necessarily such as to be G.

If there is such a property as G, then essentialism must perhaps make itself more interesting by seeking to join forces with the findings of empirical science.[11]

(γ) I note that, if we pursue the line I have just suggested, then, given the claim (i), we shall have to widen the rationale that I first announced for the *de re* 'must'. The original rationale invoked the close proximity of a *de re* property of a thing to the basis on which the object with that *de re* property was, under a whole variety of circumstances, to be individuated. But the proposition (i) is concerned with the further property of being necessarily such as to be *either* not human or G.

---

[10] See for instance the reasonable complaint of Peter Simons at note 9 on page 240 of his *Parts: a Study in Ontology* (Oxford: Clarendon Press, 1987). For a substantive contribution to this question, see Stephen Williams's Oxford DPhil thesis 'Meaning, Validity and Necessity' (1985). See also Christopher Peacocke's 'Appendix' to *Wiggins 1976b*.

[11] For the difficulties that stand in the way, see Elliott Sober, 'Evolution, Population Thinking and Essentialism', *Philosophy of Science*, 47 (1980), pp. 350–83, and Samir Okasha, 'Darwinian Metaphysics, Species and the Question of Essentialism', *Synthese*, 131 (2002), pp. 191–213.

(δ) Another point to be remarked is how in (i) above, where we have a claim in the form (∀x)(x is NEC such that x is either not human or else G), one is brought one step closer to a quite different question. This is the question of the relation of NEC read as predicate modifier to NEC read in grammatical engagement with a closed sentence. Should we take NEC as modifying the *truth* of that closed sentence? (There are paradoxes here to be avoided.) Or does NEC in adjunction to a closed sentence '...', mean that all objects are necessarily such that...? Or what? It is a good question, but maybe the right question to begin with is an earlier one, namely why the *de re* 'necessarily' that NEC introduces must mean *anything at all* in adjunction to a closed sentence. A further question I have not treated concerns the deductive relation between claims involving NEC and claims involving □.

Extract One

(FROM 'THE *DE RE* "MUST": A NOTE ON THE LOGICAL FORM OF ESSENTIALIST CLAIMS', IN GARETH EVANS AND JOHN MCDOWELL (EDS), *TRUTH AND MEANING: ESSAYS IN SEMANTICS* (OXFORD: CLARENDON PRESS, 1976B), PP. 285–9)

'Necessity does not properly apply to the fulfilment of conditions by objects (such as the ball of rock which is Venus or the number which numbers the planets), apart from ways of specifying them.' So Quine writes in 'Reference and Modality'.[12] A little later in the same article he writes 'This means adopting an invidious attitude towards certain ways of specifying x... and favouring other ways as somehow better revealing the 'essence' of the object... Evidently this reversion to Aristotelian essentialism is required if quantification into modal contexts is to be insisted upon'.

Quine mocks essentialism. But are his strictures levelled at unreflecting acceptance of the ancient Aristotelian ontology of three-dimensional changeable continuants in terms of which we are still doing our unthinking best to make sense of the everyday fabric of the world? Or does he maintain that, *even while we remain within that provincial ontology of ours*, we have the choice to discriminate or not to discriminate invidiously in favour of some of the concepts which the things we recognize fall under: that we can somehow avoid giving pre-eminence to concepts constitutive of what it is to be this or that very kind of continuant—giving

---

[12] Quine, *From a Logical Point of View*, p. 151. Note also p. 148: 'To be necessarily greater than 7 is not a trait of a number but depends on the manner of referring to the number.' For the solution to Quine's paradox of the number of the planets see A. F. Smullyan, 'Identity and Description', *Journal of Symbolic Logic*, 13 (1948), pp. 31–7 and Richard Cartwright, 'Identity and Substitutivity', in Milton K. Munitz (ed.), *Identity and Individuation* (New York: New York University Press, 1971).

prominence to 'essences', natures, and answers to Aristotle's *what is it? question*?[13]

Quine's intention is not completely clear to me. But if it were to suggest the second of these two things, then I should object that nothing less than a universally agreed and deeply rooted system of deliberate discrimination in favour of substance-concepts and/or essences, and against what are rated mere accidents, could explain the *definiteness* with which our culture has had to contrive to invest questions of persistence and identity through time.[14] Nor could anything less than this kind of discrimination account for the measure of unanimity with which scientific discoveries—in biology, zoology, ecology, for instance, as well as in everyday life—are deployed to find objective answers for questions that involve what philosophy calls substances.

In anti-essentialist writings one of the most striking admissions of the claims I have just made is to be found in Russell's chapter on 'Aristotle's Logic' in his *History of Western Philosophy*. As a statement of an archetypal idea from which so much of the anti-essentialism—and indeed the anti-Aristotelianism—of modern philosophy derives, it deserves extended quotation:

Socrates may be sometimes happy, sometimes sad; sometimes well, sometimes ill. Since he can change these properties without ceasing to be Socrates, they are no part of his essence. But it is supposed to be of the essence of Socrates that he is a man.... [But] in fact, the question of essence is one as to the use of words. We apply the same name, on different occasions, to somewhat different occurrences, which we regard as manifestations of a single 'thing' or 'person'. In fact however this is only a verbal convenience. The essence of Socrates thus consists of those properties in the absence of which we should not use the name 'Socrates'. [But this] question is purely linguistic: a *word* may have an essence, but a *thing* cannot. The conception of 'substance' like that of 'essence' is a transference to metaphysics of what is only a linguistic convenience. We find it convenient, in describing

---

[13] Cf. Willard Van Orman Quine, *Word and Object* (Cambridge, MA: MIT Press, 1960), p. 92: 'We in our maturity have come to look upon the child's mother as an integral body who, in an irregular closed orbit, revisits the child from time to time'. Question: Do we have any alternative but to see the child's mother in such a way? Maybe nothing compels us to find or apprehend the child or the child's mother. But, once we do apprehend them, there is scarcely any alternative but to see the child's mother in the way Quine describes. Some philosophers seem to suggest that we have the 'choice' of conceptualizing or not conceptualizing what we come across in our experience in such a way as to articulate such entities as women and their children. It may have been the purpose of some essentialists to deny that there is any such choice of conceptual scheme, but it is not my purpose. My chief purpose is to suggest that to confuse the question 'do we have any alternative but to see the child's mother in the way Quine describes?' with the question 'do we have the choice to conceptualize or not to conceptualize what happens to us in our experience in such as way as to articulate such substances as women and their children?'—and try then to transform a negative answer to the first into a negative answer to the second—is to perpetuate confusion.

[14] Cf. *ISTC*, Part One, p. 7 and Part Two, pp. 30–4, a passage justly criticized by Shoemaker and wholly amended for *S&S*. See also *Wiggins 1974*.

the world, to describe a certain number of occurrences as events in the life of 'Socrates' and a certain number of others as events in the life of 'Mr Smith'. This leads us to think of 'Socrates' or 'Mr Smith' as denoting something that persists through a number of years, and as in some ways more 'solid' and 'real' than the events that happen to him.... [But] he is not... really any more solid than the things that happen to him. 'Substance' when taken seriously is a concept impossible to free from difficulties... 'Substance' in fact is merely a convenient way of collecting events into bundles... What is Mr Smith apart from... occurrences? A mere imaginary hook, from which the occurrences are supposed to hang. They have in fact no need of a hook, any more than the world needs an elephant to rest upon.... 'Mr Smith' is a collective name for a number of occurrences. If we take it as anything more, it denotes something completely unknowable, and therefore not needed for the expression of what we know. 'Substance', in a word, is a metaphysical mistake due to transference to the world structure of the structure of sentences composed of a subject and a predicate. I conclude that the Aristotelian doctrines with which we have been concerned in this chapter are wholly false, with the exception of the formal theory of the syllogism, which is unimportant.

Allowing Russell 'convenience' as a name of what is a virtual necessity, and waiving several small points such as the age-old confusion of a substance with a we-know-not-what (the suppositious survivor of a hypothetical process of removal of 'mere attributes', presumably as 'not really' the substance's attributes), I find much as an essentialist to applaud in this passage. The ontology of substances, in terms of which we view ourselves and one another and the medium-sized landmarks of human existence, is indeed in the peculiar but agreed sense a convenience. For all I know, Russell and other philosophers with a powerful talent for logical construction really could dispense with this ontology and then—all across the board!—adopt in its place some purer and more homogeneous ontology of processes and events.[15] But it is the virtue of Russell's account as I see it that he has no consistent desire to deny, and does seem to assert, that, *if* we *insist* on availing ourselves of the convenience of the ontology of continuants (which strictly he thinks we should not, but *if* we do), then we shall commit ourselves to conferring a special role upon the essences that cohere with the principles of continuity of the continuants which are articulated in that conceptual scheme. That is meant to be one of the objections to the ontology of continuants. It is true that Russell's anxiety to cast doubt on the echt existence of so second-grade an existent as Mr Smith or Socrates—note the imperfectly executed project of scare-quoting all the occurrences of their names—induces him to declare that the question is purely linguistic. ('A *word* may have an essence but a *thing* cannot'—which by no means follows from

---

[15] For more on this see Chapter 1, sections 13–15.

Socrates or Mr Smith's being in the peculiar but agreed sense a convenience.) But Russell's real purpose is to advertise the claims of a *superior* ontology.

The matter is utterly different with the other and later philosophers, numbering perhaps thousands, who in middle-of-the-road fashion have resisted Russell's ontological prospectus. They have preferred to discuss ordinary continuants like Socrates or Mr Smith or his briefcase rather than, say, successions of events along a world-line, yet persisted in the idea that there is nothing more than convenience or confusion in the essential role that Aristotelean philosophers such as myself assign to *man* in the individuation of Smith or Socrates. What I am emphasizing is that their position is not Russell's position. But it is characteristic of the philosophers I have in mind to view with deep suspicion, *without* rejecting or defying Socrates or Mr Smith themselves as individual continuants, the essentialist contention that, whatever else these substances may be, they are necessarily men. If any philosophers believe in a substrate of *we know not what*, it must I think be these latter day anti-essentialists. Certainly they are bad heirs to Russell. Without even noticing what they are doing, they have shifted the question of 'convenience' to a new place. They have transferred it from the point of embracing or not embracing the continuant ontology as a whole—which is where Russell more or less put it—to the entities themselves which that world-view articulates. But, in seeming to allow that Socrates and Mr Smith—and hence they themselves?—need not be men (could then be anything?), they threaten the operation of the only ontological scheme through which they can even think of or refer to Socrates or Mr Smith.

There is of course one respect in which I sympathize with the philosophers I have just mentioned. If the three-dimensional continuant ontology must make a distinction of essence and accident, as Russell and I seem agreed that it must, then that is more than sufficient excuse for some obstinate interest—whether friendly or hostile—in what on earth it means to make claims such as *Socrates must be a man* or *Socrates is necessarily a man* or *Socrates cannot help but be a man*.

Extract Two

(FROM 'ESSENTIALISM, CONTINUITY, AND IDENTITY', SYNTHESE, 28(3-4) (1974), PP. 323-4)

Eli Hirsch remarks[16] (p. 39) that the spatio-temporal and qualitative continuity of a certain, never unoccupied, spatio-temporal path is not enough to guarantee that the path defines some one space-occupying object. 'Let Q be the space-time path traced according to the following rule: at any time *t* between 12 00 and 12 05,

---

[16] Eli Hirsch, 'Essence and Identity', in Munitz (ed.), *Identity and Individuation*, p. 39.

Q contains just that portion of some tabletop that is directly below your [constantly moving] hand at t.' His response to the problem posed by Q starts out where mine would. He draws attention to the role of sortal words. But then, instead of developing that answer—e.g. by reference to the causal and dispositional properties of the kinds that we recognize and the principles of activity or functioning that shape these kinds[17]—and instead of using that to exclude bad candidates for persistence, Hirsch moves into an attempt to fix up the whole difficulty perfectly generally, without any reference to natural kinds, by recourse to the mathematics of continuity. He instantly collides with the problems of part-subtraction and part-addition, of intermittent manifestation, and of homeomerous entities (such as the Pope's crown[18]). It is the real if unintended virtue of Hirsch's piece to reveal a quite general difficulty in any purely mathematical definition of spatio-temporal continuity with pretensions to match our intuitive notion of what it is for this f to persist, to change or to coincide with that f. It is doubtful however that any search for one single or general criterion of persistence can succeed.[19]

Extract Three

(FROM 'ESSENTIALISM, CONTINUITY, AND IDENTITY', PP. 324 FOLLOWING)

Kripke observes that some have been disturbed by the following derivation.[20] Begin with Leibniz's Law

(1) $(x)(y)(x = y \rightarrow (Fx \equiv Fy))$.

As one instance of (1), provided that the letter F may stand proxy for such modal properties of objects as *is necessarily identical with x*, we get

---

[17] Cf. *S&S*, ch. 3 and *S&SR*, ch. 3.

[18] He does consider 'dissective' entities (cf. Nelson Goodman, *Structure of Appearance* (Indianapolis, IN: Bobbs-Merrill, 1966), p. 53), *f*-entities all of whose parts are *f*. He gives them a special and separate status connected with the category of mass terms. But *f*s which are not strictly dissective but simply have *f*s as parts (cf. *ISTC*, pp. 39–40, 60–1) may be substances, and they are equally disruptive of Hirsch's revised definition of continuity. For that reads: *a* is the same *f* as *g* iff *a* is instanced on *P* at t_1 and *b* is instanced on *P* at t_2, and *f* is instanced on every point of *P*, where *P* is a continuous path in the following sense (cf. p. 41)—for any time t_0 in *P* there is a time interval *I* around t_0 such that any *t* in *I* the (extended) place for *P* at time *t* overlaps the (extended) place for *P* at time t_0.

[19] The search continues in *The Concept of Identity* (New York: Oxford University Press, 1982) where Hirsch argued for the basic rule: 'trace an object's career by following a spatio-temporally and qualitatively continuous path of the object which minimizes changes as far as possible'. Can this rule be interpreted in isolation from well-established substance concepts as we know them? I would also ask: why try to minimize change?

For my further doubts that an account of spatio-temporal continuity *as such* can assist any would-be general account of identity, see Chapter 1, sections 8 and 9, with note 17.

[20] See Saul Kripke, 'Identity and Necessity', in Munitz (ed.), *Identity and Individuation*, pp. 135–64.

(2) $(x)(y)(x = y \to (\Box(x = x) \equiv \Box(x = y)))$.

But by the truth of $(x)\Box(x = x)$—reading $\ulcorner\Box\varphi a\urcorner$ as saying that $\ulcorner\varphi a\urcorner$ is true with respect to any world containing a[21]—and by the consequent superfluity of the third clause, viz,

(3) $\Box(x = x)$,

(2) must entail

(4) $(x)(y)(x = y \to \Box(x = y))$.

But how, it has been asked, can this be accepted? If we must normally discover identities empirically, they cannot be true necessarily.

Kripke's reply may be seen as falling under two heads: (A) he shows how to find a way to accept (4); and (B) he shows why one should want to accept (4).

(A) Sentence (4) generalizes upon the case where we have a particular identity statement made by the use of names or demonstratives. Where identities are stated by means of definite descriptions, and where a sentential operator such as 'not' or 'necessarily' is present, we must according to Kripke pay careful heed to matters of scope. Consider

(5) The first Postmaster General of the United States is identical with the inventor of bifocals.

Kripke insists that it is a contingent matter that (5) is true—and that this does not count against (4).

Indeed if we treat (5) in accordance with Russell's theory of definite descriptions, then the only consequence we will draw [from (4)] is that there is an object x such that x invented bifocals, and (as a matter of contingent fact) an object y such that y is first Postmaster General of the US, and, finally, it is necessary that x is y. What are x and y here? Here x and y are both Benjamin Franklin and it can certainly be necessary that Benjamin Franklin is identical with Benjamin Franklin. So there is no problem if we accept Russell's notion of scope. That Russell's distinction of scope eliminates modal paradoxes has been pointed out by many logicians,[22] especially Smullyan.

---

[21] Cf. Kripke, 'Identity and Necessity', p. 137: 'Let us interpret necessity here weakly. We can count statements as necessary if whenever the objects mentioned therein exist, the statement would be true.'

[22] Kripke refers here to Arthur Francis Smullyan, 'Modality and Description', *Journal of Symbolic Logic*, 13 (1947), pp. 31–7, reprinted in Leonard Linsky (ed.), *Reference and Modality* (London: Oxford University Press, 1971), pp. 35–43. In this connection note also Richard L. Cartwright, 'Some Remarks on Essentialism', *Journal of Philosophy*, 65 (1968), pp. 615–26.

In other words, all (5) should lead us to expect, if we follow Russell's theory of descriptions, is

(5') $(\exists x)(\exists y) [(w)(\text{FPMG}w \equiv w = x) \& (z)(\text{IBF}z \equiv z = y) \& (\text{necessarily } (x = y))]$.

The necessity attaching to the third clause of this expansion of (5) results from intersubstituting what (4) demonstrates to be equivalents.

Most of the residual resistance to the idea of (4)'s holding will rest, according to Kripke, on a confusion of the categories of *necessity* and *a priority*. If x is necessarily y then x *must be y, cannot not be y*. But to say this last, which is a metaphysical claim, is not the same as to say that x's identity with y is *a priori*. By *a priori* is or should be meant that this can be told independently of all experience. (That is an epistemological claim and irrelevant to (4).) The supposed coextensiveness of the metaphysical and the epistemological claims would 'require some philosophical argument to establish it'.

(B) When these obstacles are cleared away, what is there positively to recommend (4)? Well, there are still (1) and (3), which on Kripke's view do no less than entail (4). Any sentence (1') or (3') which instantiates either (1) or (3) with regard to entities a, b is manifestly *about a, b* themselves, not the senses of their names, or their associated concepts, or their 'counterparts' in other worlds, or about anything at all other than a and b.

Kripke is not the first to have wished to champion (4). Ramsey supposed that true statements of the form '$a = b$' would have to be necessary truths.[23] Ruth Barcan Marcus, who was the first to present a formal derivation of (4), has long accepted this conclusion and defended it on lines strongly reminiscent of *Tractatus Logico-Philosophicus* 4.243.[24] That passage depends on a special view of proper names, however. In Kripke's argument, the proper names which are in question are common or garden ones, naturalistically viewed. His position depends not at all on the distinction between logically proper names and other proper names. It depends, he says, on the distinction between rigid designators, such as proper names or functors like '$\sqrt{25}$' (p. 144), and 'non-rigid designators'.

---

[23] Frank Plumpton Ramsey, *The Foundations of Mathematics and Other Logical Essays*, ed. R. B. Braithwaite (London: Kegan Paul, 1931), pp. 59–60.

[24] See Ruth Barcan Marcus, 'Modal Logics I: Modalities and Intensional Languages', in Marx W. Wartofsky (ed.), *Boston Studies in the Philosophy of Science: Proceedings of the Boston Colloquium for the Philosophy of Science 1961/1962*, vol. 1 (Dordrecht: Reidel, 1963), pp. 77ff.; Ruth C. Barcan, 'The Identity of Individuals in a Strict Functional Calculus of Second Order', *Journal of Symbolic Logic*, 12 (1947), p. 15.

A designator is rigid (p. 145) if and only if it designates the same object in all possible worlds. So equipped Kripke argues as follows (p. 154).

> If names are rigid designators then there can be no question about identities being necessary, because 'a' and 'b' will both refer to this same object x, and to no other, and so there will no situation in which a might not have been b. That would be a situation in which the object which we are now also calling 'x' would not have been identical with itself... One could not possibly have a situation in which... Hesperus would not have been Phosphorus.

[*Comment (2014–15)*. This argument of Kripke's quickly became canonical, and it has remained so. In the period from which the extracts that make up this chapter derive, I wanted to make two remarks about it.

First, Kripke's argument is complete without the penultimate sentence, which were best removed. See Extract Five below, second paragraph.

Secondly, the necessity of identity can be established without appeal to Kripke's however useful idea of rigid designation. See Extract Four below, the penultimate paragraph, which makes it possible to derive the necessity of the relation of identity simply and directly from Leibniz's Law without reference to theories of possible worlds or theories of reference. The argument is in the material mode. It will be exempt moreover from all doubts concerning the intensionality of 'necessarily'.]

Extract Four

(FROM 'REPLY TO THOMAS BALDWIN: CONTINGENCIES, IDENTITY, AND *DE RE* AND *DE DICTO* NECESSITY', IN JONATHAN DANCY (ED.), *PAPERS ON LANGUAGE AND LOGIC: THE PROCEEDINGS OF THE CONFERENCE ON THE PHILOSOPHY OF LANGUAGE AND LOGIC HELD AT THE UNIVERSITY OF KEELE IN APRIL 1979* (KEELE: KEELE UNIVERSITY LIBRARY, 1980), P. 40)

It would be wrong for me to write as if all contingency theorists had said exactly the same things about the Barcan proof. So I have chosen E. J. Lemmon, as he represented himself in lectures I attended in the early 1960s in Oxford (some of the relevant material appears in *APQ Monograph* No. 11, 1977, pp. 8–10) and A. J. Ayer as he still [1979] represents himself.

Lemmon objected to the conclusion of the Barcan derivation; and the 1966 *Lemmon Notes* still cite as the cause of the 'paradox' the 'intensionality' of the context 'Necessarily $(a = x)$', which Lemmon says may be true of a but not true of b even where a is b. At about the time of his Oxford lectures he wrote:

'x=y' may be true, even though x has an attribute y has not got. Thus the morning star, though it is the evening star, has the attribute of being necessarily the morning star, which the evening star does not have. This consequence will be unpalatable to many, but I believe it to be a paradox of intensionality that should be accepted on a par with the paradoxes of infinity that we have now come to accept... Indeed, in view of Quine's arguments, it may be viewed as the price we pay for quantifying into modal contexts. (*Acta Philosophica Fennica* 1963, fasc. 16)

A decade later, A. J. Ayer wrote (see his contribution to Asa Kasher (ed.), *Language in Focus: Foundations, Methods and Systems* (Dordrecht: Reidel, 1976), pp. 3-24):

If the object is designated by the numeral '9', it does satisfy the predicate [of being necessarily greater than 4]; if it is referred to simply as 'the number of the planets', it does not... Objects do not have necessary predicates except in virtue of the way that we describe them... Sentences of the form 'A is B' where 'A' and 'B' are proper names are almost invariably contingent and not necessary propositions. The explanation is very simple... those for whom the information is intended either possess answers to only one of the questions 'who or what is A?' and 'who or what is B?', or possess answers to both of them, but largely different answers... [i.e. their sense is different]... What then becomes of the argument that, since being necessarily identical with x is a property of x, it must be a property of y if x and y are identical? Since the conclusion that identity statements of the form x is y are always necessary is false, ... one of the premises must be false... I deny that being necessarily identical with x is a property of x because I deny that there is any such property as that of being necessarily identical with x... To say that a property necessarily characterizes such and such an object is just a way of saying that some sentence which predicates the property of the object expresses a necessary proposition, and whether this is so or not depends on the way in which the object is designated... The sentence 'a is necessarily identical with b' will express a necessary true proposition only if the propositions which are expressed by the sentences 'fa' and 'fb', whatever predicate 'f' may be, are also logically equivalent.

At the time of writing the pieces that Baldwin has cited, it seemed to me that the right way to proceed against these positions was to disabuse Ayer of the idea that all propositions of the form 'The F is F' are necessary propositions in the fashion presupposed to his metalinguistic reductions of the modalities of natural language; and then to present both Lemmon and Ayer with a derivation of the necessity of identity exempt from problems of intensionality or referential opacity. These problems can only arise if, as Quine supposed, the modal adverb '*necessarily*' governs a sentence rather than a constituent predicate. But let us confine the scope of the adverb to the predicate. Consider any individuals H and P (Hesperus and Phosphorus, say) such that

(7) H = P

184 THE *DE RE* 'MUST'

Then it follows by Leibniz's Law that, for all F such that F is a genuine property of P or of H,

(8) F <H> ≡ F <P>.

Now H is necessarily H. So the following is a truth about H:[25]

(9) [NEC[λxλy(x = y)]], <H, H>;

and, the scope of this NEC being confined to the abstract, there then exists the abstractable property of being necessarily identical with H or[26]

λz[NEC[λxλy(x = y)], <H, z>].

But H itself has this property. So

(10) [λz[NEC[λxλy(x = y)], <H, z>]], <H>.

and whatever applies to H applies to P. So

(11) [λz[NEC[λxλy(x = y)], <H, z>]], <P>.

Then applying the λ-conversion rule—to infer back and forth between φ(t) and (λx)(φx)< t >—we can simplify and obtain

(12) NEC[λxλy(x = y)], <H, P>

(12) is not put forward here as a necessarily true statement. It is put forward as a true statement of *de re* necessity. For a first level version of this whole inference, see (1λ)(2λ)(3λ) ⊢ (4λ) justified in the last paragraph of Part I of the Preamble to the present chapter. See p. 172.

I claimed in the writings that Baldwin reviews that this proof and its generalization to all objects x,y that are identical is unobstructed by the suspicion that 'necessarily' can create an opaque context. The proof is exclusively concerned

---

[25] The formula ensuing may be read as follows:

H and H stand necessarily in the relation in which x and y stand just where x is the same as y.

For fuller explanation, see the Preamble to the present chapter, section I, the last paragraph, where a first-level and altogether more readable version is given (λ1)(λ2)(λ2) ⊢ (λ4) of the argument (7)(8)(9) (10)(11) ⊢ (12) that is displayed here.

[26] The formula ensuing may be read as follows:

The property that z has just where z and H stand necessarily in the relation in which x and y stand just if x is the same as y.

A first level equivalent might run as follows:

z is such that z and H together are necessarily such as to be the same.

with objects and their properties. All substitutions in the proof are on manifestly extensional positions, lying outside NEC. (But the proof itself does something to relax the preoccupation with extensional position. For it sets free the modal intuition that even within a context governed by NEC we should expect NEC-identicals to be intersubstitutable.)

Extract Five

(FROM 'REPLY TO THOMAS BALDWIN', P. 36 (EDITED AND EXPANDED SUBSTANTIALLY))

Baldwin dislikes my use of the lambda notation. I used this for two separate reasons, which (since I shall persist with it) I had better recall here.

First reason. It seemed important to distinguish 'Hesperus is Hesperus' from 'Hesperus is itself'.[27] The latter distinguishes Hesperus from nothing else whatever. For everything is itself. On the other hand, following on from the first sentence 'Hesperus is Hesperus', I can add *only* Hesperus is Hesperus. Nothing else is Hesperus. When *Reference and Generality* appeared, I tried to represent such differences by using Geach's diagrammatic notation for reflexive pronouns. But Timothy Smiley pointed out in his review of *Reference and Generality* (in *Philosophical Books* IV, 1963) that one could get the same effect by λ-abstraction, and trouble the printer less. When the lambda notation is employed the truism

(14) Hesperus is Hesperus

becomes

(14′) $[\lambda x \, \lambda y \, (x = y)]$, <Hesperus, Hesperus>

whereas

(15) Hesperus is itself,

---

[27] A full commentary upon the last citation from Kripke in Extract Three would avail itself of the same distinction, as would any response to *Tractatus Logico-Philosophicus* 3.5303, where Wittgenstein wrote

> Roughly speaking, to say of two things that they are identical is nonsense, and to say of one thing that it is identical with itself is to say nothing at all.

Disregarding the ontology of simple objects which was Wittgenstein's particular context, some who still want to deny that identity is any sort of relation have availed themselves of this passage. Disregarding Wittgenstein's context in the same way as those proponents do, let us dispose first of Wittgenstein's first claim. Concerning two things, Hesperus and Neptune, for instance, I can say that they are identical. That is false. It couldn't be false if it were *nonsense*. What then of the second claim? Does one who says that Hesperus is Phosphorus (or Hesperus is Hesperus) really say that Hesperus is itself? No. It is an astronomical and interesting finding that Hesperus is Phosphorus.

arising from the truism (14), becomes

(15′) [λ*x* (*x* = *x*)], <Hesperus>.

It may be objected that it is logically impossible for (14) and (15) to diverge in truth-value. Yes. The claims are in that sense logically equivalent, but they are semantically distinct. This appears so soon as we precede each with the word 'only'. Only Hesperus is Hesperus, yes, but it is not the case that only Hesperus is itself. Everything is itself. The sentences (14) and (15) simply don't *mean* the same. Logical transformation does not have to preserve sense.

The second interest I had in abstraction was that, once it became possible to abstract upon open sentences of arbitrary complexity in the formation of non-modal predicates, one could go on to see 'necessarily' as in effect qualifying the copula and signifying the *mode of inherence* of such arbitrarily complex properties in the objects that possess them. Thus [as already remarked in the Preamble and elsewhere] we can form the sentence 'Socrates has λ*x*(Man *x*)', that is [λ*x* (Man *x*)], <Socrates>, and then form the further sentence '[NEC[λ*x* (Man *x*)]], <Socrates>' and read that as saying that Socrates necessarily has [λ*x* (Man *x*)]. Or else, even better, we can count that as saying that *for Socrates* it is necessary to be a man. The name 'Socrates' is no more within the scope of this necessity than it is within the scope of 'had' in 'Socrates had to drink the hemlock', which says (truly or falsely) that Socrates had no legal or physical alternative but to drink it. But, in the cases we are concerned with here, what we find is an *individuative* necessity, a necessity arising from the very being of Socrates, rather than a legal or physical necessity.

A supplementary and quite different advantage then came to light from lambda abstraction. This was the perspicuity with which it can mark modal asymmetries and discriminate between the claim that the class α, which has as its members the Eiffel Tower and the Crystal Palace, must contain the Eiffel Tower, which is true if α does contain it, and the false claim that the Eiffel Tower which is a member of α must necessarily be a member of α.[28] The class α needs the Eiffel Tower but the Eiffel Tower doesn't need the class α. Nec[λ*x* (Eiffel Tower ∈ *x*)],<α> but not Nec[λ*x*(*x* ∈ α)],<Eiffel Tower>. It is true that this distinction can be made more laboriously within the orthodox systems by the insertion of extra existence conditions. But these insertions can only aggravate the difficulty of relating □ to the natural language adverb 'necessarily'. Theories of modality will not flourish by postponing this sort of problem indefinitely.

---

[28] See *S&S*, pp. 112–15 and *S&SR*, p. 118–21.

Extract Six

(FROM 'ESSENTIALISM, CONTINUITY, AND IDENTITY', PP. 332–6)

What relation must x_i in possible world W_m bear to x_k in world W_n if x_i is to be identical with x_k? Hintikka spoke for many scholars when he said[29]

Each possible world contains a number of individuals with certain properties and with certain relations to each other. We have to use these properties and relations to decide which member (if any) of a given possible world is identical with a given member of another possible world.

It is this point of view which has led to the search for individual essences, haecceitates, particularized forms, etc. But it is difficult to see any reason to hope that by making predicates longer and more and more complicated we shall be able to overcome the obvious non-sufficiency, or evident non-necessity, for purposes of identity with just x_k, that infects all the other relatively simple predicates true of x_k. Disappointment in the search for a more complex and adequate specification of the essence of x_k either gives rise to 'counterpart' theory,[30] which means we are not thinking about what we suppose we are thinking about when we entertain subjunctive conditionals, or else threatens disillusionment with possible worlds as a vehicle for philosophical understanding.

Fortunately Kripke offers a striking observation which tells against Hintikka's view of the whole problem. Possible worlds are not things we discover or observe with a telescope. They are constructions which *we* who entertain and explore the suppositions to which they correspond *make for ourselves*, using our ordinary names and predicates. There is no more problem, according to Kripke, about identifying the individuals about which we are making suppositions than there is about identifying the properties and relations which enter into the supposition. If one cannot even use Julius Caesar's *proper name* to think through what would have happened if Julius Caesar (the victim of Brutus, the conqueror of Gaul, the consul of 59 BC) had not crossed the Rubicon, then what on earth can one use?

Within the possible world approach, this observation [fortified, I like to suggest, with the vindication given in Extract Four of the necessity of identity] is enough to justify Kripke's treating proper names as rigid designators. All the same, as Kripke recognizes, constructivism concerning possible worlds does not carry us to the end of the whole problem. For we cannot insert just any individual we wish into just any arbitrary role in any possible world we please. It is not open

---

[29] Jaakko Hintikka, 'The Semantics of Modal Notions', *Synthese* 21 (1970), pp. 408–24.
[30] Cf. David K. Lewis, 'Counterpart Theory and Quantified Modal Logic', *Journal of Philosophy* 65 (1968), 113–26, criticized in Kripke, 'Identity and Necessity', p. 147.

to us to construct the possible world in which Julius Caesar is a clay pipe or a paddle steamer or the number fifty-seven. Until we spell out the restrictions upon the construction of possible worlds, we shall have an incomplete understanding of them.

The required constraints on possible world construction appear to fall under two heads in Kripke, constraints of *make-up* or of *origin* and constraints of *thing-kind*. (By the *thing-kind of x* I mean the answer to the Aristotelian question 'what is x?'.)

Under the first head, Kripke claims that, given that a certain lectern is not made of ice, is in fact made of wood, one cannot conceive of any possible circumstances under which this very lectern is made of ice.

It could have been in another room...but it could not have been made from the very beginning from water frozen into ice (p. 152).

One certainly could have made a lectern of water from the Thames, frozen it into ice by some process, and put it right there in place of this thing. If one had done so [however] one would have made of course a very different object. It would not have been this very lectern...the question whether it could afterwards, say a minute from now, turn into ice is something else...In any counterfactual situation of which we would say this lectern existed at all, we would have to say that it was not made from water (p. 153).

There is a little more in Kripke's Princeton lectures about the difference between such attributes as *being in this or that room* and *not being made of ice*.[31] We also find there a discussion of the supposed necessity that a given person should have sprung from the very sperm and egg which he did spring from.

What right would we have to call this baby from completely different parents—in what sense would she be—*this very woman*? One can imagine, *given* the woman, that various things in her life could have changed. One is given, let us say, a previous history of the world up to a certain time, and from that time it diverges considerably from the actual course. This seems to be possible. It is possible, even though she were born of these parents, like Mark Twain's character who was switched off with another girl. But what is harder to imagine is her being born of different parents. It seems to me that anything coming from a different origin would not be this object. (p. 314)

The argument is more suggestive than explicit—I react to it simply as an agnostic—but it would appear to comprise two strands. The first strand seems to be this.

Ordinarily when we ask intuitively whether something might have happened to a given object, we ask whether the universe could have gone on as it actually did up to a certain

---

[31] Saul A. Kripke, 'Naming and Necessity', in Donald Davidson and Gilbert Harman (eds), *Semantics of Natural Language* (2nd edn, Dordrecht: Reidel, 1972), p. 314ff., with footnotes 56, 57, 58.

time, but diverge in its history from that time forward so that the vicissitudes of that object would have been different from that time forth. *Perhaps* this feature should be erected into a general principle about essence.[32]

Here I ask: can there really be a *general* prohibition on 'backward' conditionals? It is not even obvious that possible worlds have to be arrived at by a process of modification of states of the actual world—especially where laws of nature are respected. But very likely, Kripke's contentions are intended to touch only those backward conditionals which concern particular (and therefore actual) individuals. Here too though we are left groping for his argument. Somehow it must show that, unless we respect the prohibitions against backward conditionals, we 'lose' the very object we mean to be speculating about. What is this argument?

Kripke asks 'by what right' one would call a person sprung from different sperm and egg 'this very woman'. If this implies that every counterfactual speculation about Julius Caesar (for instance) involves the thinker who undertakes it in establishing his *title* to call the individual concerned Julius Caesar, then this is dangerously close to the positions of Hintikka and others. But this problem we have seen reason to applaud Kripke's method of avoiding. We do not have to find something *in virtue of which* the object of speculation is Julius Caesar. Let me go one step to meet Kripke however. Perhaps the speculator has to be able to *rebut* the charge that he has actually lost his subject of discourse if he changes the subject's parents or origin. But I ask can he not *rebut* the charge by claiming to speculate about how *the man whom Brutus murdered in 44 BC* would have fared if (say) Marius had been his father? To rebut the charge of losing the individual perhaps there must always be available to the speculator, *consistently with his speculation*, some such explanation of which man he means by Julius Caesar. But even if this principle were self-evidently just—which is perhaps contestable—does it favour any particular specification of who Julius Caesar is? Must it favour a specification (say) of the sperm and egg he sprang from? There is something here it would be good to understand better.

Another constraint which Kripke puts upon possible world construction (though on this he lays lighter stress) is the *thing-kind* of the individual concerned. Here the rebuttal principle which we have tentatively suggested does indeed suggest a useful way of exploiting another thought to which Kripke gives voice: 'I am not suggesting that only origin and substantial make-up are essential. For example, if the very block of wood from which the table was made had instead been made into a vase, the table never would have existed. So (roughly)

---

[32] Kripke, 'Naming and Necessity', p. 351 n. 57, l. 20.

being a table seems to be an essential property of the table'. This is a different and perhaps much more familiar thought. Suppose we extend it in the following way. A thinker who entertains a contrary-to-fact speculation about Julius Caesar must leave himself room to rebut the charge that he has lost Caesar. This Roman consul need not have been consul, need not have been Roman, need not have been male perhaps..., but, unless anything might be anything, there must be some f such that, no matter what else he is, he can be picked upon as *this f*. And what else can f stand for here than the most general sortal specification of the object which is capable of individuating it, fixing its existence or persistence condition and answering the question 'what is it?'/'which one is it?'.[33] Perhaps there must be some true description to make clear *which f* is in question, and this description must not be inconsistent with the speculation. But, as already remarked, there is no particular description which must remain available beside f and whatever is entailed by f. Or so it may seem.

---

[33] Cf. the discussion of ultimate sortals at *ISTC*, p. 23 and *S&SR*, p. 65 n. 8.

10

Mereological Essentialism and Chisholm on Parts, Wholes, and Primary Things

1. In *Person and Object* Roderick Chisholm holds that *entia per se* or primary things such as persons are the only real continuants and comprise the only substances which you can single out at different times and say of them 'in the strict and philosophical sense' that they are one and the same then and now.[1] One of Chisholm's principal extrasystematic grounds for this tenet is his general agreement with Leibniz's claim that 'we cannot say, speaking according to the great truth of things, that the same whole is preserved when a part is lost'.[2] It is Chisholm's total acceptance of this principle—later designated (A3)—that underlies his willingness to demote entities such as ships, trees, and houses, which we see pre-philosophically as continuants gaining or losing parts, to the status of *entia successiva* or *entia per aliud*. These *entia successiva* are logical constructions raised upon the mereological 'stand-ins', faithful to (A3) but ephemeral, that constitute them. *Entia successiva* have their properties derivatively from the properties of these stand-ins. The stand-in h_i for an *ens successivum* house H is succeeded by another stand-in h_j so soon as h_i loses a part. So long as there is a succession of stand-ins for H, H can persist—but only in the *loose or popular sense* that is appropriate for an *ens successivum*; appropriate, that is, for something sustained through other thing(s), an *ens per aliud*.

Chisholm has given a finished form to these doctrines in Chapter III of *Person and Object*. But the doctrines cannot be fully comprehended or appreciated without recourse to Chisholm's views on temporal parts and his mereological

---

[1] Roderick M. Chisholm, *Person and Object: A Metaphysical Study* (London: Allen and Unwin, 1976).

[2] *New Essays Concerning Human Understanding* II.27.11, where Leibniz's actual words are 'selon l'exacte vérité des choses' quoted by Chisholm at *Person and Object* p. 145; compare also the passage of Reid that Chisholm quotes at p. 96; and Leibniz to de Volder (Gerhardt, II, p. 261).

essentialism. These are explained in Appendices A and B of the same book, and the arguments of these appendices are important determinants of Chisholm's theories of these matters.

2. Chisholm's general method of argument for the Leibnizian claim about wholes and parts is to try to show (in his Appendix B) that there is no resting place between it and certain weaker principles proposed for discussion by Alvin Plantinga. (See Chisholm, *Person and Object*, p. 150.) Having shown that none of these weaker principles is quite right, Chisholm cuts matters short[3] and proposes a theory of mereology whose third axiom simply registers 'the great truth of things':

> (A3) If x is an s-part [a part which is a part in the strict and philosophical sense of part, and also a proper part] of y, then y is such that in every possible world in which y exists x is an s-part of y.[4]

Is this axiom true? What would persuade one of its truth? If the variable 'y' ranges over all entities whatever, then it appears false. For, as I shall argue and insist later on, a genuine whole substance surely *can* lose parts and still remain the very same substance, and this is a sense not standing in need of any reconstruction. That is something I shall need to argue for. Meanwhile, though, if we are to assess Chisholm's theory of *entia per se*, and his theory of *entia successiva*, then we need to search out whatever truth there may be in (A3). We need to understand its attractions. And we need to know what Chisholm's other axioms say:

> (A1) If x is an s-part of y and y is an s-part of z, then x is an s-part of z (transitivity)
> (A2) If x is an s-part of y, then y is not an s-part of x (asymmetry)
> (A4) For every x and y, if x is other than y, then it is possible that x exists and y exists and that there is no z such that x is an s-part of z and y is an s-part of z.

After reading these axioms, everyone will want to know more about how wholes are constituted from their parts. What is the conception of wholes and parts that motivates the contention that 'we cannot say that the same whole is preserved when a part is lost'? Doesn't the plausibility or implausibility of (A3) depend entirely on what whole we are considering? (A3) is plausible for the case of a set and its subsets, for a telephone number and its digits, a barcode and its bits, a tune and its principal notes, a staircase, its treads and its risers. But why must all wholes be like this? Short of annihilation even works of art have to suffer *some* depredation of their parts. (See *S&SR*, pp. 136–8.)

---

[3] See, however, *Person and Object*, pp. 221–2 n. 7.   [4] *Person and Object*, p. 151.

3. There is only one way forward, namely to start from the intuitions to which Chisholm gives voice by means of an example that he provides in his Appendix B.

Let us picture to ourselves a very simple table, improvised from a stump and a board. Now one might have constructed a very similar table by using the same stump and a different board, or by using the same board and a different stump. But the only way of constructing precisely *that* table is to use that particular stump and that particular board. It would seem, therefore, that that particular table is *necessarily* made up of that particular stump and that particular board.

But to say of the table that it is necessarily made up of the stump and board is not to say of the stump and the board that *they* are... necessarily parts of the table. And it is not to say that the stump is necessarily joined with the board. God could have created the stump without creating the board; he could have created the board without creating the stump; and he could have created the stump and the board without creating the table. But he could not have created *that* particular table without using the stump and the board.[5]

Such an asymmetry between table T and board B or stump S could be represented in quantified modal logic by distinguishing between the propositions

$\Box$((board exists and stump exists) ⊃ stump is part of table)
$\Box$(table exists ⊃ stump is part of table)
$\Box$(stump exists ⊃ stump is part of table)

while insisting upon the falsehood of the first and third propositions. But a more natural way of rendering the asymmetrical *de re* necessity that Chisholm illustrates by means of this example is this:

Table T is necessarily such as to have stump S and board B as its parts; but neither S nor B is necessarily such as to be a part of T.

More colloquially, one might say in the spirit of (A3) that T needs S and B, but S and B don't need T.

4. Chisholm does not offer table T as a candidate to be an *ens per se* or an *ens successivum*. T is just an example, designed to speak to intuitions available in advance of all theory or philosophy. But this is the closest we come in Chisholm's chapter or its appendices to any illustration of the *positive* philosophical attractions of (A3). His table T does however suggest one possible argument for (A3). The only way I know to develop that argument is to start from Tarski's paper, 'Foundations of the Geometry of Solids'.[6]

---

[5] *Person and Object*, p. 146.
[6] See Alfred Tarski, *Logic, Semantics, Metamathematics: Papers from 1923 to 1938*, trans. J. H. Woodger (Oxford: Clarendon Press, 1956), pp. 24–9. In this Appendix, Chisholm says that (A3) is a basic tenet of the theory of part and whole, but he does not say why that should be so. Nor

In Tarski's presentation we have two axioms:

POSTULATE I. If X is a part of Y and Y is a part of Z, then X is a part of Z.

POSTULATE II. For every non-empty class α of individuals there exists exactly one individual X which is a sum of all elements of α.

'Sum' is defined as follows:

An individual X is called a sum of all elements of a class α of individuals if every element of α is a part of X and if no part of X is disjoint from all elements of α.

Chisholm may complain—see his (A4)—that in his own axiom system he was careful to dispense with anything like Tarski's second postulate. For, contrary to the whole tenor of (A4), Postulate II threatens to give us far too many mereological sums—the sum, for instance, of the number two and the Trojan War, or the sum of Chisholm's left foot and the carburettor of his neighbour's car.[7] We must return to all that. But our first difficulty here is that, apart from offering the illustrative example (table, stump, and board), Chisholm says nothing else to persuade us that the same whole cannot be preserved when a part is taken away.

5. Nothing will be lost and something gained if, rather than give the argument in full generality, we apply Tarski's axiom and the argument directly to the case of Stump, Board, and Table. Consider first the non-empty class {S, B}. Then by Tarski's Postulate II there is exactly one whole X which is the sum of all the elements of {S, B}. S and B are parts of X and no part of X is disjoint from both S and B. See Tarski's definition of sum. Let us call this sum of S and B [S+B]. Conjoining Chisholm's explanations with Tarski's axiom, we reach three equivalent statements:

(*) Table T is the sum of S and B
(**) Table T = [Stump S + Board B]
(***) Table T is such as to be identical with [S+B].

Each of (*) (**) (***) says what T is, namely a sum, but says also *which* sum it is. It identifies T. The identification is no more trivial than is Postulate II. We have parts S and B fused according to that postulate into the whole [S+B]. And we have the table T. And Chisholm finds that [S+B] is the same as T. But if that holds, then let us apply the principle of the *de re* necessity of identity in the form

---

does he address the thought that, if (A3) were taken for a necessary and sufficient ground for identity, generalized and applied next as grounds for the identity of parts, then regress would threaten.

[7] See *Person and Object*, p. 219 n. 4 and p. 222 n. 11.

for all *x* and all *y*, if *x* is such as to be the same as *y*, then *x* is necessarily such as to be the same as *y*.⁸

Conjoining this with (***) we now have the necessity *de re*

T is necessarily such as to be identical with [S+B]

and this implies, given the definition of 'sum',

(****) T is necessarily such as to have as its parts S and B.

Compare now (A3) and the so-called 'great truth of things'. What we have here is a sort of argument for (A3).

In this argument, what is the underlying conception of parts and wholes? In the light of Chisholm's discussion one might say: T is S and B simply assembled together or simply thought of together, and conceived as making up a whole thing, something larger but on the same ontological level as its constituents. T is the simple aggregation of S and B. The only way to recognize or reidentify such an aggregation is by its members.

At this point, one remarks that, if (A3) is secured in *this* way, then (A4) is a lost cause. For the justification of (A3) just given promises no limit to aggregation. Whatever *x* and *y* may be we can always dream up (conceive of) something that is their aggregation within some *further* thing. Witness Tarski's Postulate II. So if our concern is to secure (A4), then the part–whole relation will have to be made more demanding than we conceived it to be when giving the argument for (A3).

6. Can one get closer to what Chisholm wanted, namely the truth of (A3) *and* (A4), if we give 'part' a more specific sense while formulating some restriction of Postulate II? Shall we say in the interests of (A4) that the existence of Table T depends upon S and B's being such as to allow and invite their being *fitted together*? On this construal of 'part', it becomes harder to conceive of anything being made from and having as its parts the number two and the Trojan War or Chisholm's left foot and a carburettor. These are not things to be fitted together. Then (A4) becomes more plausible. How does the new construal affect (A3)? Maybe we can try to restrict Postulate II to components that go together but still let Chisholm have his way with T and [S+B]. Maybe there is no T without precisely S and B, where S and B go together. Perhaps so much still holds good for that particular case. But in the effort to attain greater generality, consider now a new object U whose parts do cohere but cohere in a more complex structure than T subserving a more demanding purpose than the table T subserves.

---

⁸ See *S&SR*, ch. 4.

Suppose that U is the sort of structure that can be serviced, repaired, refurbished as well as traced, stored, inventoried, etc. Suppose U is a machine. Can the structure U really not be individuated without reference to *each and every* component? Do we really lose U by changing a bearing or two or a wheel or a coil? It may be insisted that *most* of the original parts must (strictly speaking) remain for the structure to remain. But even that is not enough to guarantee (A3) or the 'great truth of things'.

7. In a word, the more undemanding the part–whole relation we are concerned with, the better the prospect for Tarski's Postulate II and the better the prospect for (A3) but the worse for (A4). The more specifically the part–whole relation is understood, the better the prospect for (A4) but the worse for (A3) and the worse for the idea that no whole can persist through the loss of any of its parts. The sad thing is that (A3), which is the foundational principle for Chisholm's whole philosophical theory, now seems mismatched with the ontology of primary things or primary wholes, or genuinely continuant substances or artefacts such as U. The natural companion of the alleged great truth of things appears to be an ontology of aggregations or Tarskian sums of elements. Mereological essentialism as Chisholm conceives it is the natural ally not of the philosophy of substance but of classical extensional mereology.[9]

Consider now a human being. A human being is not an *ens per aliud* or *ens successivum*. A human being is not a logical construction or something raised upon a whole sequence of distinct stand-ins, but a proper continuant. As Chisholm says,

> there is no reason whatever for supposing that I hope for rain in virtue of the fact that some *other* thing hopes for rain—some stand-in which, strictly and philosophically, is not identical with me but happens to be doing duty for me at this particular moment.[10]

A human being is a primary being or an *ens per se.* But is a human being subject to Chisholm's (A3) or to (****)? How can it be? A human being can lose a finger or a leg—the finger or leg can be amputated and, if you insist, incinerated or annihilated—without prejudice to the human being's being singled out or individuated, without prejudice to persistence, and without prejudice to survival as

---

[9] This affinity becomes further apparent in David Lewis, *Parts of Classes* (Oxford: Blackwell, 1991). Lewis affirms a principle cognate with (A3) which he calls uniqueness of composition ('it never happens that the same things have different fusions'). But the difficulty that I have urged against Chisholm will not apply to Lewis because in Lewis's ontology there are no primary things such as Chisholm postulates. Lewis's ontology allows no endurance, only perdurance. (See in this volume Chapter 1, section 12, and Chapter 3, section 10.) Where Lewis differs from Chisholm is in his careful rejection of (A4) and his insistence upon the Axiom of Unrestricted Composition. That insistence is all of a piece with Lewis's single and uniform conception of the part–whole relation.

[10] Chisholm, *Person and Object*, p. 104.

the same human being or *ens per se*. It might be claimed that a finger or a leg is really an *appendage*—that the *ens per se* for which (A3) holds good has a lesser extent than the whole human body. But how small is one prepared to make the *ens per se*? And how can proper sense be made of characteristic human activities, dancing, playing the piano, hitting a ball..., if the great truth of things commits us to see hands, fingers, or legs as mere appendages? It is a high price to pay for (A3) if it requires us to see a hand, a finger, or a leg as metaphysically speaking a sort of *prosthesis*.

8. The mismatch between (A3) and Chisholm's philosophical aims extends further. For (A3) shapes and motivates not only his conception of *entia per se* but also his conception of the *entia successiva* which are sustained or 'constituted' at each moment by stand-ins that do obey (A3). The result is a theory of *entia per aliud* that bears an uncanny resemblance to something that Chisholm firmly and convincingly rejects, namely the theory of temporal parts. (See Chisholm's Appendix A.) How different can the stand-ins be from temporal parts?

In so far as one is not convinced by (A3)—the great truth of things—or by Chisholm's theory of *entia per aliud*, one may want to persist in the conviction that there are countless favourable cases where ships, trees, houses, etc. lose a part yet persist and remain the same ship, tree, house in as strict and philosophical a sense as you will of the words 'persist' and 'same'.

9. Chisholm began his account of identity and persistence by rehearsing a whole sequence of philosophical puzzles, among them Heraclitus' river, Theseus' ship, the Carriage (involving the gradual but complete exchange of parts between two similar conveyances), and the Mississippi river. Then on the basis of these perplexities Chisholm says approvingly

> Bishop Butler suggested that it is only in a 'loose and popular sense' that we may speak of the persistence of such familiar things as ships, plants and houses. And he contrasts this 'loose and popular sense' with 'the strict and philosophical sense' in which we may speak of the persistence of persons.[11]

Anyone who chooses to quarrel with Chisholm's theory of continuants or the use that he makes of his axiom (A3) incurs an obligation to reveal their own response to the puzzles that shape Chisholm's positive theory and motivate his insistence on the distinction between the strict or philosophical and the loose or popular uses of 'same', 'not the same', 'persist' and the 'is' of identity. I shall seek to

---

[11] Chisholm, *Person and Object*, p. 92. Compare Chisholm's words at the top of page 92: 'Each of us knows with respect to himself that he now has properties he did not have in the past and that formerly he had properties he doesn't have now'.

discharge this obligation by considering from among Chisholm's examples the river of Heraclitus and the Mississippi river, interposing a brief discussion of another even less puzzling example.

10. Heraclitus is commonly reported as saying that you could not step twice into the same river. Chisholm reports him so in his chapter III. But what Heraclitus wrote was this:

> Upon those who step into the same rivers different and again different waters flow. The waters scatter and gather, come together and flow away, approach and depart.[12]

Heraclitus' actual words—once we heed them—show the way forward. Rivers persist through time and stretch across space as 'the same rivers'. Their waters change constantly. You can say, if you like, that rivers are flowing waters. But what that means is that rivers are made up (constituted in a certain way) by water. Better, the river is a changeable but long-persistent feature of a terrain that extends between mountain and sea. It has a lawlike mode of activity by reference to which its several tendencies and varying states can be understood. Helpfully—but neither in his chapter called 'Identity through Time' nor anywhere else where he says that we can only speak in 'a loose and popular way' of a river's persistence or identity over time—Chisholm quotes from Aquinas words about the river Seine that will serve very well in lieu of further commentary:

> 'The Seine river is not "this particular river" because of "this flowing water" but because of "this source" and "this bed" and hence is always called *the same river*, although there may be other water flowing into it; likewise a people is [continues] the same, not because of sameness of soul or of man, but because of the same dwelling place, or rather because of the same laws and the same manner of living.'[13]

11. One further example may serve to reinforce the importance of the *what is it?* question. A man is asked what he treasures above everything else in the world. He replies by embracing one of his own possessions, embracing seemingly a figurine of Athena. Hearing of a fire in his house, you enquire whether the thing that he treasured above all else survived. Yes, he says. It is true that the graven image of Athena was destroyed, but none of the gold it was made from was lost. The ingot which survives is not the same as the figurine but it is the same gold. What we come to realize is that in embracing his dearest possession, the man

---

[12] Fragments 12 and 91, as reunited by Geoffrey Kirk in G. S. Kirk, *Heraclitus: The Cosmic Fragments* (Cambridge: Cambridge University Press, 1954). See this volume Chapter 6, section 2.5.

[13] See Chisholm, *Person and Object*, p. 220 n. 13.

was intentionally and deliberately embracing not the Athena but the gold it was made from.[14]

12. So much for the temporal lifespan of that which persists and that which ceases to exist. Before I conclude, I must say something about one of the spatial puzzles to which Chisholm alludes:

> Puzzles about the persistence of objects through periods of time have their analogues for the extension of objects through places in space. Consider the river that is known in New Orleans as 'the Mississippi'. Most of us would say that the source of the river is in northern Minnesota. But what if one were to argue instead that the source is in Montana, where it is known as 'the Missouri'? Or that its source is in Pittsburgh, where it is known as 'the Ohio', or that its source is further back where it is called 'the Allegheny' or in still another place where it is called 'the Monongahela'?[15]

Chisholm then imagines a lively argument breaking out about where the Mississippi rises, between what points it flows, and about the status of various tributaries—are they or are they not the Mississippi?—remarking that these disputes are 'analogous in significant respects to the problem of the ship of Theseus' and suggesting that, as in so many other cases, our anxieties result from our unfortunate habit of using 'A is B' or 'A is identical with B' in a loose sense but looking for answers that seek to invoke the strict or philosophical sense.

Is there room for another approach? As always we begin by asking *what sort of thing is the thing in question?* Until that is made clearer there is no point in disputation. Is a river such as the Mississippi to be just one stream, or a single stream whose waters rise in different places? Or is it a causally connected system of *many* streams that debouches, either in a single stream or via a delta, into a sea distant from its source or sources? What kind of thing do we *want to talk about* here?

Once we recognize the possibility of different conceptions of Mississippi... or of Nile or Amazon..., and once we review the different hydrological possibilities, there is simply no problem if different thinkers conceive of the running water they see in front of them in different ways and find different answers to the identity question concerning that of which they take these waters to be a part. Once that last is clearer, it will be apparent that they need not be contradicting one another or using 'the same' in a loose sense. Even if some conceptions are more useful or natural than others, there is room within rational thought for

---

[14] The gold in question is a quantity in the sense well explained by Helen Morris Cartwright, 'Quantities', *Philosophical Review*, 79 (1969), pp. 25–42. We have the same gold when there is no addition or subtraction.

[15] Chisholm, *Person and Object*, pp. 90–1.

different conceptions of what sort of thing 'Mississippi', 'Nile' or 'Amazon' stand for. (See Introduction, section 5.) But once the relevant conception is decided upon—and once we find and explore the thing that answers to it—nothing prevents the finding of identity from being at once absolute *and* philosophical *and* popular.

13. *Coda.* Chisholm speaks of an analogy between (say) the ship problem and the Mississippi problem. But there is also a disanalogy or a difference.

In the Mississippi case, there is a choice to be made in the light of hydrological or geographical considerations and these considerations determine what it is most useful to single out. The choice affects the reference. (The shape or extent of what is referred to varies with the thinker's purpose.) In the case of Theseus' ship it is exactly not like that. In 650 BC (say), when Theseus first sailed it, *working ship* and *trireme*[16] subsumed one and the same ship. The working ship *was* a trireme. What we do not have here is a mere aggregate co-occupying a space with an artefact-substance. We have one ship under two descriptions.

Under the auspices of the *what is it?* question we must separate at least two sorts of inquiry:

(1) what sort of thing is it most useful to single out if we are to understand the phenomena we are interested in? Under what concepts shall we search for substances? This is the Mississippi case. (See also Introduction, section 4.)

(2) Having singled something out, how are we to conceive it specifically enough in order to track it, to reidentify it, to find it, to recognize it again? This is the case of the ship.[17]

---

[16] 'Trireme' is an anachronism for the seventh century, but never mind.
[17] See Chapter 2, Postscript and Commentary, and Chapter 1, footnote 38.

11

Sortal Concepts
A Reply To Xu

1. Introduction

Fei Xu argues, in opposition to claims I have made, that 'object' glossed as 'bounded, coherent, three-dimensional, physical object that moves as a whole' stands for a sortal concept in the repertoire of both infants and adults.[1] She says that it plays a foundational role in the formation of the understanding of more specific sortal concepts such as *dog* or *cup*. So far so good (though I shall try to replace her gloss). And in saying this, she commits herself to the idea that, in making sense of the world, infants and adults can deploy an autonomous or self-sufficient understanding of this concept of an object, and that their grasp upon it suffices—and suffices without the tacit or implicit support of any incipient understanding of more specific concepts—for the tracing of objects through space and time and the making of judgements of identity and difference. (Another claim she enters is that this concept of object suffices for purposes of counting. But this last contention, because of the complexity and indirectness of the relationship between counting and making judgements of identity or difference—see *ISTC*, p. 40 and *S&S*, p. 73—I shall adjourn.)

I agree with Fei Xu that the idea of an object plays a foundational role in the emergence of ideas of specific sortal concepts. I agree that it is indispensable to individuative agency and thought. Indeed, saluting her experimental findings, I am prepared to assert on my own behalf that the idea of object is nothing less than an innate idea—in the Leibnizian sense. That is to say that I am ready to number the possession of this idea among our fundamental unlearned or given 'inclinations, dispositions, tendencies or natural potentialities' and our earliest

---

[1] Fei Xu, 'From Lot's Wife to a Pillar of Salt: Evidence that *Physical Object* is a Sortal Concept', *Mind and Language*, 12 (1997).

'endeavours towards action'.[2] I cannot however agree that *object* is a sortal concept. It is rather a *determinable* or *formal* concept and, in that role or function, best not glossed quite as Xu glosses it.

2. What Is At Issue

The chief questions that Fei Xu's various contentions point towards are these, or so I think: could adults—could we, could anyone who was placed outside the special circumstances of Xu's experimental subjects—really operate with the idea of *object* explicated in the way she explicates it (rather than in the way I shall shortly recommend); and (secondly), in so far as they succeed in this, could they really be operating with *object* in a manner entirely independent of incipient understanding of any more specifically sortal concepts?

I say that these must be the important questions because otherwise there is scarcely anything at issue between Xu and the philosophers whom she says she disagrees with—at least in so far as I am one of those. (See further section 5 below.) The formulation of the question at issue is a matter of some delicacy, however, because, according at least to the version that I myself defend of the doctrine that Xu says she disagrees with, any picking a thing out and tracing it through space and time is part and parcel with coming to see it as a thing with some specific way of behaving that needs to be gradually discovered; and according to this neo-Aristotelian version of the sortal doctrine I defend, so soon as one does treat the thing in that way, one is already somewhere en route to a full-blown grasp of some properly sortal concept or other, namely some sortal concept that gathers up some class of things that *tend to move and behave* in certain specific ways, *come into being* in a certain specific way, *survive* certain sorts of change, *tend to be qualified* in certain specific ways, and *tend to cease to be* in certain specific ways...[3] That is the direction in which we are headed (I say) simply as a direct or indirect result of our innate possession of the idea of object. In this framework, which I adapt from Aristotle and Leibniz, specific information under these heads is correlative with increasingly specific answers to the *what is it?* question—'dog', 'snail', 'horse', 'tea cup', 'bottle', or whatever. Compare *S&S*, chapter 3; compare also my *1995d* (= Chapter 3); and

---

[2] See G. W. Leibniz, *New Essays on Human Understanding*, trans. and ed. Peter Remnant and Jonathan Bennett (Cambridge: Cambridge University Press, 1981), pp. 51, 52, 106, 110. As we shall see, it is from the nature and *direction* of the said tendencies, dispositions, endeavours... that the content of the a priori idea is to be determined.

[3] Here I spell out the Aristotelian understanding in more ways than are strictly needed at this point.

compare Aristotle, *Metaphysics*, 5, 1015a following, from which I shall quote here just one sentence. 'The nature [or way of being] of something is that source of change [including motion] in natural objects [substances] which is somehow inherent in them, either potentially or actually.'

In sum, grasping a sort involves (I say) grasping the mode of activity exemplified by this or that kind of thing; such grasp is in part irreducibly practical; and it is graduated. Why does this heighten the delicacy of formulating the question? Because, according to me at least, and according to the works of mine that Xu touches upon, a subject does indeed begin with the innate idea of an object but that innate idea leads straight into the idea of the object as possessed of *some* specific nature or other (to be discovered) and with some particular mode of activity or other (to be further determined). The object kept track of is not (*pace* Xu) kept track of as a thing whose particular nature is irrelevant to its individuation.

It will promote mutual understanding to clarify the role of 'concept' in this dispute. In my normal or deliberate usage (modelled on Frege's), a concept is what a predicate stands for (a property) and a sortal concept is what a sortal predicate stands for (a sortal property). Fei Xu uses the words 'concept' and 'sortal [concept]' differently. By 'concept' she means more or less what I mean by 'a conception' or (non-imagistic) 'idea'. For the time being, I can go along with her usage however. I only insist that, in our shared converse, room must be kept for the answer to the question whether a concept (= conception of some particular concept) is present or not, involved or not, and implicit or not in an individuative practice... to be a matter of degree. We miss something important if we treat as open or shut the question whether a particular subject's capacity at a particular moment in their life to trace what is in fact a duck or a dog or a car involves full mastery of the concept *duck, dog, car*. Such as it is, the success here of some subject, once continued outside the closely delimited conditions that Xu describes, must suggest that, however inchoately, he or she is in the process of getting hold of these concepts (even if not yet of names for these sorts) and is seeking to grasp the correlative natures of particular kinds of thing.

3. One More Preliminary

I note that Fei Xu's gloss on 'object', namely 'bounded, coherent, three-dimensional physical object that moves as a whole' definitely excludes all sorts of things that we certainly need to be able to pick out (and to recognize again and again) so soon as we seek to situate ourselves in the frame of reference with respect to which the things that she calls objects move. Her gloss excludes from objecthood rooms, walls, floors, ceilings, corridors, staircases, trees, verges, ditches, roads, hedges, footpaths, ponds, hills, slopes. Is it not strange to take all these things for granted and *then* raise questions about the grasp of identity and individuation of things that move? Why, one might then wonder, does Fei Xu's gloss read in the way in which it reads? Why is it so restricted? It reads as it does because its author is engaged and preoccupied in a particular sort of empirical inquiry into infant conceptualization. This inquiry is based on offering visual displays of smallish moveable objects to an infant who is not exploring or experimenting or stumbling about finding his way around the world, but is at rest in one part of it, settled on a bench, I suppose, or on someone's knee. About this I would ask: is there not something artificial about this set-up? Xu's findings illustrate the power of an innate idea. But a philosopher of individuation will want the human subject to progress to the point where s/he can experience the mutual involvement of striving, experimentation and judgement, and the essential interdependency of individuation and spatial orientation. In anticipation of that, I shall shortly propose another gloss upon *object*, more general than Xu's and better reflecting the way in which the possession of the concept of object prompts us to advance. The gloss I shall suggest will not obstruct any of Xu's experimental purposes. Contrast some of the philosophical conclusions into which she is led by her experimental results.

4. Adult Response to Various Individuative Challenges

Back now to the however delicate primary or chief question. Imagine first that one with an entirely innocent eye witnesses not an experimental array devised by Xu or her colleagues but a bun-fight in which, because of some oversight or devious stratagem of the organizers, the buns themselves have not been baked and, in irritation and disappointment at this, the participants take sides and pelt one another vigorously with balls of sticky white dough. In the struggle there are occasional mid-air collisions of dough balls, which sometimes then coalesce and fall to earth. Soon a wicked person on one side of the struggle produces from his pocket a golf ball. In its flight towards the enemy, this golf ball shatters or burrows through anything else that gets in its way and then continues (a little less dangerously) towards the other side. A referee halts the struggle, however, and calls for the second scene. In this, the innocent eye is confronted with a dozen india rubber balls, outsize and of wonderful elasticity, which are being thrown around rapidly and hard in a walled enclosure. In some of the mid-air collisions that take place, two balls will meet head-on. In others they will glance off at an angle. Judging with an absolutely innocent eye from the appearance of a head-on collision—while carefully disentangling from this appearance all the empirical information or hypothesis that is part and parcel with grasp of the sortal concept *india rubber-ball*—either what appears to that innocent eye is that one ball-object passes through another ball-object and each continues on its journey, or else the thing that appears to the innocent eye is that ball-objects collide, bounce apart and then return, each one, into the hands perhaps of the very person who flung it. That these are each possibilities—until empirical assumptions or hypotheses are tacitly adduced about what kind of thing these ball-objects are—is marked by the next scene.

For the next scene, the decks are cleared and the innocent eye is confronted with a set of rubber ducks of ingenious construction. These ducks are powered to expand and contract rapidly. When they are in the expanded state, however, these ducks offer a membrane through which alien objects can pass. (In some cases, however, this membrane, immediately anything broaches it, seals itself instantly, in the manner in which a fighter aircraft's fuel tank seals itself instantly when punctured by a bullet.) For this scene, re-enter the same teams of jaculators, still lively, still throwing, as happy as ever to make missiles collide, but equipped now with rubber duck-objects. In due course, however, this scene is cleared too. Finally, re-enter the same teams, still jaculators, still jumpers, still happy to achieve missile collisions, but equipped now with rubber ball objects *and* rubber duck objects. When a duck-object hits a duck-object mid-air, the one object may under the right conditions pass through the other. Similarly, under the right conditions, with a ball-object hitting a duck-object. But ball-objects rebound from ball-objects.

Because events happen so quickly in these scenes, involving cases of rebound, of apparent coalescence, and of apparent passing through, epistemological problems press. But no adult need normally despair of bracketing these problems entirely or of saying what is *at issue* in making the distinction between rebounding, passing through, coalescence, or fusion followed by fission. The thing that is at issue has to be what *kind or kinds* of thing they are concerned with. Suppose though that an adult availed himself *only* of Fei Xu's notion of an object. The bare idea of 'bounded, coherent three-dimensional physical object that moves as a whole', when deployed in a manner truly innocent of all assumptions about what kind of thing with what manner of motion is moving in a given case, cannot prompt its possessor to look for an effective demarcation of the difference between (say) X's rebounding from Y and X's passing through Y.

Is there any way forward here using only Xu's concept of object? If there is to be anything much at issue between her and the philosophers she disagrees with, then her philosophical claim must be that, even for adults' judgements of identity and difference, the (supposedly sortal) concept *object* need not compel us to look for further determinations. My claim is that, *unless* our grasp upon it prompts us to look for further determinations of the determinable idea of object, there will be real difficulties for the observer in arriving at the question what constitutes the difference between a rebound and a passing through. After all, both cases give a dense unbroken sequence of objects at places. How is one to credit the supposition that an innocent observer in these set-ups could advance the problems that they pose without even starting to excogitate more specific concepts of various different kinds of object?

Let me put the same thought in a different way. However simple it may appear, the intuitive cum pre-theoretical idea of an object's moving from one place to another has half-hidden conceptual complexities (as well as physical complexities). For an object X to move from point a to point b over d seconds it is not enough for there to be a dense succession of X-like objects at a dense succession of points between a and b at a dense succession of moments during the period d seconds. There is more than that to moving. To move, X needs to have a *way* of behaving—and any putative motion by X needs to cohere with that way of behaving. These necessities arise directly from the need for something to count as X's moving, for something to count as X's rebounding from things that lie on its path, and for something else to count as X's passing through what lies in its way.

5. Another Gloss upon 'Object'

What is the content of the concept *object*? Reaching out to Xu's paper, the determinable that I offer in the place of hers is 'bounded, coherent, three-dimensional thing *with some particular way of behaving*'. Aristotelians may want to add here: '*of coming to be, being qualified and passing away*'. But what matters here is that the words that I have italicized in this characterization lead straight into the need for anyone who would explore the world to arrive at more specific and properly sortal conceptions. If Xu were to embrace this suggestion, that might have the effect of releasing her discussion from some of the restrictions I mentioned at section 3 above. But another reason why I say it is important for the concept of *object* to be explained in the way that I have just proposed is that we do not properly grasp *dog, horse, ball* as giving principles of tracing for such objects unless we understand the relation between tracing and identity or between identity and Leibnizian community of predicates. (See *S&S*, p. 5.) We need to grasp *dog, horse, ball* as determinations of a properly determinable concept of *object* (as understood with my gloss not Xu's, or some further generalization of my gloss).

I should explain that, where I have said in the various books or articles that Xu refers to, that 'thing' or 'object' or 'substance' are *dummy* sortal concepts, I have never meant to disparage these concepts. ('Formal' would have been better than 'dummy'.) If thinkers need sortal *and* determinable concepts, can anything be added to my philosophical guesswork about their acquisition? There is an empirical question here. But at this point I want to remark that there is no reason to suppose that, in the intellectual development of human beings, a grasp of any of these devices is formed either in isolation, or completely, or at some set moment in a predetermined schedule. That may or may not be the case. It has seemed much more likely that the grasp of each kind of device is formed either in concert or in reciprocity with the grasp of others. Maybe it is only when the totality is in place that the grasp of any one of them can count as complete.

6. 'Identification'

In her section 3.3, Fei Xu mentions an example of Kahneman, Treisman, and Gibbs: 'As something approaches from a distance, one might hear the sentence, "It's a bird, it is an airplane, it is Superman".' Then she comments: 'Here the reference of the pronoun "it" does not change; it refers to the same physical object.' Then Xu claims that 'physical object' in her narrow sense will sufficiently define the sort the thing belongs to. Similarly, with regard to Eli Hirsch's example of a child who grows up on a farm, who has never seen a car before, and then sees one move across an open field—demonstrating thus that he can track something he knows no kind for— Xu's suggestion is that 'it's the concept of physical object [under her gloss upon 'object'] that guides the child's judgement in this case. The child applies the criteria for being the same *object*.' I have already argued against *object*'s qualifying (glossed in either Fei Xu's way or mine) as a properly sortal concept. My present obligation is not to do all that over again but to say how I should treat these examples myself.

I can readily agree that in the case of the claim (responsibly uttered) 'it is a bird, it is an airplane, it is Superman', the reference of 'it' remains constant. (Why, on anyone's view, should it not?) The conclusion I do not draw from that, however, is that, given 'the novelty of the thing presented', the words 'it is an object' will count as an 'identification' and an identification which is 'acceptable' (Fei Xu's word). Rather, it *leads* to the identification.

One who asks what a thing is does not need to have answered the 'what is it' question *already* in order to ask the question. (That would create a paradox. Cf. Plato, *Meno* 71d.) Rather, one who asks such a question in genuine puzzlement is *fumbling* for the completion of an identification only partly begun. But this is not to say that there is another kind of identification he or she has already completed. What the inquirer wants to know is what he or she has not yet got, namely the particular substantial sort the thing belongs to. In the interim he or she picks out the thing tentatively as a bounded, coherent, three-dimensional physical object with a particular way of behaving, which is yet to be discovered but can be provisionally-cum-analogically specified, trying at the same time, from one moment to the next, to keep track of the thing supposedly behaving in that way.

Very similar remarks apply to the child and car case. The determinable 'object', as understood with my gloss, guides the child's success in tracking the car. But the gloss that I have proposed for 'object' precisely points to the need to *find out* the thing's nature or way of behaving. Enough of this car-thing's mode of behaviour is immediately apparent for tracking to be possible. But even as other things happen to the car in its immediate environs the child has to start out on the *what is it?* question concerning the car-thing.

7. Further Advantages of Taking 'Object' as Standing for a Determinable

The determinable concept *object*, glossed as I gloss it, not only makes possible the thoughts of those who are inquiring or fumbling. It will also show a way out from the impasse Xu seems to have entered in her discussion of the formula (∃x) (person (x) and tall (x)).[4] Here Fei Xu commits herself to the claim that 'in this formulation x is a bare particular—it is an individual with no properties of its own but it still supports properties such as "being a person" or "is tall"'. Here Xu seems to say that, because we have an unspecified x that makes the formula (∃x) (person (x) and tall (x)) true, the object x will have no properties of its own. It will have no properties of its own yet it will be a person? That is hard, indeed impossible. But there is no need to say it.

Again, we misunderstand the determinable *object* and the part it plays in our thought if, along with Xu, we see it as defining some unspecific sort of sort that Lot's wife belonged to both before and after being turned into a pillar of salt. The incoherence that I attributed in *S&S* to the Lot story flowed from the impossibility of assigning any *one way* of behaving, coming to be, being, and passing away to Lot's wife as she figures in the biblical narrative. (There is no comparable difficulty of course in the idea that she is *replaced* by the pillar.) The story is incoherent. But incoherence does not entail unintelligibility. We perfectly understand countless

---

[4] Xu, 'From Lot's Wife to a Pillar of Salt', section 1.2, p. 366.

stories that correspond to no possible world. We can understand *War and Peace*, for instance, despite the fact (if it is a fact) that (as some say) there are radically incurable chronological anomalies in the story. (Understanding stories is a whole subject. No need to begin on it here.)

8. Some Questions

Finally, I venture a remark about infants and their supposed 'conceptual system'. Consider for instance Xu's statement: 'The infant's conceptual system... bears no resemblance at all to [the] adult's, for it has no individuals that persist through time and space, and the infant has no criteria for individuation and numerical identity.'[5]

Infants are creatures who are en route by exploration, trial and error, by probation, by tâtonnement, to the full human conceptual system. Why is crediting them with an alternate fully-fledged *interim system* the best way to make sense of their strivings? I do not understand why this is a better way to see things than it would be to see infants as simply en route to a larger framework of thinking. Still less do I understand the assumption, if Fei Xu is making it, that this is somehow mandatory.

Uneasily, I sense that there is some connection between the question last mentioned and the reservations that I mentioned in Section 3 above. Maybe there is also a link with another kind of question that has troubled me. What does Xu mean when she says (as she frequently does) things like this?: 'infants [do/do not] represent specific sortals such as *rod, box, rabbit*';[6] 'for *ball* or *bottle* to be a sortal, the infant should be able to use the difference between a bottle and a ball to set up representations of two numerically distinct individuals';[7] 'infants [do/do not] represent basic level *kinds/sortals*'.[8]

Maybe there is no reader of *Mind and Language* who will take exception to these turns of phrase. But let me who am no sort of a behaviourist (not even a reconstructed one) say that I for one have only a dim sense of what they mean. Does 'Infant X represents [does not represent] *rod* [or *box* or *rabbit*]' mean anything more or less than 'Infant X, in handling/tracing/identifying/re-identifying things, does/does not deploy some understanding of what sort of thing a rod [or box or rabbit] is'?

---

[5] Xu, 'From Lot's Wife to a Pillar of Salt', section 2.4, p. 380.
[6] Xu, 'From Lot's Wife to a Pillar of Salt', section 2.1, p. 375.
[7] Xu, 'From Lot's Wife to a Pillar of Salt', section 2.1, p. 374.
[8] Xu, 'From Lot's Wife to a Pillar of Salt', section 2.4, p. 380 (emphasis added).

Is the key to the 'represents' terminology as follows?:

The infant Matthew represents *box* if and only if Matthew has reached a point where a box can strike him, or can appear to be presented to him, *as a box*.

If this is the proper key, and the right hand side is ordinarily understood as entailing that Matthew grasps what sort of thing a box is, then I shall place on the record two points:

(1) the left-hand side is inhospitable to vagueness, indeterminacy, or questions of degree in a way in which 'Matthew grasps what sort of thing a box is' is not inhospitable to vagueness or to matters of degree;
(2) the left-hand side seems to add something to the right, something supposedly explanatory—yet what it adds is utterly mysterious. To commit oneself to the right-hand side is of course to commit oneself to something about the infant's being capable of *awareness*. Awareness is mysterious, perhaps deeply mysterious. But the left-hand side does not *demystify* the ideas of awareness and differentiated readiness. Rather it mystifies further that which the right hand side has registered already as something about Matthew's mental capacities.

12

Activity, Process, Continuant, Substance, Organism

1. In a manifesto entitled 'A Process Ontology for Biology' and issuing from the Centre for the Study of Life Sciences, University of Exeter, John Dupré has proposed the question whether *things* or *processes* provide a better framework for interpreting science. He says that this question should be 'a central concern for everyone interested in the metaphysics of science'.[1] He is ready to think that it is a real option to abandon the substance-theorist's preoccupation with 'the changes that occur to an entity and the conditions under which an entity can remain the same thing through change'[2] and to embrace instead a process-theorist's concern with 'how a combination of processes can maintain the appearance of stability and persistence in an entity that is fundamentally only a temporary eddy in a flux of change'.

Dupré is not alone in his readiness to embrace an ontology of processes.[3] But my own response to the question he has raised is not to disagree over the importance of processes. It is rather to contend that, if the idea of persistence is to have even a toehold within a scientific world-view that extends to the realm of organisms—if that world-view is ever to afford the option to make the barest cross-reference between some x or other at this time and some y at another time—then there is need for an ontology not simply of *event*, *process*, and *activity* but also and equally of *material things*, things that persist however temporarily from one time to the next. For present purposes it will suffice to call these latter,

---

[1] <http://thebjps.typepad.com/my-blog/2014/08/a-process-ontology-for-biology-john-dupré.html>.
[2] Speaking for substance-theorists, let me insist that the words 'remain the same thing' be replaced by the word 'persist', unless our preoccupation is to be misdescribed.
[3] See for instance Alexandre Guay and Thomas Pradeu (eds), *Individuals Across the Sciences* (New York: Oxford University Press, 2016). But these authors state their aims differently: '[We] suggest a shift from an ontology of *substances*, *invariance* and *laws* to an ontology centred on *processes* and *change*'.

with W. E. Johnson, continuants.[4] Continuants exist in time, have material parts, and pass through phases. But such phases are not the material parts of the continuant. The phases are parts of the continuant's span of existence. Contrast processes. The phases of a particular historically dateable process *are* its parts.

There are further differences between processes and things. A process can be rapid or regular or staccato, or steady. It can even be cyclical and lifelong. Consider the Krebs cycle. Talk of organisms certainly demands talk of the processes by which they are maintained. But how is talk of organisms to be replaced altogether by talk of processes which submit to attributions such as rapid, regular, staccato, steady, or cyclical? Organisms themselves cannot submit to these attributions. Meanwhile an organism can be the proud possessor of eight fingers and two thumbs. Can a process? In pressing these points, I shall appear to hark back to the archaic style of disputation proprietary to 'linguistic philosophy'. Yet, archaic or not, difficulties of this sort are suggestive of real distinctions—distinctions that are crucial perhaps for the philosophy of individuation. Does it not help towards the understanding of what an item is to ask what one can truly say about it?

2. Such arguments move much too swiftly, I fear, to carry full conviction among those who need convincing. Dupré himself is more interested in the radical redescription of biological reality, or so I surmise, than in the emendation of existing accounts of it. So let me begin afresh upon the effort of persuasion and invite the reader to try to imagine a world of pure process—of process without anything else. Let us try, for instance, to imagine a world consisting only of weather—a world where hurricane struggles with tornado for supremacy and powerful winds constantly oppose or cut across one another or combine to overwhelm all the other forces of the heavens. Such a world might seem to approximate to a world of pure process. But in a vacuum there is no weather. If there is to be weather, there must be not only process but also air or earth or water or ... some material principle which is other than process. (Could matter itself amount to no more than a process?) And, once there is any material principle at all, the collision of one process with another cannot help under some circumstance but make some quantities of matter collide and occasionally

---

[4] Johnson defines a continuant to be 'that which continues to exist throughout some limited or unlimited period of time, during which its inner states or outer connections with other continuants may be altering or may be continuing unaltered'. W. E. Johnson, *Logic*, Part III: *The Logical Foundations of Science* (Cambridge: Cambridge University Press, 1924), pp. xx–xxi. It should go without saying that on these terms *continuant* is a determinable notion—the most that can be available in advance of empirical experience or inquiry.

concresce with other matter. Not all the results of such concrescence need be momentary. To judge by the report of Diogenes Laertes IX.7 [Diels-Kranz A1], the thought is at least as old as Heraclitus: 'the totality of things is harmoniously joined together through *enantiodromia* [the running of this against that]'. In a world properly of process *and* matter, moreover—in a world such as can be the object of biological science—there wants at least one other thing, namely the possibility to refer twice to one and the same material concretion.

Here, in the world where we are, that condition is satisfied. Indeed our worldview has long since committed us to the existence not only of atoms and the rest, but also of re-identifiable organisms and micro-organisms. At the subatomic and subsubatomic level all sorts of problems arise about the identification and reidentification of individual entities. Such problems have been thought to threaten the whole ontology that we try to apply there. But only a rather special kind of fanatic would claim that problems of *this* kind must undermine the possibility of genuine identity or difference of continuants at the macroscopic level. The subatomic level is not the level at which we have to account for the identification and reidentification of most of that which we know about from biology. The subatomic is not the level at which we enquire how living things relate to the processes that combine to enable or constitute their continuing existence.

3. In the effort to master these questions, some theorists of process without substance are apt to invoke the idea of *genidentity*. Alexandre Guay and Thomas Pradeu[5] write

> What does the concept of genidentity say? In a nutshell, [genidentity] says that the identity through time of an entity X is nothing more than the continuous connection of the states through which X goes. For example a 'chair' should be understood in a purely historical way, as a connection of spatio-temporal states from its making to its destruction. The genidentity view is thus utterly *anti*-substantialist in so far as it suggests that the identity of X through time does not in any way presuppose the existence of a permanent 'core' or 'substrate' of X. It also leads one to replace the question 'what *is* X, fundamentally?' by the question 'How should I *follow* X through time?'... In this context, the notion of individual becomes derivative... [I]t will not be unreasonable to [contend] that processes are ontologically prior, and individuals should be conceived of as specific temporary coalescences of processes.

In response to this I protest first that, according at least to my own avowedly 'substantialist' account of what it takes to find a thing X and then find X again

---

[5] See Alexandre Guay and Thomas Pradeu, 'To Be Continued: The Genidentity of Physical and Biological Processes', in Guay and Pradeu (eds), *Individuals Across the Sciences*, pp. 317–47.

later, it is only required that in tracking X one should attend to the activity of X—attend that is to X's way of being and behaving.[6] Such a principle (I insist) need not invoke any 'permanent core' or 'substrate'. The operation of a principle of activity for X's kind of thing will involve matter, but it is not excluded that that matter be exchanged constantly. Everything depends here on what kind of thing X is. Let me add that, among the proper parts or constituents of continuants of a given kind, nothing excludes the possibility that there be further continuants. Indeed, in the case of a continuant with the principle of activity of something alive, it may be discovered that it is essential to the life and survival of that continuant that it have within it certain other continuants, microbes, symbionts, etc. This I learn from Dupré and Pradeu themselves. But in this connection everything depends on the empirically discoverable demands of the particular principle of the activity that sustains the stability and persistence of the sort of organism in question.

The second point I put to Guay and Pradeu relates to what they mean by 'temporary coalescences of processes'. Do they mean the coalescence of *matter* with *matter*, a coalescence brought about by distinguishable processes? Or do they mean the process that results from the confluence or concurrence of the various processes which sustain the something or other that is some organism? On a literal reading of what they say, it seems they must mean the second. They must mean that the organism is *itself* a process. Only this literal reading distinguishes their position from the 'substantialist' position from which they seek to distance themselves.[7] But are they content for this to be what they mean? The

---

[6] See Chapter 1, sections 8–10.

[7] In a further effort to reconcile Guay and Pradeu to 'substantialism' in the form in which I have tried to present it, let me quote (yet again—see S&S, p. vii) from a text I have long revered:

> The essence of a living thing is that it consists of atoms of the ordinary chemical elements we have listed, caught up into the living system and made part of it for a while. The living activity takes them up and organizes them in its characteristic way. The life of a man consists essentially in the activity he imposes upon that stuff... It is only by virtue of this activity that the shape and organization of the whole is maintained. (J. Z. Young, *Introduction to the Sciences of Man* (Oxford: Oxford University Press, 1971))

Another text by which I might seek to distance Guay and Pradeu from their reading of substantialism comes from Aristotle himself (*Metaphysics* 1050b2):

Substance or form is *energeia*

Perhaps this is to say, not without some grammatical obscurity, that substance or form is active being. What I should *like* Aristotle to be saying here is that for *x* to be a substance is for *x* to have a principle of activity (in the sense I give these words in Chapter 1). But it will be for the scholars of the *Metaphysics* to unwind the syntactical and interpretive intricacies of Aristotle's sentence.

discomforts of taking such a position (see again section 1 above, *ad finem*), would be out of all proportion with any real difficulties in the philosophy of continuants.

4. Where the idea of genidentity is concerned, I am drawn to a rival account:

> [An] examination of the concepts and principles of relativity...shows that they rest squarely on the ontology of things and events. A *world-line* is a sum of events all of which involve a single *material* body; any two events on the same world line are *genidentical*. That which cannot be accelerated up to or beyond the speed of light is something with a non-zero mass. But only a continuant can have mass. In like fashion, the measuring rods and clocks of special relativity, which travel from place to place, are as assuredly continuants as the emission and absorption of light signals are events. Nor does relativity entail that large continuants have temporal as well as spatial parts... We suggest that that rejection of the old (substantialist) ontology be postponed until such time as the promised alternative is in a much more liveable state.[8]

Genidentity thus explained depends on the idea of a world-line and that idea depends on the idea of a material body. It is a relation between the events that involve a material body. On these terms—genidentity being glossed as Simons glosses it—it is simply impossible to reconstrue genidentity as a link between physical states whose concatenations can *stand in* for material bodies. We needed material bodies from the outset in order to say what a world-line was.

5. Guay and Pradeu may try to show that there is another way to say what a world-line is. But this is the moment for me to turn to their admirable suggestion that the philosophy of biology needs to focus upon the question 'How should I follow X through time?'. No proposal could be more welcome. I have long promoted the very same question—not because I have wanted to show the notion of individual continuant to be derivative in the way that Guay and Pradeu propose, but because I have wanted not to strain and strain in scholastic fashion after the idea of the singular essence of a thing. There had to be another way. The thought was that, in order to understand identity and individuation, one needs to study the way in which we track continuants of any particular sort—at the same time, in the course of doing this, exploiting and extending our knowledge of how and why these things, of this or that sort, behave as they do.

Applying the question 'How should I follow X through time?' to the context of biological science, Guay and Pradeu make a whole wealth of suggestions about how the competent inquirer must proceed: by consulting considerations of 'causally significant process'; by reference to considerations relevant to 'internal organization as measured in terms of intensity of interactions'; and by consulting considerations relating to 'well-specified metabolic interactions' that contribute

---

[8] Peter Simons, *Parts: A Study in Ontology* (Oxford: Oxford University Press, 1987), p. 127.

to the 'cohesiveness' and unity of a whole organism, as well as to 'higher level interactions', some of them on the part of the immune system, which themselves 'exert control over metabolic interactions at a lower level'.

6. I have three kinds of doubt whether these proposals—interesting and enlightening though they are, and illuminating as they are of the ways in which scientists have tried to understand the secret life-cycles of strange creatures—can in the end help to vindicate any theoretical preference for a simplified ontology of process over the larger ontology that I advocate.

The first doubt concerns how well the thoughts, ideas, and scientific practices of the numerous investigators who have created the branches of biology that Guay and Pradeu appeal to could cohere and consist with the claim that the concept of individual organism is 'derivative'. Could some revision of the research practice of these investigators amount to their dispensing altogether with all implicit reliance on the determinables *continuant* and *organism*? Could these investigators really think of the organisms they study as simply concatenations of states? If they were asked what concatenates the states in question, they would surely refer to their however provisional account of the life-cycle of a given organism. There is more to this preference than meets the eye. A concatenation, being defined by its membership, has its members necessarily. To imagine the smallest difference in a concatenation is to imagine a different (non-identical) entity. Is this not a special disadvantage? We need a connection between states—a connection that is more specific moreover than undifferentiated succession or causation.

My second doubt concerns cohesiveness, unity, wholeness...I submit that, au fond, such ideas depend for their application on a context that is framed by the kinds or kinds of kind in question. They need to be glossed in context as 'one f', 'a whole f', 'something cohesive in the manner of an f', 'unitary f'...and in the presence of some adumbration at least of the concept f. Is it all right for the concatenation-of-states construal of continuants to wait for its implementation upon the *prior* operation of criteria informed by thoughts about the nature of the bearers of those states, namely (as I should say) the organisms themselves?[9]

The third doubt relates to something we all three agree about, namely the role of principles in the reidentification/tracking/following of a particular continuant

---

[9] Suppose the putative parts of a putative thing are all present but in the wrong array. Is the entity 'cohesive' or 'unitary'? If not, why not? Well, constituted so, the entity cannot participate in the mode of activity that is proprietary to it and definitive of its kind. Is it not in the light of *this* that 'cohesiveness' has to be interpreted and determined?

(as I should say) or concatenation-of-states (as they would say). It relates also to something we do not agree about. I say that these principles depend not on the idea of a concatenation of states but on the idea of some continuant or other.

I begin upon this by remarking that simple logic requires that such tracking principles should respect both the reflexivity of identity and the indiscernibility of identicals. These imply the symmetry or reversibility and the transitivity of the relation which must hold between X and the this-or-that to which we trace it. Suppose that some putative principle P carries us from X to Y and carries us from Y to Z. Then P gives us a path back and forth between X and Z. Suppose however that P also gives a path between X via Y to Z' but P offers no path between Z and Z'. Then we shall have a contradiction. Z and Z' are distinct—there is no identificatory direct route between them—and yet also identical. For, via Y, P carries us back from Z to X and carries us back from Z' to X. So Z = Z'. But on the basis of P we had *also* supposed that Z ≠ Z'.

Any tracking principle P that gives such a result in any of its applications will need to be reconsidered. I am uncertain what Guay and Pradeu will say that that involves. But anyone who takes the idea of a continuant in the way I do as primitive—and not as reducible to the account of a mere concatenation of states—will say that any workable tracking principle must arise from some however provisional conception of the particular kind of thing that is to be followed or tracked. In the face of contradiction it is this conception, the conception that animates principle P, which needs to be reshaped. Suppose, for instance, that in the sort of case we began with the conception was the conception of *human being*; and suppose that, as it stood, this conception allowed us to think of a human being as starting its existence as a zygote. The trouble would be that, as is well known, the human zygote may divide at any moment before the twelfth day after conception and give rise to two separate embryos (twins). It follows that the principle corresponding to the conception of human beings that we began with cannot stand. It is a mistake to think of a human being's existence as starting before the formation of the embryo (see Chapter 1, section 10). The conception we began with needs correction. The earliest moment a human being can begin is with the embryo. I am not sure how that point will come out on the concatenation of states conception.

7. Here, arising from the last point but moving on to something else, someone may offer an interesting objection. '*Genetically* speaking surely Z and Z' really are the same. And, in that case, is it completely clear that P can offer no direct path between Z and Z'?' Such an objection is highly instructive. Anyone who is a sortalist about identity in the same way as I am will insist that, if P is meant to

track *human beings*, then **P** cannot stand. On the other hand, if **P** is a principle deriving from the non-singular idea of some [*individual*] *human genotype* or *lineage*, then there ought indeed to have been a path back and forth between Z and Z'.

The point I want to make now is that, where identity is concerned, everything depends on what *category* of thing and what *kind* of thing one is to single out from the rest of reality. Is the item in question concrete or abstract, is it a thing or a nature, a particular animal or an animal species, something singular or something plural, a member or a class, a plant or a plant-colony, a clone (specimen) or a clone (group), a token or a type, a continuant or an aggregate...? And is it a continuant or a process?[10]

8. Having now, in this way, more or less reinvented the sortalist conception of identity, let me try to apply it to some part of the area where philosophers of biology such as Dupré, Pradeu, and Guay experience the doubts that prompt them to try to dispense (or dispense initially) with continuants proper or cause them to long for a purer ontology of processes. Let me apply the sortalist approach to some of the remarkable creatures that Jack Wilson describes in *Biological Individuality*.[11] I am not entirely sure how process-theorists such as Dupré or Pradeu and Guay will prefer to describe such organisms. But what I hope to show is that these creatures need not especially daunt a substance-theorist who embraces the pluralist ontology that I have sought to advocate.

(1) 'A colonial siphonophore begins as a zygote. The zygote divides and forms a larva. The larva's ectoderm thickens and buds off zooids... [which] remain attached together... New zooids are budded off from one of the two growth zones located at the end of the nectophore region. Each colony is composed of a variety of zooids that closely resemble the parts of a normal jellyfish. The top of the colony is a gas-filled float. Below the float are the nectophones that move the colony by pumping water... Their action is coordinated... The colony can swim and feed like a single organism... Is a siphonophore colony an individual or is each single zooid an individual?' (p. 7)

---

[10] A word more about the logical adequacy requirement upon principles such as P. It demands more than respect for symmetry, reflexivity, and transitivity. It demands that grounds for the identity of x and y be grounds for the indiscernibility of x and y. That is, x and y must share all their properties. They must have the same life-history. If that seems implausible in a given case, then the fault (if there is one) lies with the conception of the kind that regulates the formulation of the principle P.

[11] Jack Wilson, *Biological Individuality: The Identity and Persistence of Living Entities* (Cambridge: Cambridge University Press, 1999).

(2) 'At one point in the life-cycle of a certain species of cellular slime-moulds, a number of independent, amoeba-like single cells aggregate together into a grex. The grex is a cylindrical mass of these cells that behaves much like a slug. It has a front and a back, responds as a unit to light, and can move as a cohesive body. The cells that compose a grex are not always genetically identical or even related. They begin their lives as free-living single-cell organisms. The grex has some properties of an individual and behaves very much like one.' (p. 8)

(3) 'Blackberry plants reproduce both by sexual means resulting in seeds and also through vegetative growth. Some stands of blackberries are hundreds of years old and trace their origin back to a single sexually produced seed. The seed grows into a plant which send out runners. Some of the runners and roots remain connected underground and others have become detached. What should we count when we count blackberry plants?' (p. 8)

9. I begin with the problem (3). If there is a problem here, it is nothing special to biology. Consider the concept *crown*. It is clear enough how a thing has to be in order to count as a crown, and clear enough what it takes for crown C_1 to be the same as crown C_2. But there is no universally applicable definite way of counting crowns. The Pope's crown is made of crowns. When the Pope wears his crown there is no unique or definite answer to the question how many crowns he has on his head.[12] If we want to count under a concept f then either we must choose a concept that does not permit division of what falls under it or else f must be further qualified. Is our interest in counting genetically uniform stands (colonies) of blackberry, or in counting individual blackberry plants whether or not connected below ground to other plants, or what...? There is nothing reasonable in the idea that reality allows only one choice—one ontology and one ideology, one domain of individuals and one domain of properties of those individuals. Compare the distinction Hilary Putnam proposes between ordinary realism and 'metaphysical' realism.[13] A reasonable inquirer has to be prepared to attend to these things or to those different things. However palpable the things we refer to may be—no matter how strong their claim to be 'there anyway'—they may require the one who attends to them to look for *this* sort of thing or for *that* sort of thing, whether singular or non-singular. Reality itself need not dictate what we are to heed. Still less will it forbid us to heed one kind of thing and *then* another kind. (See also Introduction, section 4.)

---

[12] Compare S&S, pp. 72–3 and S&SR, pp. 74–5.
[13] Hilary Putnam, *Philosophy in an Age of Science: Physics, Mathematics, and Skepticism*, ed. Mario De Caro and David Macarthur (Cambridge, MA: Harvard University Press, 2012), ch. 2.

10. I revert now to case (1). The idea of an individual or individual organism is the idea of a determinable. To ask whether something X is an individual is to ask whether there is some fully determinate kind *f* such that X is an individual *f*. In the case of the siphonophore colony it is indeed a particular kind of (quasi-jellyfish) creature with a specific principle of activity. There is nothing wrong with *siphonophore* as a specific kind. Let us forget the obsolescent idea that a substance is something that lacks substantial parts and is viable without parts that are substances. Nothing in the idea of a continuant demands this. Among the constituents of a siphonophore are numerous sortally further specified continuants, each of them with its very own principle of activity, co-ordinated and subordinated in important respects—but why not?—to the activity principle of the whole siphonophore.

I venture to think that there is nothing to forbid a similar treatment of the remarkable creature, the *grex*, which is the second puzzle-case.

11. Over the millennia, the philosophy of substance has created all sorts of mysteries and obscurities of its own. My claim is that, slimmed down in the form of a logically informed philosophy of continuants, taking each continuant not as indivisible but as possessed of its own determinate principle of activity, the philosophy of substance is ready and equipped to cohere and combine with any equally clear and coherent philosophy of process, activity, and event. There must be room within any such philosophy for the idea of a continuant.

At the outset (see section 2 above), I allowed that Dupré may be more interested in the possibility of a radical redescription of biological phenomena than in any scheme for the translation of existing descriptions into a language of pure process. So let me acknowledge that the very most I can achieve by the arguments I have advanced here is to suggest that radical redescription is not so urgent or so necessary as it has appeared.

Bibliography

Writings of David Wiggins

Books

ISTC Identity and Spatio-Temporal Continuity (Oxford: Blackwell, 1967).
S&S Sameness and Substance (Oxford: Blackwell, 1980; a second impression appeared in 1981 with errata and addenda).
NVT Needs, Values, Truth: Essays in the Philosophy of Value (Oxford: Blackwell, 1987; rev. 2nd edn, Oxford: Blackwell, 1991; 3rd edn with extra chapter (cf. 1998a), Oxford: Clarendon Press, 1998; amended 3rd edn, Oxford: Oxford University Press, 2002; unluckily and by mistake, a subsequent reprint of the book followed the 1998 text instead of this amended impression of 2002).
S&SR Sameness and Substance Renewed, an extended and heavily revised edition of S&S (Cambridge: Cambridge University Press, 2001).
ETL Ethics: Twelve Lectures on the Philosophy of Morality (Cambridge, MA: Harvard University Press, 2006).

Other writings by David Wiggins

1963 'The Individuation of Things and Places', *Proceedings of the Aristotelian Society*, suppl. 37, pp. 177–202; reprinted in corrected form, in the first edition only, of M. Loux (ed.), *Universals and Particulars* (New York: Doubleday, 1967).
1965 'Identity-Statements', in R. J. Butler (ed.), *Analytical Philosophy: Second Series* (Oxford: Blackwell); reprinted in German as 'Identitätsaussagen', trans. Matthias Schirn, in Kuno Lorenz (ed.), *Identität und Individuation*, Band 1: *Logische Probleme in historischem Aufriß* (Stuttgart-Bad Cannstatt: Frommann-Holzboog, 1982). (The chief contention and error of this paper was recanted at *ISTC* note 7, and 1971a, 17 note b.)
1968 'On Being in the Same Place at the Same Time', *Philosophical Review*, 77, pp. 90–5 (see also 1997c). [See also this volume, Chapter 2.]
1969 'Reply to Mr Chandler', *Analysis*, 29, pp. 175–6.
1970 'Freedom, Knowledge, Belief and Causality', in G. Vesey (ed.) *Knowledge and Necessity* (London: Macmillan), pp. 132–54.
1971a 'On Sentence Sense, Word Sense and Difference of Word Sense: Towards a Philosophical Theory of Dictionaries' and 'Reply to Mr Alston', in Danny D. Steinberg and Leon A. Jakobovits (eds), *Semantics: An Interdisciplinary Reader in Philosophy, Linguistics and Psycholinguistics* (Cambridge: Cambridge University Press); translated into Greek in *Deucalion: A Quarterly Review*, 31 (1980), pp. 35–52.
1971b 'Sentence Meaning, Negation, and Plato's Problem of Non-Being', in Gregory Vlastos (ed.), *Plato I* (New York: Doubleday).

1973 'Towards a Reasonable Libertarianism', in Ted Honderich (ed.), *Essays on Freedom of Action* (London: Routledge & Kegan Paul), pp. 270–302. (Also in amended edition 1979, and rewritten for *NVT* and rewritten again for 2003b.)

1974 'Essentialism, Continuity, and Identity', *Synthese*, 28, pp. 321–59.

1975 'Identity, Designation, Essentialism and Physicalism', *Philosophia*, 5, pp. 1–30.

1975–6 'Deliberation and Practical Reason', *Proceedings of the Aristotelian Society*, 76, pp. 29–51; reprinted in Amélie Oksenberg Rorty (ed.), *Essays on Aristotle's Ethics* (Berkeley, CA: University of California Press, 1980), pp. 221–40. (Rewritten for *NVT*. An excerpt was rewritten for 1978c. Rewritten again for 2008b.)

1976a 'Truth, Invention and the Meaning of Life', *Proceedings of the British Academy*, 62, pp. 331–78; reprinted in Geoffrey Sayre-McCord (ed.), *Essays on Moral Realism* (Ithaca, NY: Cornell University Press, 1988). (Rewritten for *NVT*.)

1976b 'The *De Re* "Must": A Note on the Logical Form of Essentialist Claims', in Gareth Evans and John McDowell (eds), *Truth and Meaning: Essays in Semantics* (Oxford: Clarendon Press). [See also this volume, Chapter 9.]

1976c 'Locke, Butler and the Stream of Consciousness: and Men as a Natural Kind', *Philosophy*, 51, pp. 131–58; reprinted in Amélie Oksenberg Rorty (ed.), *The Identities of Person* (Berkeley, CA: University of California Press, 1976); also reprinted in Harold W. Noonan (ed.), *Personal Identity* (Aldershot: Dartmouth Publishing, 1993).

1976d 'Frege's Problem of the Morning Star and the Evening Star', in M. Schirn (ed.), *Studies on Frege II: Logic and Philosophy of Language* (Stuttgart-Bad Cannstatt: Frommann-Holzboog).

1976e 'Identity, Necessity and Physicalism' and 'Reply to Professor Marcus and Mr Hacking', in Stephan Körner (ed.), *Philosophy of Logic* (Oxford: Blackwell).

1978a 'Are the Criteria of Identity that hold for a Work of Art in the Different Arts Aesthetically Relevant? Reply to Richard Wollheim', *Ratio*, 20, pp. 52–68.

1978b 'Aurel Thomas Kolnai (1900–1973)': Introduction (written with Bernard Williams) to Aurel Kolnai, *Ethics, Value, and Reality: Selected Papers of Aurel Kolnai*, ed. Francis Dunlop and Brian Klug (London: Athlone Press).

1978c 'Deliberation and Practical Reason', in J. Raz (ed.), *Practical Reasoning* (Oxford: Oxford University Press), pp. 144–52.

1978–9 'Weakness of Will, Commensurability, and the Objects of Deliberation and Desire', *Proceedings of the Aristotelian Society*, 79, pp. 251–77; reprinted in Amélie Oksenberg Rorty (ed.), *Essays on Aristotle's Ethics* (Berkeley, CA: University of California Press, 1980), pp. 241–66. (Rewritten and corrected for *NVT*.)

1979a 'Ayer on Monism, Pluralism and Essence', in G. F. MacDonald (ed.), *Perception and Identity: Essays Presented to A. J. Ayer with his Replies to them* (Ithaca, NY: Cornell University Press), pp. 131–60. (Badly mistaken with respect to Leibniz. Superseded entirely by 1987c.)

1979b 'The Concern to Survive', *Midwest Studies in Philosophy*, 4, pp. 417–22. (Rewritten for *NVT*.)

1979c 'On Knowing, Knowing that One Knows and Consciousness', in E. Saarinen, R. Hilpinen, I. Niiniluoto, and M. B. Provence Hintikka (eds), *Essays in Honour of Jaakko Hintikka: On the Occasion of His Fiftieth Birthday on January 12, 1979* (Dordrecht: Reidel), pp. 237–48.

1979d 'Mereological Essentialism: Asymmetrical Essential Dependence and the Nature of Continuants', in Ernest Sosa (ed.), *Essays on the Philosophy of Roderick M. Chisholm*, Grazer Philosophische Studien, 7/8 (Amsterdam: Rodopi), pp. 297–315. (In this volume, Chisholm makes a response. See his 'Objects and Persons: Revisions and Replies' at pp. 317–88.) [See also this volume, Chapter 10.]

1980a '"Most" and "All": Some Comments on a Familiar Programme, and on the Logical Form of Quantified Sentences', in Mark Platts (ed.), *Reference, Truth and Reality: Essays on the Philosophy of Language* (London: Routledge & Kegan Paul), pp. 318–46.

1980b 'What would be a Substantial Theory of Truth?', in Zak van Straaten (ed.), *Philosophical Subjects: Essays Presented to P. F. Strawson* (Oxford: Clarendon Press), pp. 189–221.

1980c 'Contingency, Identity, and *de re* and *de dicto* Necessity', in Jonathan Dancy (ed.), *Papers on Language and Logic: Proceedings of the 1979 Keele Conference on Language and Logic* (Keele: Keele University Library), pp. 35–53.

1980d 'Truth and Interpretation', in R. Haller and W. Grassl (eds), *Language, Philosophy and Logic: Proceedings of the 4th International Wittgenstein Symposium, Kirchberg am Wechsel, 1979* (Vienna: Hölder-Pichler-Tempsky), pp. 36–50.

1981 'Public Rationality, Needs, and What Needs are Relative to', in David Banister and Peter Hall (eds), *Transport and Public Policy Planning* (London: Mansell), pp. 198–219.

1982 'Heraclitus' Conceptions of Flux, Fire and Material Persistence', in Malcolm Schofield and Martha Nussbaum (eds), *Language and Logos: Essays for G. E. L. Owen* (Cambridge: Cambridge University Press), pp. 1–32. [See also this volume, Chapter 6.]

1984 'The Sense and Reference of Predicates: A Running Repair to Frege's Doctrine and a Plea for the Copula', *Philosophical Quarterly*, 34 (136), pp. 311–28. Also in Crispin Wright (ed.), *Frege: Tradition and Influence* (Oxford: Blackwell, 1984), pp. 126–43.

1985 'Claims of Need', in Ted Honderich (ed.), *Morality and Objectivity: A Tribute to J. L. Mackie* (London: Routledge & Kegan Paul), pp. 149–202. (Rewritten for *NVT*.)

1985–6 'Verbs and Adverbs and some other Modes of Grammatical Combination', *Proceedings of the Aristotelian Society*, 86, pp. 273–304.

1986a 'On Singling Out an Object Determinately', in Philip Pettit and John McDowell (eds), *Subject, Thought, and Context*, Oxford: Clarendon Press. (Corrected on one important point by the reply to Williamson among 'Replies' in Lovibond and Williams: 1996d.) See also *S&SR*, chapter six.

1986b 'Teleology and the Good in Plato's *Phaedo*', *Oxford Studies in Ancient Philosophy* (December 1986), 4, pp. 1–18.

1987a 'The Person as Object of Science, as Subject of Experience, and as Locus of Value', in Arthur Peacocke and Grant Gillett (eds), *Persons and Personality: A Contemporary Inquiry* (Oxford: Blackwell), pp. 56–74. [See also this volume, Chapter 4.]

1987b 'Needs, Need, Needing' (with Sira Dermen), *Journal of Medical Ethics*, 13, pp. 62–68.

1987c 'The Concept of the Subject contains the Concept of the Predicate: Leibniz on Reason, Truth and Contingency', in Judith Jarvis Thomson (ed.), *On Being and Saying: Essays for Richard Cartwright* (Cambridge, MA: MIT Press), pp. 263–84; reprinted in Roger Woolhouse (ed.), *Leibniz: Critical Assessments*, 4 vols (London: Routledge & Kegan Paul, 1994), vol. 2, pp. 141–63. [See also this volume, Chapter 7.]

1990-1 'Moral Cognitivism, Moral Relativism and Motivating Moral Beliefs', *Proceedings of the Aristotelian Society*, 91, pp. 61–85.

1991a 'Categorical Requirements: Kant and Hume on the Idea of Duty', *The Monist*, 74, pp. 83–106.

1991b 'Ayer's Ethical Theory: Emotivism or Subjectivism?', *Philosophy*, suppl. 30, pp. 181–96. (This is an abbreviation of 1992a. The same Supplement of *Philosophy* was published as A. Phillips Griffiths (ed.), *A. J. Ayer: Memorial Essays* (Cambridge: Cambridge University Press, 1991).)

1991c 'Temporal Necessity, Time and Ability: A Philosophical Commentary on Diodorus Cronus' Master Argument as Given in the Interpretation of Jules Vuillemin', in Gordon G. Brittan Jr (ed.), *Causality, Method, and Modality: Essays in Honor of Jules Vuillemin* (Dordrecht: Kluwer). (Superseded by 1993c.)

1991d 'Pourquoi la notion de substance paraît-elle si difficile', *Philosophie*, 30, pp. 77–89.

1992a 'Ayer on Morality and Feeling: from Subjectivism to Emotivism and Back?', in Lewis Edwin Hahn (ed.), *The Philosophy of A. J. Ayer* (LaSalle, IL: Open Court).

1992b 'L'éthique et la raison', *Studia Philosophica*, 51, pp. 75–87.

1992c 'Meaning, Truth-Conditions, Proposition: Frege's Doctrine of Sense Retrieved, Resumed and Redeployed in the Light of Certain Recent Criticisms', *Dialectica*, 46, pp. 61–90.

1992d 'Remembering Directly', in Jim Hopkins and Anthony Savile (eds), *Psychoanalysis, Mind and Art: Perspectives on Richard Wollheim* (Oxford: Blackwell).

1993a '*Sinn, Bedeutung*, et les mots d'espèce', *Revue de Theologie et de Philosophie*, 24, pp. 225–37. (Translated and substantially rewritten as 1993d.)

1993b 'Cognitivism, Naturalism, and Normativity: A Reply to Peter Railton' and 'A Neglected Position?', in John Haldane and Crispin Wright (eds), *Reality, Representation, and Projection* (New York: Oxford University Press), pp. 301–13, 329–36.

1993c 'Time, Ability and Real Choice', in Petr Horák and Josef Zumr (eds), *La Responsibilité/ Responsibility: Entretiens de Prague: Actes de l'Assemblée générale de l'Institut International de Philosophie, Prague du 5 au 9 septembre 1990* (Prague: Institute of Philosophy of the Czechoslovak Academy of Sciences). (Some misprints and mis-edits.)

1993d 'Putnam's Doctrine of Natural Kind Words and Frege's Doctrines of Sense, Reference and Extension: Can they Cohere?', in A. W. Moore (ed.), *Meaning and Reference* (Oxford: Oxford University Press), pp. 192–207; also (with an answer by Putnam) in Peter Clark and Bob Hale (eds), *Reading Putnam* (Oxford: Blackwell, 1994), pp. 201–15; and in John Biro and Petr Kotatko (eds), *Frege: Sense and Reference One Hundred Years Later* (Dordrecht: Kluwer, 1995), pp. 59–74. [See also this volume, Chapter 8.]

1994a 'The Kant–Frege–Russell View of Existence: A Rehabilitation of the Second Level View', in Walter Sinnott-Armstrong with Diana Raffman and Nicholas Asher (eds), *Modality, Morality, and Belief: Essays in Honor of Ruth Barcan Marcus* (Cambridge: Cambridge University Press), pp. 93–113.

1994b 'Vérité et morale', trans. Monique Canto-Sperber from 1990-1, in Monique Canto-Sperber (ed.), *La philosophie morale britannique* (Paris: Presses Universitaires de France).

1995a 'Preface', in Aurel Kolnai, *The Utopian Mind and Other Papers: A Critical Study in Moral and Political Philosophy*, ed. Francis Dunlop (London: Athlone Press).

1995b 'Eudaimonism and Realism in Aristotle's Ethics: A Reply to John McDowell', in Robert Heinaman (ed.), *Aristotle and Moral Realism* (London: UCL Press), pp. 219-31.

1995c 'Categorical Requirements', in Rosalind Hursthouse, Gavin Lawrence, and Warren Quinn (eds), *Virtues and Reasons: Essays in Honour of Philippa Foot* (Oxford: Clarendon Press). (The longer version of 1991a, corrected.)

1995d 'Substance', in A. C. Grayling (ed.), *Philosophy: A Guide through the Subject* (Oxford: Oxford University Press), pp. 214-49. [See also this volume, Chapter 3.]

1995e 'Objective and Subjective in Ethics, with Two Postscripts about Truth', *Ratio*, 8, pp. 243-58; also in Brad Hooker (ed.), *Truth in Ethics* (Oxford: Blackwell, 1996), pp. 35-50. There is another version in Monique Canto-Sperber (ed.), *Dictionnaire de philosophie morale* (3rd edn, Paris: Presses Universitaires de France, 2001). See 2001a.

1996a 'Meaning and Truth Conditions: From Frege's Grand Design to Davidson's', in Bob Hale and Crispin Wright (eds), *A Companion to the Philosophy of Language* (Oxford: Blackwell), pp. 3-28.

1996b 'Natural and Artificial Virtues: A Vindication of Hume's Scheme', in Roger Crisp (ed.), *How Should One Live? Essays on the Virtues* (Oxford: Clarendon Press), pp. 131-40.

1996c 'Language: The Great Conduit', *Times Literary Supplement*, 12 April 1996, p. 15.

1996d 'Replies', in Sabina Lovibond and S. G. Williams (eds), *Identity, Truth and Value: Essays for David Wiggins* (Oxford: Blackwell), pp. 219-84.

1996e 'Sufficient Reason: a Principle in Diverse Guises Ancient and Modern', *Acta Philosophica Fennica*, 61, pp. 117-32.

1996f 'From Piety to a Cosmic Order' (review), *Times Higher Education Supplement*, 4 October 1996, p. 22.

1997a 'Sortal Concepts: A Reply to Xu', *Mind and Language* 12, pp. 413-21. [See also this volume, Chapter 11.]

1997b 'Natural Languages as Social Objects', *Philosophy*, 72, pp. 499-524.

1997c 'On Being in the Same Place at the Same Time', a reprint with corrections and postscript of (1968), in Michael C. Rea (ed.), *Material Constitution: A Reader* (Lanham, MD: Rowman & Littlefield), pp. 3-9.

1997d 'Editor's Preface', in Michael Woods, *Conditionals*, ed. David Wiggins with a commentary by Dorothy Edgington (Oxford: Clarendon Press), pp. i-vii.

1998a 'Incommensurability: Four Proposals', in Ruth Chang (ed.), *Incommensurability, Incomparability, and Practical Reasoning* (Cambridge, MA: Harvard University Press, 1997), pp. 52-66.

1998b 'In a Subjectivist Framework, Categorical Imperatives and Real Practical Reasons', in Christoph Fehige and Ulla Wessels (eds), *Preferences* (Berlin: De Gruyter), pp. 212-32.

1998c 'Railways, Settlement and Access', in Anthony Barnett and Roger Scruton (eds), *Town and Country* (London: Jonathan Cape).

1998d '*The Right and the Good* and W. D. Ross's Criticism of Consequentialism', *Utilitas*, 10, pp. 3-24; reprinted in Royal Institute of Philosophy Supplement, 47 (September 2000), pp. 175-95.

1998e 'What is the force of the claim that one needs something?', in Gillian Brock (ed.), *Necessary Goods: Our Responsibilities to Meet Others' Needs* (Lanham, MD: Rowman & Littlefield), pp. 33-55 (an edited version of 1985).

1999a 'C. S. Peirce: Belief, Truth, and Going from the Known to the Unknown', *Canadian Journal of Philosophy*, suppl 24, pp. 9–29 (superseded by 2004a).
1999b 'Names, Fictional Names and "Really"', *Proceedings of the Aristotelian Society*, suppl 73, pp. 271–86.
1999–2000 'Nature, Respect for Nature and the Human Scale of Values', *Proceedings of the Aristotelian Society*, 100, pp. 1–32. (The correct text of this paper was given only in the bound *Proceedings of the Society*.)
2000 'Sameness, Substance and the Human Animal' (an interview), *Philosophers' Magazine*, 12, pp. 50–3. [See also this volume, Chapter 5.]
2001a French version of 1995e in M. Canto-Sperber (ed.) *Dictionnaire de Philosophie Morale* (3rd edn, Paris: Presses Universitaires de France).
2001b 'Valediction for a Subfaculty', *Oxford Magazine*, 191 (4th week, Trinity 2001).
2002a 'An Indefinibilist cum Normative View of Truth and the Marks of Truth', in Richard Schantz (ed.), *What is Truth?* (Berlin: de Gruyter), pp. 316–32.
2002b 'Identity and Supervenience', in Andrea Bottani, Massimiliano Carrara, and Pierdaniele Giaretta (eds), *Individuals, Essence and Identity: Themes of Analytic Metaphysics* (Dordrecht: Kluwer), pp. 247–66.
2003a 'Existence and Contingency: A Note', *Philosophy*, 78, pp. 483–94.
2003b 'Towards a Reasonable Libertarianism', in Gary Watson (ed.) *Free Will* (2nd edn, Oxford: Oxford University Press), pp. 94–121 (a corrected and extended version of 1973).
2004a 'Reflections on Inquiry and Truth arising from Peirce's Method for the Fixation of Belief', in Cheryl Misak (ed.), *The Cambridge Companion to Peirce* (Cambridge: Cambridge University Press), pp. 87–126. (Misprints and the like will be corrected in a collection forthcoming from OUP.)
2004b 'Aurel Kolnai on Utopia', in Zoltán Balázs and Francis Dunlop (eds), *Exploring the World of Human Practice: Readings in and about the Philosophy of Aurel Kolnai* (Budapest: Central European University Press), pp. 219–30.
2004c 'That which is inherently Practical: Some Brief Reflections', in Fátima Évora, Paulo Faria, Andrea Loparic, Luiz Henrique Lopez dos Santos, and Marco Zingano (eds), *Lógica e Ontologia: Ensaios em Homenagem a Balthazar Barbosa Filho* (São Paulo: Discurso Editorial), pp. 461–71.
2004d 'Reply to Shoemaker' and 'Reply to Shoemaker's Reply', *The Monist*, 87, pp. 594–609, 614–15.
2004e 'Wittgenstein on Ethics and the Riddle of Life', *Philosophy*, 79, pp. 363–91.
2004f 'Neo-Aristotelian Reflections on Justice', *Mind*, 113, pp. 477–512.
2005a 'Objectivity in Ethics; Two Difficulties, Two Responses', *Ratio*, 18, pp. 1–27.
2005b 'An Idea We Cannot Do Without: What difference will it make (e.g. to moral, political and environmental philosophy) to recognize and put to use a substantial conception of need?', in Soran Reader (ed.), *The Philosophy of Need* (Cambridge: Cambridge University Press), pp. 25–50.
2005c 'Précis of *Sameness and Substance Renewed*' and 'Replies (to Book Symposium contributors)', *Philosophy and Phenomenological Research*, 71, pp. 442–8, 470–6.
2006–7 'Three Moments in the Theory of Definition or Analysis: its Possibility, its Aim or Aims and its Limit or Terminus', *Proceedings of the Aristotelian Society*, 107, pp. 73–109.

2008a 'Deux conceptions d'identité', in Edgardo D. Carosella, Bertrand Saint-Sernin, Philippe Capelle, and S. E. Marcelo Sanchez Sorondo (eds), *L'identité changeante de l'individu: La constante construction du Soi* (Paris: L'Harmattan), pp. 17–28.

2008b 'Deliberação e Razio Práctica', in Marco Zingano (ed.), *Sobre a Ética Nicomaqueia de Aristóteles* (São Paulo: Odysseus), pp. 155–82. (A translation from a newly revised English version of 1975–6, 'Deliberation and Practical Reason'.)

2008–9 'Solidarity and the Root of the Ethical', *Tijdschrift voor Filosofie*, 71, pp. 239–69 (corrected and expanded version of Lindley Lecture published by the Philosophy Department, University of Kansas).

2009a 'What is the Order among the Varieties of Goodness? A Question posed by von Wright; and a Conjecture made by Aristotle', *Philosophy*, 84, pp. 175–200.

2009b 'Knowing How To and Knowing That', in Hans-Johann Glock and John Hyman (eds), *Wittgenstein and Analytic Philosophy: Essays for P. M. S. Hacker* (Oxford: Oxford University Press), pp. 263–77.

2010 'The Paradox of Analysis and the Paradox of Synonymy', in Gilles-Maurice de Schryver (ed.), *A Way with Words: Recent Advances in Lexical Theory and Analysis. A Festschrift for Patrick Hanks* (Kampala: Menha Publishers), pp. 119–32.

2011a 'Platonism and the Argument from Causality', in Benjamin Schneider and Moritz Schulz (eds), *Themes from Early Analytic Philosophy: Essays in Honour of Wolfgang Künne*, Grazer Philosophischen Studien, 82 (Amsterdam: Editions Rodopi), pp. 315–28.

2011b 'A Reasonable Frugality', in A. O'Hear (ed.), *Philosophy and the Environment*, Royal Institute of Philosophy Supplement, 69 (Cambridge: Cambridge University Press), pp. 175–200.

2012a 'Identity, Individuation and Substance', *European Journal of Philosophy*, 20, pp. 1–25. [See also this volume, Chapter 1.]

2012b 'Practical Knowledge: Knowing How To and Knowing That', *Mind*, 121, pp. 97–130.

2012c 'From A Humanities Perspective: New Public Management and the Universities', in Jenny Manson (ed.), *Public Service on the Brink* (Exeter: Imprint Academic), pp. 136–52.

2013 'Truth, Pragmatism and Morality', *Philosophy*, 88, pp. 351–68.

2013–14 'Hilary Putnam's Philosophy of Morals and Values', an extended version of 2013, with a reply by Putnam, in M. Frauchiger (ed.), *Themes from Putnam* (Lauener Library of Analytical Philosophy, ed. W. K. Essler and M. Frauchiger, vol. 5) (Berlin: de Gruyter).

2014 'Work, its Moral Meaning or Import', *Philosophy*, 89, pp. 477–82; also in Virginia Mantouvalou (ed.), *The Right to Work, Legal and Philosophical Perspectives* (Oxford: Hart Publishing), pp. 11–15.

2016 'Activity, Process, Continuant, Substance, Organism', *Philosophy*, 91, pp. 269–80.

Other writings referred to

Adams, Robert Merrihew (1982), 'Leibniz's Theories of Contingency', in Michael Hooker (ed.), *Leibniz: Critical and Interpretive Essays* (Manchester: Manchester University Press), pp. 243–83.

Anscombe, G. E. M. (1959), *An Introduction to Wittgenstein's Tractatus* (London: Hutchinson).
Aristotle, *Aristotle: the Revised Oxford Translation*, ed. Jonathan Barnes (Princeton, NJ: Princeton University Press, 1994).
Aristotle, *Categories and De Interpretatione*, trans. and ed. J. L. Ackrill (Oxford: Clarendon Press, 1974).
Aristotle, *Metaphysics Books Z and H*, trans. with commentary by David Bostock (Oxford: Clarendon Press, 1994).
Austin, J. L. (1950), 'Truth', *Proceedings of the Aristotelian Society*, suppl. 24, p. 121.
Austin, J. L. (1962), *Sense and Sensibilia*, reconstructed from the manuscript notes by G. J. Warnock (Oxford: Clarendon Press).
Austin, J. L. (1970), *Philosophical Papers*, ed. J. O. Urmson and G. J. Warnock (2nd edn, Oxford: Clarendon Press).
Ayers, M. R. (1975), 'The Ideas of Power and Substance in Locke's Philosophy', *Philosophical Quarterly*, 25, pp. 1-27; revised for I. C. Tipton (ed.), *Locke on Human Understanding: Selected Essays* (Oxford University Press, 1977), pp. 77-104.
Ayers, Michael (1991), *Locke*, 2 vols (London: Routledge, 1991).
Ayers, Michael (2005), 'Ordinary Objects, Ordinary Language and Identity', *The Monist*, 88, pp. 534-70.
Barcan Marcus, Ruth (1961), 'Modalities and Intensional Languages,' *Synthese*, 13, pp. 303-22; reprinted as 'Modal Logics I: Modalities and Intensional Languages', in M. W. Wartofsky (ed.), *Proceedings of the Boston Colloquium for the Philosophy of Science 1961/1962*, Boston Studies in the Philosophy of Science, 1 (Dordrecht: Reidel, 1963), pp. 77-96.
Burnet, John (1908), *Early Greek Philosophy* (2nd edn, London: A. & C. Black).
Burnyeat, Myles (2001), *A Map of Metaphysics Zeta* (Pittsburgh, PA: Mathesis).
Carnap, Rudolf (1958), *Introduction to Symbolic Logic and its Applications* (New York: Dover).
Cartwright, Helen Morris (1970), 'Quantities', *Philosophical Review*, 79, pp. 25-42.
Cartwright, Richard L. (1968), 'Some Remarks on Essentialism', *Journal of Philosophy*, 65, pp. 615-26.
Cartwright, Richard (1971), 'Identity and Substitutivity', in Milton K. Munitz (ed.), *Identity and Individuation* (New York: New York University Press), pp. 119-33.
Chisholm, Roderick M. (1976), *Person and Object: A Metaphysical Study* (London: Allen and Unwin).
Clark, Peter, and Bob Hale (eds) (1994), *Reading Putnam* (Oxford: Blackwell).
Crombie, I. M. (1962-3), *An Examination of Plato's Doctrines*, 2 vols (London: Routledge & Kegan Paul).
Dancy, Jonathan (ed.) (1980), *Papers on Language and Logic: The Proceedings of the Conference on the Philosophy of Language and Logic Held at the University of Keele in April 1979* (Keele: Keele University Library).
Davidson, Donald (1973), 'Radical Interpretation', *Dialectica*, 27, pp. 313-28.
Davidson, Donald (1980), *Essays on Actions and Events* (Oxford: Clarendon Press).
Descartes, René, *Œuvres de Descartes*, ed. Charles Adam and Paul Tannery, 12 vols (Paris: Vrin, 1964-76).

Martin, C. B., and Max Deutscher (1966), 'Remembering', *Philosophical Review*, 75, pp. 161–96.
Dicks, D. R. (1970), *Early Greek Astronomy to Aristotle* (London: Thames & Hudson).
Diels, H., and W. Kranz (eds) (1952), *Die Fragmente der Vorsokratiker* (6th edn, Berlin: Weidermann).
Dummett, Michael (1958–9), 'Truth', *Proceedings of the Aristotelian Society*, 59, pp. 141–62.
Dummett, Michael (1973), *Frege: Philosophy of Language* (London: Duckworth).
Evans, Gareth (1982), *The Varieties of Reference*, ed. John McDowell (Oxford: Clarendon Press, 1982).
Evans, Gareth, and John McDowell (1976), *Truth and Meaning: Essays in Semantics* (Oxford: Clarendon Press).
Fine, Kit (2006), 'In Defence of Three-Dimensionalism', *Journal of Philosophy*, 103, pp. 699–714.
Føllesdal, Dagfinn (1986), 'Essentialism and Reference', in Lewis E. Hahn and Paul Arthur Schilpp (eds), *The Philosophy of W. V. Quine* (La Salle; IL: Open Court, 1986), pp. 97–113.
Frede, Michael (1987), 'Substance in Aristotle's *Metaphysics*', in *Essays in Ancient Philosophy* (Oxford: Clarendon Press), pp. 72–80.
Frege, Gottlob (1884), *The Foundations of Arithmetic: A Logico-Mathematical Enquiry into the Concept of Number*, trans. J. L. Austin (Oxford: Blackwell, 1980) [Ger. orig. *Die Grundlagen der Arithmetik: Eine logisch mathematische Untersuchung über den Begriff der Zahl* (Breslau: Koebner, 1884)].
Frege, Gottlob (1952), *Translations from the Philosophical Writings of Gottlob Frege*, ed. P. T. Geach and M. Black (Oxford: Blackwell).
Frege, Gottlob (1979), *Posthumous Writings*, ed. Hans Hermes, Friedrich Kambartel, and Friedrich Kaulbach, trans. Peter Long and Roger White (Oxford: Blackwell).
Frege, Gottlob (1891), Letter to Husserl 24.5.1891, in *Philosophical and Mathematical Correspondence*, trans. Hans Kaal (Oxford: Blackwell, 1980). pp. 61–4.
Gerhardt, C. I. (ed.) (1875–90), *Die philosophischen Schriften von G. W. Leibniz*, 7 vols (Berlin: Weidmannsche Buchhandlung).
Grandy, Richard (1973), 'Reference, Meaning, and Belief', *Journal of Philosophy*, 70, pp. 439–52.
Grice, H. P. (1962), 'The Causal Theory of Perception', *Proceedings of the Aristotelian Society*, 35, pp. 121–52.
Hacking, Ian (1975), 'All Kinds of Possibility', *Philosophical Review*, 84, pp. 321–37.
Hacking, Ian (1976), 'Reply to David Wiggins's "Identity, Necessity & Physicalism"', in Stephan Körner (ed.), *Philosophy of Logic* (Oxford: Blackwell), pp. 147–8.
Harman, Gilbert H. (1965), 'The Inference to the Best Explanation', *Philosophical Review*, 74, pp. 88–95.
Hawthorne, John (2006), *Metaphysical Essays* (Oxford: Oxford University Press).
Helme, Mark (1979), 'An Elucidation of *Tractatus* 3. 262', *Southern Journal of Philosophy*, 17, pp. 323–34.
Higginbotham, James (1998), 'Adverbs', in E. Craig (ed.), *Routledge Encyclopaedia of Philosophy* (London: Routledge).

Higginbotham, James (1995), *Sense and Syntax: An inaugural lecture delivered before the University of Oxford on 20 October 1994* (Oxford: Clarendon Press).
Hintikka, Jaakko (1970), 'The Semantics of Modal Notions', *Synthese*, 21, pp. 408–24.
Hirsch, Eli (1971), 'Essence and Identity', in Milton K. Munitz (ed.), *Identity and Individuation* (New York, New York University Press), pp. 31–49.
Hirsch, Eli (1982), *The Concept of Identity* (New York: Oxford University Press).
Hume, David (1739–40), *A Treatise of Human Nature*, 3 vols (London: John Noon).
Hume, David (1751), *An Enquiry Concerning the Principles of Morals* (London: A. Millar).
Hussey, Edward (1972), *The Presocratics* (London: Duckworth).
Ishiguro, Hidé (1972), *Leibniz's Philosophy of Logic and Language* (London: Duckworth).
Ishiguro, Hidé (1978), 'Pre-established Harmony versus Constant Conjunction: A Reconsideration of the Distinction between Rationalism and Empiricism', *Proceedings of the British Academy*, 63, pp. 239–63.
Ishiguro, Hidé (1980), 'On the Primitiveness of the Concept of Person', in Zak van Straaten (ed.), *Philosophical Subjects: Essays Presented to P. F. Strawson* (Oxford: Clarendon Press), pp. 62–75.
Ishiguro, Hidé (1981), 'Contingent Truths and Possible Worlds', in R. S. Woolhouse (ed.), *Leibniz: Metaphysics and Philosophy of Science* (Oxford: Oxford University Press), pp. 64–76.
Johnston, Mark (1987), 'Is there a Problem about Persistence?', *Proceedings of the Aristotelian Society*, suppl. 61, pp. 107–55.
Kahn, Charles H. (1960), *Anaximander and the Origin of Greek Cosmology* (New York: Columbia University Press).
Kahn, Charles H. (1964), 'A New Look at Heraclitus', *American Philosophical Quarterly*, 1, pp. 189–203.
Kahn, Charles H. (1979), *The Art and Thought of Heraclitus: An Edition of the Fragments with Translation and Commentary* (Cambridge: Cambridge University Press).
Kant, Immanuel (2004), *Prolegomena to Any Future Metaphysics*, trans. and ed. Gary Hatfield (rev. edn, Cambridge: Cambridge University Press) [German orig. 1783].
Kasher, Asa (ed.) (1976), *Language in Focus: Foundations, Methods and Systems: Essays in Memory of Yehoshua Bar-Hillel* (Dordrecht: Reidel).
Kirk, G. S. (1951), 'Natural Change in Heraclitus', *Mind*, 60, pp. 38–42.
Kirk, G. S. (ed.) (1954), *Heraclitus: The Cosmic Fragments* (Cambridge: Cambridge University Press).
Kripke, Saul A. (1971), 'Identity and Necessity', in Milton K. Munitz (ed.), *Identity and Individuation* (New York: New York University Press), pp. 135–64.
Kripke, Saul A. (1972), 'Naming and Necessity', in Donald Davidson and Gilbert Harman (eds), *Semantics of Natural Language* (2nd edn, Dordrecht: Reidel), pp. 253–355.
Kripke, Saul A. (1972), *Naming and Necessity* (Oxford: Blackwell).
Leibniz, G. W. (1875–90), *Die philosophischen Schriften von Gottfried Wilhelm Leibniz*, ed. C. I. Gerhardt, 7 vols (Berlin: Weidmannsche Buchhandlung).
Leibniz, G. W. (1973), *Philosophical Writings*, ed. G. H. R. Parkinson (London: Dent, 1973).
Leibniz, G. W. (1969), *Philosophical Papers and Letters*, trans. and ed. Leroy R. Loemker (2nd edn, Dordrecht: Reidel).

Leibniz, G. W. (1903), *Opuscules et fragments inedits de Leibniz: Extraits des manuscrits de la Bibliothèque royale de Hanovre*, ed. Louis Couturat (Paris: Alcan, 1903).
Leibniz, G. W. (1948), *Textes Inedits d'après les manuscrits de la Bibliothèque provinciale de Hanovre*, ed. Gaston Grua, 2 vols (Paris: Presses Universitaires de France).
Leibniz, G. W. (1704), *Nouveaux essais sur l'entendement humain*, in *Samtliche Schriften und Briefe*, Series VI, vol. 6 (Berlin: Akademie Verlag, 1923-).
Leibniz, G. W., *New Essays on Human Understanding*, trans. and ed. Peter Remnant and Jonathan Bennett (Cambridge: Cambridge University Press, 1981).
Leibniz, G. W. (1953), *Discourse of Metaphysics*, trans. Peter G. Lucas and Leslie Grint (Manchester: Manchester University Press, 1953) [Ger. orig. 1686].
Leibniz, G. W., 'Meditations on Knowledge, Truth, and Ideas', Gerhardt vol. IV, pp. 422-6.
Leibniz, G. W. (1956), *The Leibniz–Clarke Correspondence* [1715-16], trans. and ed. H. G. Alexander (Manchester: Manchester University Press).
Lemmon, E. J. (1963), 'A Theory of Attributes Based on Modal Logic', *Acta Philosophica Fennica*, 16 (*Proceedings of a Colloquium on Modal and Many-valued Logics, Helsinki, 23-26 August, 1962*), pp. 95-122.
Lenzen, Wolfgang (1986), '"Non est" non est "est non" - Zu Leibnizens Theorie der Negation', *Studia Leibnitiana*, 18, pp. 1-37.
Lévy, J. R. (1973), 'Le Verrier', in Charles Gillespie (ed.), *The Dictionary of Scientific Biography* (New York: Scribner's), vol. 8, pp. 276-9.
Lewis, David (1968), 'Counterpart Theory and Quantified Modal Logic', *Journal of Philosophy*, 65, pp. 113-126.
Lewis, David (1986), *On the Plurality of Worlds* (Oxford: Blackwell).
Lewis, David (1991), *Parts of Classes* (Oxford: Blackwell).
Lewis, David (1993), 'Many, but almost one', in Keith Campbell, John Bacon, and Lloyd Reinhardt (eds), *Ontology, Causality and Mind: Essays on the Philosophy of D. M. Armstrong* (Cambridge: Cambridge University Press), pp. 23-37.
Lewis, David (2002), 'Tensing the Copula', *Mind*, 111, pp. 1-14.
Linsky, Leonard (ed.) (1971), *Reference and Modality* (London: Oxford University Press).
Locke, John (1689), *An Essay Concerning Human Understanding*.
Mackie, J. L. (1977), *Ethics: Inventing Right and Wrong* (Harmondsworth: Penguin).
Mauss, Marcel (1938), Huxley Memorial Lecture: 'Une Categorie de l'Esprit Humain: la Notion de Personne, celle de "Moi"', *Journal of the Royal Anthropological Institute*, 68, pp. 263-81.
McDowell, J. (1976), 'Truth Conditions, Bivalence and Verificationism', in Gareth Evans and John McDowell (eds), *Truth and Meaning: Essays in Semantics* (Oxford: Clarendon Press), pp. 42-66.
Mill, James (1829), *Analysis of the Phenomena of the Human Mind* (London: Baldwin and Cradock).
Nussbaum, Martha C. (1972), '*Psuchē* in Heraclitus, 1', *Phronesis*, 17, pp. 1-16.
O'Meara, Dominic (ed.) (1981), *Studies in Aristotle* (Washington, DC: Catholic University of America Press).
Okasha, Samir (2002), 'Darwinian Metaphysics, Species and the Question of Essentialism', *Synthese*, 131, pp. 191-213.

Owen, G. E. L. (1953), 'The Place of the *Timaeus* in Plato's Dialogues', *Classical Quarterly*, n.s. 3, pp. 79–95.

Owen, G. E. L. (1966), 'Plato and Parmenides on the Timeless Present', *The Monist*, 50, pp. 317–40.

Owen, G. E. L. (1983), 'Particular and General', in *Logic, Science and Dialectic: Collected Papers in Greek Philosophy*, ed. Martha Nussbaum (Ithaca, NY: Cornell University Press).

Parfit, Derek (1984), *Reasons and Persons* (Oxford: Clarendon Press).

Peacocke, Christopher (1976), 'An Appendix to David Wiggins' "Note"' ['The *De Re* "Must": A Note on the Logical Form of Essentialist Claims'], in Gareth Evans and John McDowell (eds), *Truth and Meaning: Essays in Semantics* (Oxford: Clarendon Press, 1976), pp. 313–24.

Putnam, Hilary (1970), 'Is Semantics Possible?', *Metaphilosophy*, 1 (1970), pp. 187–201, and in Howard E. Kiefer and Milton K. Munitz (eds), *Language, Belief and Metaphysics* (Albany, NY: State University of New York Press, 1970), pp. 50–63.

Putnam, Hilary (1975), 'On Properties', in *Philosophical Papers*, vol. 1: *Mathematics, Matter and Method* (Cambridge: Cambridge University Press), pp. 305–22.

Putnam, Hilary (1975), 'The Meaning of "Meaning"', in *Philosophical Papers*, vol. 2: *Mind, Language and Reality* (Cambridge: Cambridge University Press), pp. 215–71.

Putnam, Hilary (1988), *Representations and Reality* (Cambridge, MA: MIT Press).

Putnam, Hilary (2012), *Philosophy in an Age of Science: Physics, Mathematics, and Skepticism*, ed. Mario De Caro and David Macarthur (Cambridge, MA: Harvard University Press).

Quine, W. V. (1940), *Mathematical Logic* (Cambridge, MA: Harvard University Press).

Quine, W. V. (1953), *From a Logical Point of View: Nine Logico-Philosophical Essays* (Cambridge, MA: Harvard University Press).

Quine, W. V. (1956), 'Quantifiers and Propositional Attitudes', *Journal of Philosophy*, 53, pp. 177–87.

Quine, W. V. (1960), *Word and Object* (Cambridge, MA: MIT Press).

Quine, W. V. (1972), 'Review of Milton K. Munitz (ed.), *Identity and Individuation*', *Journal of Philosophy*, 69, pp. 488–97.

Ramsey, Frank Plumpton (1931), *The Foundations of Mathematics and Other Logical Essays*, ed. R. B. Braithwaite (London: Routledge & Kegan Paul).

Rundle, Bede (2009), *Time, Space, and Metaphysics* (Oxford: Oxford University Press).

Russell, Bertrand (1900), *A Critical Exposition of the Philosophy of Leibniz* (Cambridge: Cambridge University Press).

Russell, Bertrand (1927), *An Outline of Philosophy* (London: Allen and Unwin).

Russell, Bertrand (1956), *Logic and Knowledge: Essays 1901–1950*, ed. Robert Charles Marsh (London: Routledge).

Russell, Bertrand (1961), *History of Western Philosophy* (London: Allen and Unwin).

Ryle, G. (1937–8), 'Categories', *Proceedings of the Aristotelian Society*, 38, pp. 189–206.

Schoenheimer, Rudolf (1942), *The Dynamic State of Body Constituents* (Cambridge, MA: Harvard University Press).

Shoemaker, Sydney (1963), *Self-Knowledge and Self-Identity* (Ithaca, NY: Cornell University Press).

Shoemaker, Sydney (2004), 'Brown–Brownson Revisited', *The Monist*, 87, pp. 571–93, 610–13.
Simons, Peter (1987), *Parts: A Study in Ontology* (Oxford: Clarendon Press).
Smiley, T. J. (1963), 'Review of *Reference and Generality: An Examination of Some Medieval and Modern Theories*', *Philosophical Books*, 4(3), pp. 6–7.
Smullyan, Arthur Francis (1948), 'Modality and Description', *Journal of Symbolic Logic*, 13, pp. 31–7.
Sober, Elliott (1980), 'Evolution, Population Thinking, and Essentialism', *Philosophy of Science*, 47, pp. 350–83.
Spinoza, Benedictus de, *Spinoza Opera*, ed. C. Gebhardt, 4 vols (Heidelberg: Carl Winter, 1925).
Strawson, P. F. (1959), *Individuals: An Essay in Descriptive Metaphysics* (London: Methuen).
Suppes, Patrick (1957), *Introduction to Logic* (New York: Van Nostrand).
Tarski, Alfred (1956), *Logic, Semantics, Metamathematics: Papers from 1923 to 1938*, trans. J. H. Woodger (Oxford: Clarendon Press).
Thagard, Paul R. (1978), 'The Best Explanation: Criteria for Theory Choice', *Journal of Philosophy*, 75, pp. 76–92.
Torretti, Roberto (1999), *The Philosophy of Physics* (Cambridge: Cambridge University Press).
Vlastos, Gregory (1955), 'On Heraclitus', *American Journal of Philology*, 76, pp. 337–68.
Weil, Simone (1973), *The Iliad, or the Poem of Force*, trans. Mary McCarthy (Iowa City, IA: Stone Wall Press).
Wheelwright, Philip (1959), *Heraclitus* (Oxford: Oxford University Press).
Williams, Bernard (1973), 'Strawson on Individuals', in *Problems of the Self: Philosophical Papers 1956–1972* (Cambridge: Cambridge University Press), pp. 101–26.
Williamson, Timothy (1995), *Vagueness* (London: Routledge).
Williamson, Timothy (1996), 'The Necessity and Determinacy of Distinctness', in Sabina Lovibond and S. G. Williams (eds), *Essays for David Wiggins: Identity, Truth and Value* (Oxford: Blackwell), pp. 1–17.
Winch, P. (1980–1), 'Eine Einstellung zur Seele', *Proceedings of the Aristotelian Society*, 81, pp. 1–15.
Wittgenstein, Ludwig (1922), *Tractatus Logico-Philosophicus*, trans. D. F. Pears and B. F. McGuinness (London: Routledge 1961).
Wollheim, Richard (1964), 'On Expression and Expressionism', *Revue Internationale de Philosophie*, 18, pp. 270–89.
Woodger, J. H. (1952), *Biology and Language: An Introduction to the Methodology of the Biological Sciences including Medicine* (Cambridge: Cambridge University Press).
Xu, Fei (1997), 'From Lot's Wife to a Pillar of Salt: Evidence that *Physical Object* is a Sortal Concept', *Mind and Language*, 12, pp. 365–92.

Index

activity, principle of x, xiii, 10–11, 12, 13, 20–1, 26–7, 29–30, 31, 46, 48–9, 57, 69, 98, 167, 179, 198, 202–3, 206, 208, 211, 214, 214n, 220
adequacy requirement (grounds for asserting the identity of x and y must be grounds for the indiscernibility of x and y) xi, xiii, 5, 6, 11, 14, 27, 97n, 218n
aggregates xvii, 14, 23–4, 33–4, 40, 69, 200, 218–9; like concatenations or sums, and unlike substances, they have the parts (elements) they have necessarily, 194, see also 'the great truth of things'
'almost identical' vi, 5n, 6n, 7n, 25
analytic judgement 129, 134–5, 161
Anaximander 100–4, 109
Anscombe, G. E. M. 151
a priori proof (Leibniz) 132–5, 142, 164n
Aristotelian syllogism 135
Aristotle 1–2, 15, 49–51, 56–8, 103, 104n, 107, 116–17, 214n
   distinction between substance and quality 1, 54–5, 121–2
   first account of substance 41–7, 56
   hylomorphic account of substance 59–70
   secondary substance 47–9
   syllogistic 135–8, see also hupokeimenon; phusis
   'What is it?' question xix, 1, 10–11, 121, 166, 176, 188, 199–200, 219
artefacts x–xi, xiii, xv–xvi, 7n, 20–1, 23–6, 32, 34n, 67–9
   distinguished from natural things 89–92
Austin, J. L. xix, 124, 152n, 155
Ayer, A. J. xii, 56, 167, 169, 182–3
Ayers, Michael xv–xviii, 40, 52n

Babylonians 168
bar of soap xi, 6–7 n.14
Barcan theorem 167–73, 181–2
bare particular 12, 56, 208
Bernoulli, J. 113
best explanation, argument to 100–2, 104
biological individuality, see Thymus praecox, slime mould, bramble
bramble, blackberry stand 219

brain transfer, see Brown/Brownson
Brouwersche principle 4n, 25
Brown/Brownson (Shoemaker) x–xi, 26–31, 97–8

chess board (Strawson) 8–9
Chisholm, Roderick xii, xiv, 191–200
chrysalis 12
Cicero 95
clear vs distinct ideas xix (n), 11–12, 55, 163–4
clone 28
concatenation, see aggregate, sum
concept xii, xiii, xviii, 4, 124–6, 135–41, 160, 175, 203, 205–6, 219
   of an artefact-kind 89
   complete concept (Leibniz) 131, 133, 148
   concept as the reference of a predicate, DW's Fregean usage xii
   determinacy/indeterminacy of identity 5–6, 6n
   distinction between concept and essence (Leibniz) 141
   distinction between concepts and objects that fall under them 141
   formal concept xix, 12n, 202
   individual concept 146–8
   of a natural kind 89
   of a person 87, 89, 92, 94, 97–8
   of the predicate (Leibnitz) 128, 134
   primitive concept 76
   sortal concept xix, 201–7
   of the subject (Leibnitz) 128, 134
   of substance 50, 96, 130–1
   of thing-kind 89–90, see also concept-word; determinable extension of concept; indeterminacy; conception/idea
concept-word 72–4, 157–9
   predicative character of 73
conception/idea xii–xv, 218, 219, 220
conceptual realism xvi–xvii
conceptualism, see conceptual realism
conclusory concept, see fundamental sort
concrete universal, corporate being xiv, 28, 92
conscious subject, see person
constitution relation, is not the relation of identity 12n
containment principle (Leibniz) 128–46

contingency 128-9, 137, 142, 145-6, 169-71, 180, 183
continuant xii, 13-14, 16-17, 25, 32, 40, 44, 57-8, 68, 106, 108-10, 120-2, 175, 177-8, 191, 196-7, 211-20
continuity 13
corporate being, *see* concrete universal
creative definition 17n, 38

Darwin, Charles 99
deixis 153-4, 162
de re necessity 166-72, 174-5, 182-4, 193-5
Descartes, René 50, 113
determinable xix, 12n, 26, 111, 174, 202, 206-8, 212n, 216, 220
dialectic of same and other 22, *see also* activity, principle of
Dicks, D. R. 105
difference, necessity of 4, 4n, 24-5
Diogenes Laertius 108, 111, 114-15, 213
Dummett, Michael 122, 151, 157
Dupré, John xii, 211-12, 218, 220
elemental forms (Heraclitus) 114-15

enantiodromia 108, 213
energy, conservation of 113-14
essence 41, 52n, 54, 59, 61-2, 67, 130, 140-1, 164, 165, 175-6, 177-8, 187, 189, 214n, 215
essentialism 141, 166, 169-70, 173-8, 187-90, *see also* individuative essentialism; mereological essentialism
entia per aliud 191, 197
entia per se 191-2, 197
entia successiva 191-2, 197
examples, *see* Brown/Brownson; bar of soap; bramble; chess board; grex; Hesperus (=Phosphorus); lump of clay; maggot; Mississippi; Pope's crown; rivers; Seine; siphonophore, colonial; table, board, and stump; teletransportation; Theseus, ship of; Tib/Tibbles; wood and tree
extension of concept 72, 73n, 75, 79, 82, 98, 131, 135, 138n, 140n, 151, 152, 154, 156, 160, 162-3, 164n
extrinsic properties 15-16, 57

first-order logic 56
flux 2, 3, 6, 44, 106-8, 110, 117-21, 211
formal concept 202, *see also* determinable
four-dimensionalism 17-20, 213
Frege, Gottlob xii, 72-4, 82n, 118, 125, 135-6, 138n, 151-2, 156-61, 203
fumble xix, 207, 208
fundamental sort 22, 23, 48, 68

Geach, P. T. ix, 37-8, 151, 185
genidentity 213-15

grex, *see* slime moulds
Guay, Alexandre 211n, 213-18

Hacking, Ian 167, 169n
Heraclitus xii, 3, 99-127, 213
  barley drink 109
  flux 105-10
  fire 110-13
  river 3, 108, 197-8
Hesperus (=Phosphorus) 4n, 73, 167-8, 170-3, 182-6
Hintikka, J. 187
Hirsch, Eli 166, 178-9, 207
Hobbes, Thomas 20-2
human beings and their nature 80-3, 96
Hume, David 41-3, 49-50, 53, 56, 69, 89, 95
Hussey, Edward 102
hupokeimenon 41n, 50, 54, 60-2

idea (as conception, not image) xii
identity 1
  absoluteness of 6
  'almost' 6-7, 25
  brain-continuity sufficient? 32, 97
  constitution relation, is not identity 12n
  criterion of identity for material objects 36
  determinacy of 5-6, 23-6, 48-9
  necessity of 5-7
  permanence 5, 6
  persistence ix-x, 3, 11, 22, 24, 30, 34, 44, 57-8, 67, 91, 97-8, 109, 176, 179, 196-9, 211, 214
  reflexivity 3
  sufficient conditions x, 7, 10-11, 13
  symmetry 4
  transitivity 4, *see also* person; sortal concept; substance; remnant
identity of indiscernibles (Leibniz) x, 7-10, 148
indeterminacy 6, 23, 32, 45, 210
indexicality 27n, 87, 94, 98, 153
indiscernibility of identicals (Leibniz) 3-4, 12
individuation 1, 212, 215
  artefacts xiii, 20-26
  individual continuant 215
  natural substances 12-13
  and persistence of identity 196
  persons 26-31, 83, 85-6, 96
  sortalist account xv-xx, 1-2, *see also* single out
individuative essentialism 165-6, 170n
individuative necessity 166, 186, *see* necessity *de re*
infants, conceptual scheme of 209-10
'interpret' 80-2
innate idea 8n, 201, 202, 203
intrinsic properties 15-17, 57-8

Jenkins, G. v
Johnson, W. E. 212
Joule, James Prescott 113-14

Kahn, Charles 99n, 117, 124n
Kant, Immanuel 49-50, 129, 134-5
Kirk, G. S. 107n
Krebs cycle 212
Kripke, Saul xii, 4n, 13, 25, 156, 167-8, 171-3, 179-82, 187-9

lambda abstraction 171, 184-6
Leibniz, Gottfried Wilhelm xi, xii, xviii, 7-8, 11, 13, 68, 113, 117, 146-9, 173, 191-2, 201-2
  Discourse of Metaphysics 129, 131-2, 133, 137, 140, 142-6
  letter to De Volder 50
  New Essays on Human Understanding 51-5
  predicative 'is' 36
  principle of contradiction 142
  principle of sufficient reason 102, 129, 131
  principle of the best 129, 137, 144
  substance, concept of 51-3, 130-3, *see also* clear v. distinct ideas, a priori proof; containment principle; identity of indiscernibles; indiscernibility of identicals; Leibniz's law; reference
Leibniz's law xvii, 22, 34-5, 37, 48, 97, 170, 172, 179, 182, 184
Lemmon, E. J. 167, 182-3
Lewis, David 6n, 15-16, 21, 57-8, 173, 187n, 196n
Locke, John 34-5, 36, 38, 51-5, 79-80, 124n
logic, philosophy of 59, 122-3, 126
logical possibility, not enough x, 30
lump of clay 6-7n

Mach, Ernst 17, 32, 56
Mackie, J. L. 85n
maggot 45
Marcus, Ruth Barcan 4, 167, 171, 181, *see also* Barcan theorem
Mauss, Marcel 88-9
maximal set of substance (Leibniz) 130-1, 148
memory 27, 28, 77-8
mereology and mereological essentialism xii, 7, 18, 21, 191-3, 197
  the (alleged) great truth of things, 21, 191, 196
  the principle of unique composition 6-7n, 21
  sum axiom 194
  see also aggregates, quantities
metamorphosis 12
metaphysical realism distinguished from ordinary realism xiii-xv, 219
Mississippi xiv, 197-200
modal logic 4n, 147, 166-9, 173-5, 179-86, 193
mountains 23

natural kinds x, xii, 13, 56, 68, 89-91, 110, 120, 151-2, 154, 156, 159-62, 179
necessity *de re* 169-71, 178, 184, 193
nomological grounding 15, 26, 45, 47, 202
'object' as formal concept xix, 201-9, *see also* determinable
only a and b rule 5-6, 11, 14, 97, 218n, *see also* adequacy requirement
ontology xiii, 44, 57, 166, 175, 185n, 213, 219
  Aristotelian 175
  of continuants 177-8
  pluralism 218
  of processes xii, 177, 216
  of substances xii, 108, 166, 177
organism 13, 214, 216, 218
Owen, G. E. L. 100-1, 109n, 119

Parmenides 15, 59-60, 101, 102, 109, 122
Parfit, Derek 29n, 91-3, 93-4n
part and whole 43, 220, *see also* mereology
perdurance 15, 17, 58, 196n
periodicity 104n, 105-6, 114-17
permanence of identity 6-7, 21, 24, 25
person/persons, *see also* Brown/Brownson; remnants of a substance
  as bearer of moral attributes 71, 94-5
  concept of 72-3
  as conscious subject 71, 76, 80-2, 84, 86
  as distinct from a mere succession of events 18-19
  human being xv, xvii, 71, 74-6
  identity of 6, 26-30, 48, 92-4, 96-8
  indexicality of the idea of 80, 87, 94
  living body of xv, xvii
  as a 'material' thing 77-8
  as natural kind 91-2
  non-human persons? 47n, 88-9, 94-6
  as object of science 71
  as our fellow creature 83-6, 87-8
  primitiveness of the concept of 76-80
  as rational being 71, 82, 94-6
  and reciprocity and solidarity 87
  reductionism 35
  stereotype of 87, 96
  substantialist view of xi, 26
phases, *see* part and whole
Phosphorus, *see* Hesperus (=Phosphorus)
physiognomy 29-30, 87, 91
Plato xiv, 61, 101, 107-8, 111, 116-17, 118-21, 134, 207
pluralism, *see* realism
Pope's crown 219
possible worlds 173, 187-90
  fatally different purposes informing Leibniz's construction of 147-8

Pradeu, Thomas 211n, 213–18
praedicatum inest subjecto, see containment principle
predicate xiin, xv, 13, 16, 36–7, 45, 50, 52–3, 56, 58, 60–4, 68, 70, 72–4, 76–81, 122–3, 125, 128, 131–40, 143–5, 154, 156, 158–61, 169, 174–5, 177, 183, 186, 187, 203, 206
Price, H. H. 154n
Principle of Unique Composition 21, *see also* mereology and 'the great truth of things'
processes xii, 2–3, 107–11, 211–12, 214, 214n, 218
psychological continuity 26, 27, 28
Putnam, Hilary xii–xiv, 13, 56, 75n, 150–6, 159–64, 219
phusis xi, 10–11, 13, 21, 46, 90
psychological continuity 26–9

quality 1, 46
  distinct from substance 54, 62, 122
quantities 2, 7n, 198
quasi-memory 27–9, 93, 93–4n
Quine, W. V. xii, xiii, 3n, 155–6, 168–73, 175–6, 183

realism, not the same as metaphysical realism xiii–xv, 199, 200, 218, 219, 220, *see also* conceptual realism
reference 72–3, 148, 157, 158, 161, 168n, 187, *see* singular term; deixis
referential opacity 171–3
relational state 13, 16
relative identity ix
remnants of a substance 21n, 24, 31, 98
rivers 3, 108, 121, 197–8, 199, 200
Rundle, B. 16n
Russell, Bertrand 35n, 41, 47, 56, 120, 130n, 135, 136, 138, 142, 154n, 166, 176–8, 180–1

same place at same time xi, xv, 22–3, 23n, 32–40, 70, 200
'same what?' x, 218
Schoenheimer, Rudolf 2–3, 117n
Seine 198
Seneca 99
Shoemaker, Sydney x, 26, 97, 176n, *see also* Brown/Brownson
Simons, Peter 39–40, 174n, 215
single out (or 'track') xviii–xix, 39, 159, 202, 215–18
singular term 72–3, 135, 140n, 151, 157–9
siphonophore, colonial 218, 220
slime moulds 219, 220
Smiley, Timothy 185
Smullyan, A. F. 170–1, 180
solidarity 83–5

sortal concept and sortal conceptions xi, xiii, xvi, xix, 6, 10, 13, 21, 25, 201–3, 205–7, 218
sortalism x–xv, xvii, xviii–xix, 1, 6, 10, 13, 21, 25–6, 31–2, 56, 68, 98, 179, 190, 201–7, 217–18, *see also* principle of activity
space-time, events in 18
Spinoza 50, 128
statue 12–13
stereotype 75, 87, 96, ch. 3, 151, 159, 162–4
Strawson, P. F. 8–9, 76–9
subject 28, 42, 49, 50–4, 60–4, 70, 128, 130, 132, 134–7, 143–5, 169, 177
substance x–xviii, xxi, 1, 6, 8, 12–15, 17–23, 25–8, 30–2, 34–6, 39–40, 41–70, 85, 89, 91, 96, 97, 105, 108–10, 117, 120–2, 130–3, 137–44, 147–9, 155, 166, 176–9, 190, 192, 196, 200, 203, 207, 213–14, 220
  Aristotle's first account 43–4
  empiricist rejection of 41–2, 49, 51, 54, 56
  primary substances 43–9, 61–2, 66, 67n, 191, 196
  secondary substances 44–8, 66
sufficient reason, principle of 8, 101–2, 106–7, 114, 129, 132, 134, 139, 142, 142, 144, 149
substratum 51–4, 60–3, *see also hupokeimenon*
sum of elements of a class 194, *see also* mereology
superposition 39–40
symmetrical object 5

table, board, stump (Chisholm) 193–5
Tarski, Alfred 143n, 193–4, 196
teletransportation 91–3
temporary intrinsic properties 16, 57–8
'the great truth of things', 191, 196–7, *see* mereological essentialism
Theseus, ship of x, xvii, 20–4, 40, 197, 199–200
thing-kind xiii, 11–12, 26, 32, 89–90, 151, 153, 162–3, 188–9
Thymus praecox xiv
Tib/Tibbles 37–8
twins 14

unity xv–xvii, xviii, 52n, 216, 218
universal xiv, 92–3, 97, *see also* corporate being

Vlastos, Gregory 112

way of behaving, *see* principle of activity
Weil, Simone 83–4
William of Sherwood 37
Williams, S. G. 114
Williamson, Timothy 4n, 25
Wilson, Jack 218
Winch, Peter 83n

Wittgenstein, L. 84, 181
Woodger J. H. 79n
wood and tree 33–6
world-line, *see* genidentity; four-dimensionalism

Xu, Fei xii, 201–9

Young, J. Z. 214n

zygote x, 12n, 14n, 217